PETER SHAFFER

GARLAND REFERENCE LIBRARY
OF THE HUMANITIES
(VOL. 916)

PETER SHAFFER
An Annotated Bibliography

Eberle Thomas

GARLAND PUBLISHING, INC. • NEW YORK & LONDON
1991

Library of Congress Cataloging-in-Publication Data

Thomas, Eberle.
    Peter Shaffer : an annotated bibliography / Eberle Thomas.
        p.   cm. — (Garland reference library of the humanities ; vol.
    916)
    Includes index.
    ISBN 0-8240-7645-1 (acid-free paper)
    1. Shaffer, Peter, 1926–   —Bibliography. I. Title.
    II. Series.
    Z8809.6.T56   1991
    [PR6037.H23]
    016.822'914—dc20   90–14052
                                                                   CIP

Printed on acid-free, 250-year-life paper
Manufactured in the United States of America

CONTENTS

Foreword by Howard Millman   xi

Acknowledgments   xiii

Introduction   xv

    The Scope of This Book   xv
    The Special Case of the Screen Adaptations   xvii
    A Brief Biographical Note   xviii
    Shaffer and His Audience   xx
    Shaffer and His Critics   xxi

Chronology of Shaffer's Works   xxiii

Chapter 1. GENERAL WORKS   3

    Bibliographies   3
    Book-Length Studies   4
    Biographical Sketches   5

Critical Compilations   7
Feature Stories and News Reports   8
Book Chapters, or Sections, on Shaffer   10
Reviews of Two or More Plays   14
Scholarly Essays on Two or More Plays   15
Dissertations and Theses   20

Chapter 2. INTERVIEWS AND OTHER
   "SHAFFER ON SHAFFER" MATERIALS   21

   1958-1962   21
   1963-1967   25
   1968-1972   31
   1973-1977   33
   1978-1982   38
   1983-1990   40

Chapter 3. EARLY WORKS—NOVELS, RADIO AND
   TELEVISION PLAYS, PANTOMIME   45

   [Texts or Descriptions of the Works:]
      Mystery Novels   45
      Works for Television   46
      Work for Radio   46
      Christmas Entertainment with Music   46
   Reviews of the Mystery Novels   47
   Review of Teleplay   47
   Reviews of the Pantomime   48

Chapter 4. FIVE FINGER EXERCISE   51

   The Text   51
   Play Reviews:
      A. Original London Production   52
      B. New York Production   56
   News Reports and Feature Stories   64

Scholarly Essays   65
The Film   66
Film Reviews   66

**Chapter 5. THE PRIVATE EAR and
THE PUBLIC EYE**   **69**

The Text   69
Play Reviews:
  A. Original London Production   69
  B. New York Production   73
News Reports and Feature Stories   79
Scholarly Essay   80
The Films   80
Film Reviews:
  The Pad (And How to Use It)   81
  The Public Eye   82

Chapter 6. THE ROYAL HUNT OF THE SUN   **85**

The Text   85
Play Reviews:
  A. Original Chichester Production   86
  B. London Production   90
  C. New York Production   95
News Reports and Feature Stories   104
Scholarly Essays   106
The Film   108
Film Reviews   109

**Chapter 7. BLACK COMEDY and WHITE LIES
(THE WHITE LIARS/WHITE LIARS)**   **111**

The Text   111
Play Reviews:

A. *Black Comedy*, Original
   Chichester Production   112
B. *Black Comedy*, First
   London Production   115
C. *Black Comedy* and *White*
   Lies (premiere), New York Production   116
D. *Black Comedy* (second London
   production) and *The White Liars*
   (first London production)   123
E. *Black Comedy* and *White*
   Liars (third revision),
   London Revival   125
F. Other Productions   127
News Reports and Feature Stories   127

Chapter 8. THE BATTLE OF SHRIVINGS   **129**

The Text   129
Play Reviews   129
News Reports and Feature Stories   134

Chapter 9. EQUUS   **137**

The Text   137
Play Reviews:
   A. Original London Production   138
   B. New York Production   142
   C. Other Productions   156
News Reports and Feature Stories   157
Scholarly Essays   162
Letters to the Editor   175
Dissertations and Theses   176
The Film   176
Film Reviews   176
Film Version—Feature Stories   182

Chapter 10. AMADEUS   **185**

   The Text   185
   Play Reviews:
      A. Original London Production   186
      B. New York Production   190
      C. London Revival   200
      D. Other Productions   203
   News Reports and Feature Stories   205
   Scholarly Essays   210
   Letters to the Editor   214
   The Film   215
   Film Reviews   215
   Film Version—News and Feature Stories   224
   Film Version—Letters to the Editor   227

Chapter 11. YONADAB   **231**

   The Text   231
   Play Reviews   231
   News Reports and Feature Stories   241
   Scholarly Essay   241

Chapter 12. LETTICE AND LOVAGE   **243**

   The Text   243
   Play Reviews:
      A. Original London Production   243
      B. New York Production   252
   News Reports and Feature Stories   257
   Scholarly Essay   259

Index   **261**

Foreword

This book offers a comprehensive and creative approach to the works of one of the English theatre's most provocative and substantial playwrights.

A playwright, director, and actor himself, Eberle Thomas has produced a remarkable resource for both the theatre and the classroom. As an artist who has also taught in a university setting, he sees where the viewpoints of the artist and the educator merge and where they separate. It is his awareness of this distinction which should make the bibliography an invaluable tool for directors, actors, designers, literary managers, educators, and writers. An unusual feature of this reference work—and a tribute to Eberle—is that it seems likely not only to serve the intellect but also to spark the imagination.

> *Howard J. Millman*
> *Producing Artistic Director*
> *GeVa Theatre*
> *Rochester, New York*
> *August 20, 1990*

Acknowledgments

The research for this project was conducted over the course of almost three years, during which a succession of jobs as a freelance director and actor took me to various parts of the country. As a result, a great many librarians lent assistance. I shall not attempt to thank them by name, for, in many cases, those who gave most freely of their time and expertise did so anonymously. Thanks, then, to the staffs of the following: The Bryant Library, Michigan State University Library, The New York Public Library (Central Research Facility, Newspaper Collection Annex, and The Billy Rose Theatre Collection), Queensborough Public Library, St. John's University Library, University of Connecticut Library, University of Rochester Library, and University of Houston Library.

Special thanks are due to Brother Emmett Corry, Director of the Division of Library and Information Science at St. John's University, who first suggested that I expand my preparatory research for directing a production of *Equus* into a comprehensive bibliography.

I am also especially grateful for the advice of my editor, Paula Ladenburg. Among other contributions, it was her pleasant insistence on considering the reader's needs that led to the present organizational scheme of this book.

Finally, I thank my wife, actress and director Barbara Redmond, who read versions of the manuscript at all stages of its completion and lent invaluable counsel on every aspect.

Eberle Thomas
New York City
July 4, 1990

Introduction

The Scope of This Book

This bibliography is intended to provide a reasonably comprehensive guide to published materials concerning Peter Shaffer and his works. A few unpublished items also appear, such as Shaffer's early television and radio scripts, as well as the six motion picture versions of his plays. The chronological span of the entries is March, 1956 through May, 1990.

The materials have been assembled as a guide not only for teachers and students of dramatic literature but also for such theatre professionals as literary managers, directors, designers, and publicists. To serve the needs of both classes of readers, the annotations are more heavily larded with direct quotations than is usual in works of this kind.

It is impossible to predict the full range of those who may consult this volume. Nevertheless, it seems safe to assume that no reader's needs would be well served by arranging materials in a strictly chronological pattern, with 35 chapters devoted to each publication year from 1956 through 1990. On the other hand, it appears likely that a typical reader will be

looking for two basic types of information: (a) biographical
and general works on Shaffer, and (b) reviews and articles
devoted to individual plays or films. With this in mind, the
first three chapters of this work are meant to assist those
seeking general information:

1. General works, including bibliographies, book-length
   works on Shaffer, biographical sketches, and articles
   dealing with more than one play.

2. Interviews and other autobiographical materials.

3. The early, "minor" works, such as mystery novels, radio
   and television scripts, and the Christmas pantomime
   Shaffer wrote for Joan Littlewood's company.

Chapters 4 through 12 provide easy access for those wishing to
find reviews, scholarly studies, news articles, discussions of the
film versions, and similar materials on each of Shaffer's nine
stage presentations. [Though the playwright has actually
produced a total of eleven plays to date, a single chapter is
devoted to the paired one-acts *The Private Ear* and *The
Public Eye*; likewise to *Black Comedy* and *White Lies*.]

In each chapter, materials are arranged in appropriate
sections and sub-sections ("Reviews: New York Production").
Within sub-sections arrangement is alphabetical by author,
with successive entries under a single author's name arranged
chronologically. There are a few exceptions to this general
rule in cases where strict chronological arrangement seemed
to be clearly preferable (as in Chapter Two).

For a bibliography, no organizational principle can be
entirely satisfactory. There are always items which logically
belong in more than one location. Many interviews, for
instance, could have been entered in either the "General
Works" chapter or in one of the chapters devoted to individual
plays. The reader will similarly find a number of reviews of

single plays which go on to discuss the entire body of Shaffer's works. Cross-references have been supplied to facilitate the process of locating obviously related pieces of information. In addition, the index aims at providing access to a wide range of connections, such as tracking a single critic's ongoing "dialogue with Shaffer" over the course of many years.

Inevitably, there are limitations as to the degree of comprehensiveness which is practical. In the present work, it was necessary, for example, to decide whether materials relating to the filmed versions of Shaffer's plays should be included at all and, if so, how extensive the coverage of such items should be. A separate note on this issue follows.

The Special Case of the Screen Adaptations

To date, six of Shaffer's eleven plays have been converted to film:

> *Five Finger Exercise* [film version, 1962]
> *The Private Ear* [film version, under the title
>   *The Pad (And How to Use It)*, 1966]
> *The Royal Hunt of the Sun* [film version, 1969]
> *The Public Eye* [film version, released as *The
>   Public Eye* in the U.S. and as *Follow Me* in
>   England, 1972]
> *Equus* [film version, 1977]
> *Amadeus* [film version, 1984]

At first the job of adapting the plays was assigned to veterans of the screenwriting trade: Frances Goodrich and Albert Hackett (*Five Finger Exercise*), Thomas C. Ryan and Ben Starr (*The Private Ear*), and Philip Yordan (*The Royal Hunt of the Sun*). However, Shaffer's increasing dissatisfaction with the treatment his works received at other hands led him, beginning in the 1970s, to take over the task of adapting his stage works for film. His first two efforts as his own adaptor, for *The Public Eye* and *Equus*, proved less than successful. However, his determination to excel in the new, and not altogether congenial medium, finally paid off. His third outing as a screenwriter, *Amadeus*, won him enormous new audiences worldwide and an Academy Award.

Despite the overwhelming success of the film *Amadeus*, Shaffer has steadfastly maintained that his natural medium is the stage and has hinted that he may never write for the screen again. In any case, he is chiefly known for his stage works, and the primary concern of the present bibliography is Shaffer the playwright.

The decision has been made, therefore, to provide representative, rather than comprehensive, coverage of materials concerning Shaffer's efforts as a screenwriter. In instances where his plays were translated to film by others, only a few reviews are covered. For Shaffer's own adaptations of *The Public Eye* and *Equus*, the reader will find a larger number of entries. *Amadeus*, the most successful and most widely discussed of the films, is given still greater coverage.

A Brief Biographical Note

Peter Shaffer was born, along with twin Anthony, on May 15, 1926, in Liverpool. He attended St. Paul's, a prestigious London public school (which would be called a "private school" in the U.S.), until he was conscripted in 1944 as a "Bevin Boy" to work in the coal mines of Yorkshire and Kent. In 1947 he was released from service and entered Cambridge, where he received his B.A. at Trinity College, in 1950.

Over the next eight years he drifted through a variety of jobs on two continents. During the early 1950s he clerked in a Manhattan book store until he found what proved to be unsatisfactory employment in the acquisitions department of the New York Public Library. Returning to England in 1954, he took a short term job in the London office of music publishers Boosey and Hawkes and then served as literary critic for *Truth*. In his spare hours during this period, he managed to write three mystery novels (two in collaboration with his brother Anthony) as well as two teleplays and a radio play which were produced by the British networks. However, none of Shaffer's early writing efforts achieved the kind of success which would have led an observer to anticipate the extraordinary phase he entered next.

In 1958 Shaffer submitted the unsolicited manuscript of his first play, *Five Finger Exercise*, to a London producer. A Cinderella-story sequence of events followed. The fledgling playwright received a telephone call from the producer and was offered for his debut not only a West End production with a stellar cast but also, as his director, one of the British theatre's most illustrious figures, John Gielgud. Thus was made, as the saying goes, theatrical history.

This constitutes virtually all the recorded facts concerning Shaffer's off-stage existence. The playwright, once described by director Peter Hall as "endlessly talkative," has been less than forthcoming about his personal life, a fact which has proved disappointing to critics looking for autobiographical references in the plays. Critic John Russell Taylor succinctly sums up the case: "As a person, Shaffer . . . has remained one of the most mysterious figures of his generation."

Shaffer and his Audience

Peter Shaffer has achieved enormous popular success throughout a lengthy, though not especially prolific, career. During the past 32 years, beginning in 1958, when he made his debut with *Five Finger Exercise*, through 1990, he has produced eleven plays. As four were paired one-acts, these actually comprise nine "entertainments." Here is the astonishing box-office scorecard on Shaffer's output to date:

3 tremendous hits

> *The Royal Hunt of the Sun*, 1964
> *Equus*, 1973
> *Amadeus*, 1979

4 solid successes

> *Five Finger Exercise*, 1958
> *The Private Ear* and *The Public Eye*, 1962
> *Black Comedy* and *White Lies*, 1965-67
> *Lettice and Lovage*, 1987

1 work generally considered unsuccessful

> *Yonadab*, 1985

1 disastrous failure

> *The Battle of Shrivings*, 1970

This record of 7 successes in 9 attempts is unmatched among serious dramatists writing in English. It might also be noted that Shaffer has been spurred by his rare failures toward his brightest accomplishments. He followed up his heartbreaking setback with *The Battle of Shrivings* (1970) by turning out *Equus* (1973), which earned a place among the 50 longest-running plays in Broadway history. After the disappointment of *Yonadab* (1985), he rebounded with the highly popular *Lettice and Lovage* (1987).

Shaffer and His Critics

While Shaffer's popularity with playgoers is undeniable, his standing among critics has been, from the first, hotly debated.

A persistent attack against Shaffer's plays has been waged by certain critics. Among the prominent detractors have been John Simon, Martin Gottfried, Benedict Nightingale, Ian Christie, Robert Cushman, Steve Grant, and (especially in regard to *Amadeus*) Frank Fenton. They have complained of Shaffer's "pretentious philosophical claptrap" (Christie, *Daily Express*), his "shoddy invention" (Simon, *New York*), his "fair-to-indifferent prose" (Cushman, *Observer*), and have dismissed him as "perhaps the worst serious English dramatist since John Drinkwater" (Fenton, *Times*).

These barbs, however, have not only been outweighed by voluminous ticket sales but also countered by extravagant praise from other critics. *Equus*, for example, has been termed "pure theatre at its best" (Jack Kroll, *Newsweek*), "a triumph" (Harold Hobson, *Sunday Times*), "a sensationally good play" (Michael Billington, *Guardian*), "brilliantly crafted, handsomely written, and unusually compelling" (Harold Clurman, *Nation*), as well as "one of the most powerful and provocative theatrical experiences of our time" (Edwin Wilson, *Wall Street Journal*). An especially faithful and eloquent admirer of Shaffer's work has been Bernard Levin of the *Daily Mail*, who hailed *The Royal Hunt of the Sun* as "the greatest play in my lifetime" and defended *Amadeus* against fellow critics by upholding it as a play with a "colossal theme [clothed] in language of great beauty."

For almost thirty years, Shaffer has been a controversial playwright. The basis of the controversy has been neither the content nor the form of his works, but rather, quite simply, his stature as a dramatist. His antagonists, unable to deny his overwhelming success at the box office, have continued to question, often with overt hostility, his intellect and his integrity. Recent examples of the anti-Shaffer tone include *Times* critic John Peter's dismissal of *Yonadab* as "a long, louche literary entertainment which relates to serious drama as Little Red Riding Hood relates to anthropology" and Michael Feingold's review of *Lettice and Lovage*, which congratulates Shaffer for abandoning "serious and important art" and applying his "middle-brow, light-entertainer's sensibility" to suitably trivial material.

Though we cannot predict the status which future theatre historians will assign to Shaffer, we can be sure that they will cite him as the most widely produced and most popular of England's playwrights during the post-World War II era. We can be equally certain that the plays will continue to be produced and that Peter Shaffer will continue to be written and talked about for many years to come. The present volume seeks to provide the first steps along an information trail for those who will be doing the producing, the writing, and the talking.

Chronology

1951

The Woman in the Wardrobe: A Light-hearted Detective Story. Mystery novel by Peter Shaffer, is published under the pseudonym "Peter Anthony."

1952

How Doth the Little Crocodile?: A Mr. Verity Detective Story. Mystery novel by Peter Shaffer and Anthony Shaffer, is published under the pseudonym "Peter Anthony."

1955

Withered Murder. Mystery novel by Peter Shaffer and Anthony Shaffer, is published as "by A. and P. Shaffer."

The Salt Land. Teleplay, is produced by ITV.

1957

The Balance of Terror. Teleplay, is produced by BBC-TV.

The Prodigal Father. Radio play, is produced by BBC.

1959

Five Finger Exercise. Play, original production opens in London.

1960

Five Finger Exercise opens in New York.

1962

The Private Ear and *The Public Eye.* One-act plays, original production opens in London.

Five Finger Exercise. Film version of Shaffer's play premieres, screenplay by Frances Goodrich and Albert Hackett.

1963

The Private Ear and *The Public Eye* open in New York.

"The Merry Roosters Panto." Christmas Entertainment, is produced by Joan Littlewood's Theatre Workshop.

"That Was the Week That Was." Television sketches, published in England. Two sketches by Shaffer included.

1964

The Royal Hunt of the Sun. Play, original production opens at the Chichester Festival in July; re-opens in London in December.

1965

The Royal Hunt of the Sun opens in New York.

Black Comedy. One-act play, original production opens at The Chichester Festival in tandem with Strindberg's *Miss Julie.*

1966

Black Comedy (with *Miss Julie*) opens in London.

The Pad (And How to Use It). Film version of *The Private Ear* premieres, screenplay by Thomas C. Ryan and Ben Starr.

1967

White Lies. Play, original production opens in New York, paired with *Black Comedy.*

1968

Black Comedy and *The White Liars* (revised version) are produced as a double bill in London.

1969

Royal Hunt of the Sun. Film version of Shaffer's play premieres, screenplay by Philip Yordan.

1970

The Battle of Shrivings. Play, is produced in London.

1972

The Public Eye (British title: *Follow Me!*). Film version of the play premieres, screenplay by Shaffer.

1973

Equus. Play, original production opens in London.

1974

Equus opens in New York.

Shrivings, substantially revised version of *The Battle of Shrivings*, is published.

1976

Black Comedy and *White Liars* (a third version, with fresh revisions) are revived in London.

Equus. Film version of the play premieres, screenplay by Shaffer.

1979

Amadeus. Play, original production opens in London.

1980

Amadeus opens in New York.

1981

Amadeus, with New York revisions, re-opens in London.

1984

Amadeus. Film version of the play premieres, screenplay by Shaffer.

1985

Yonadab. Play, original production opens in London.

1986

Yonadab, with revisions, re-opens in London.

1987

Lettice and Lovage. Play, original production opens in London.

1990

Lettice and Lovage opens in New York.

Peter Shaffer

Chapter One

General Works

BIBLIOGRAPHIES

1. Carpenter, Charles A., compiler. "Bond, Shaffer, Stoppard,
   Storey: An International Checklist of
   Commentary." *Modern Drama* 24.4 (Dec. 1981):
   546-556.
   A brief, selective bibliography of articles
   dealing with Shaffer, pages 550-551.

2. Klein, Dennis A. *Peter and Anthony Shaffer: A
   Reference Guide.* Boston: G.K. Hall, 1982.
   80 pages of this annotated bibliography are
   devoted to Peter Shaffer, including reviews
   through the New York opening of *Amadeus.*

3. Palmer, Helen H. *European Drama Criticism,
   1900-1975.* 2nd ed. Folkestone, England: Shoe
   String Press, 1977.
   Contains a selective listing of reviews of
   Shaffer's plays through *Equus*, pages 476-478.

4. Page, Malcolm (compiler). "Peter Shaffer: Bibliography,
   Biography, Playography." *Theatre Checklist No.
   16.* London: TQ Publications, 1978.
   A reprint of a brief, selective bibliography
   originally published in 1978 in the periodical
   Theatrefacts.

BOOK-LENGTH STUDIES

5. *File on Shaffer.* Compiled by Virginia Cooke and
   Malcolm Page. London: Methuen, 1987.
   This slim (88 page) paperback proves to be an
   excellent resource. It reprints excerpts, ranging
   from a single paragraph to a page in length, from
   a wide variety of materials. These include several
   reviews of each play (through *Yonadab*) plus a
   large number of interviews and assorted examples
   of "the writer on his work." *File on Shaffer* also
   supplies a chronology, production and publication
   data, and information on the playwright's
   non-theatrical works.

6. Klein, Dennis A. *Peter Shaffer.* Twayne English Author
   Series, no. 261. Boston: Twayne, 1979.
   An extensive (163 page) report of Shaffer's
   career through *Equus.* Klein devotes separate
   chapters to each of the full-length plays and a
   single chapter to the one-acts *The Private Ear,
   The Public Eye, Black Comedy,* and *White
   Lies/White Liars.* The opening section provides
   an outline of Shaffer's life and discusses his early
   and minor works (mystery novels, a pantomime,
   teleplays, and a radio play).

7. Plunka, Gene A. *Peter Shaffer: Roles, Rites and Rituals in the Theatre*. Rutherford, NJ: Fairleigh Dickinson University Press, 1988.
 Plunka examines each play through *Amadeus*. After an introduction which supplies biographical material, two opening chapters are devoted to an analysis of Shaffer (1) as a "sociologist of the theatre," who investigates the nature, uses, and abuses of conformity; and (2) as a craftsman who experiments with ritualistic and other devices in order to locate suitable forms for his purposes. Scattered throughout the body of the text and its following "Notes" section are references to an interview with Shaffer, conducted by Plunka on April 19, 1986, apparently unpublished.

8. Taylor, John Russell. *Peter Shaffer*. [Writers and Their Work Series, no. 244] Harlow, England: Longman House, 1974.
 Taylor analyzes each of Shaffer's plays through *Equus*, for which he has high praise: " . . . after *Equus*, there is just no guessing what [Shaffer] may do next, but it seems inevitable that it will be grand and glorious."

BIOGRAPHICAL SKETCHES

9. *Contemporary Authors: A Bio-Bibliographical Guide to Current Writers*. Ed. by Hal May and Deborah A. Straub. New Revision Series. Vol. 25. Detroit: Gale Research Co., 1986.
 On pages 409-413 are (1) a biographical sketch, (2) a chronology of Shaffer's works through the London opening of *Lettice and*

Lovage, (3) a capsule history of the critical
responses to the plays, and (4) a bibliography.

10. *Contemporary Dramatists.* Ed. by James Vinson. 2nd
ed. London: St. James Press, 1977.
    Biographical and other information about
    Shaffer is included on pages 710-713.

11. *Critical Survey of World Drama: English Language
    Series.* Ed. by Frank N. Magill. Englewood
    Cliffs, New Jersey: Salem Press, 1985.
    Pages 1676-1688 of Volume 4 contain
    biographical notes and an essay on Shaffer's
    works through *Amadeus.* A brief reference also
    appears on page 2789 of Volume 6, in an article
    on "Twentieth Century British Drama": "The
    contemporary theatre is dominated by a number
    of playwrights; among them, Peter Shaffer and
    Tom Stoppard are perhaps the most noteworthy."

12. *Current Biography Yearbook 1988.* New York: H.W.
    Wilson Co., 1988.
    The entry on Shaffer, pages 521-525, provides
    the most recent comprehensive biographical data
    on the playwright. It covers his career through the
    London opening of *Lettice and Lovage* and his
    subsequent receiving of the award of the title,
    "Commander of the British Empire," in 1988.

13. *McGraw-Hill Encyclopedia of World Drama.* Vol. 4.
    New York: McGraw-Hill, 1972.
    Notes on Shaffer and his plays, pages 83-85.

14. Taylor, John Russell. "Peter Shaffer." Pages 313-328 in
    *British Writers; Supplement I: Graham
    Greene to Tom Stoppard.* New York: Charles
    Scribner's Sons, 1987.

This essay, though published in 1987, contains
no mention of *Yonadab*, which opened in 1985.
In fact, it is a barely retouched excerpt from
Taylor's 1974 book, *Peter Shaffer* [see #8].
Here he concludes that Shaffer's "gradual,
unsparing exploration of the expressive
possibilities of his chosen form . . . has little by
little established him as a major figure in world
drama."

15. *Who's Who in the Theatre: A Biographical Record
   of the Contemporary Stage.* 15th ed. London:
   Pitman & Sons, 1972.
   Contains an entry on Shaffer, page 1397.

16. *World Authors 1950-1970.* Ed. by John Wakeman. New
   York: H.W. Wilson Co., 1975.
   A biographical sketch on Shaffer is included
   on pages 1289-1290.

CRITICAL COMPILATIONS

17. *Contemporary Literary Criticism.* Vols. 5, 14, 18, 37.
   Detroit, Michigan: Gale Research Company,
   1976-1986.
   Contains excerpts from works cited in the
   present volume, as follows: Vol. 5, pages 386-390:
   entries #312, #505, #24, #536, #504, #511,
   #530, #534, #537, #546; Vol. 14, pages 484-488:
   entries #40, #48, #8, #447, 583; Vol. 18, pages
   473-478: entries #49, #661, #672, #109; Vol. 37
   [in which the materials relate to the film version
   of *Amadeus*], pages 381-389: entries #798,
   #116, #790, #813, #807, #806, #795, #815, #50.

18. *Modern British Literature*; Vol. 4: Supplement; Vol 5: Second Supplement. New York: Ungar Publishing Company, 1975, 1985.
    Contains excerpts from works cited in the present volume, as follows: Vol. 4, pages 457-462: entries #192, #213, #304, #313, #410, #499; Vol. 5, pages 482-484: entries #49, #6, #763.

19. *Twentieth-Century British Literature*. Vol. 4. General Editor, Harold Bloom. New York: Chelsea House, 1987.
    Reprints, on pages 2485-2496, entire articles cited in the present volume as follows: entries #78, #63, #624, #763.

FEATURE STORIES AND NEWS REPORTS

20. Bolton, Whitney. "London-versus-N.Y. Comparisons of Shaffer Plays Are Invidious." *New York Morning Telegraph* 14 Oct. 1963: 2.
    This feature story follows up the recent Broadway opening of *Private Ear/Public Eye*. Its proposition: is it true, as inter-continental theatre-goers often maintain, that Shaffer's (and other British playwrights') works receive superior productions in London and inferior ones in New York? After several playful paragraphs, Bolton concludes that the British have not "kept the goodies home and sent us stale biscuits."

21. Dallas, Ian. "The Naturalists." *Encore* 10 Sept. 1958: 24-28.
    Discussing the "new naturalist" playwrights, Dallas expresses little hope for Osborne, Bolt, [Doris] Lessing, or Delaney and wonders why they

bother to write plays at all, since their attitudes
toward audiences seem negative or negligent. He
sees only two with promise: Michael Hastings and
Shaffer ("a born dramatist because he is first and
foremost an architect").

22. Messina, Matt. "Peter Shaffer's TV Script Shelved by CBS
Playhouse." *New York Daily News* 29 July
1967: 10.
Reports that a Shaffer teleplay, whose title is
not mentioned, has been cancelled. It was to have
starred John Gielgud as a "middle-aged
Englishman who has a bitter-sweet liaison with a
swinging young American cutie."

23. Rogoff, Gordon. "Richard's Himself Again: Journey to an
Actors' Theatre." *Tulane Drama Review* 11
(Winter 1966): 29-40.
This report on the 1966 National Theatre
season comments briefly on *Royal Hunt* and
Black Comedy. Rogoff mentions a rarely
publicized fact: Shaffer wrote bridging passages
and short scenes for the National Theatre
production of Congreve's *Love for Love.*

24. Schickel, Richard. "Showman Shaffer." *Time* 11 Nov.
1974: 117, 119.
A story on Shaffer's career through *Equus*,
based in part on an interview with the playwright.
Shaffer is said to have completed a rough draft of
a "light comedy" called "The Syllabub Saloon."

25. Taylor, John Russell. "Tomorrow's Elder Statesmen?"
Plays and Players 337 (Oct. 1981): 11-15.
Taylor evaluates Shaffer's position among
established British playwrights. The verdict is
mixed. He complains that "the inventiveness (or
gimmickry if you like)" of the productions—rather

than the quality of the writing—has been
responsible for the success of Shaffer's plays.
Amadeus, however, is applauded as an example
of Shaffer's ability to learn through his mistakes
and mend them through re-writes. Taylor, who
considers comedy to be the playwright's true
metier, describes *Amadeus* as "one of Shaffer's
best plays, second only to *Black Comedy*."

BOOK CHAPTERS, OR SECTIONS, ON SHAFFER

26. Beckerman, Bernard. "The Dynamics of Peter Shaffer's
    Drama." In *The Play and Its Critic: Essays
    for Eric Bentley*. Ed. by Michael Bertin.
    Lanham, MD: University Presses of America,
    1986.
       Beckerman's study of Shaffer's themes and
    techniques appears on pages 199-209.

27. Chiari, J. *Landmarks of Contemporary Drama*.
    London: Herbert Jenkins, 1965.
       Includes a discussion of Shaffer's works
    through *Royal Hunt*, pages 210-211.

28. Elsom, John. *Post-War British Theatre*. London:
    Routledge & Kegan Paul, 1976.
       Contains comments on Shaffer's plays
    through *Equus*, pages 96-98.

29. Gassner, John, and Edward Quinn, eds. *The Reader's
    Encyclopedia of World Drama*. New York:
    Thomas Y. Crowell, 1969.
       Notes on Shaffer's life and his plays through
    Black Comedy are found on pages 759-760.

30. Glenn, Jules. "Twins in the Theater: A Study of Plays by
    Peter and Anthony Shaffer." Pages 277-299 in
    Blood Brothers: Siblings as Writers. Ed. by
    Norman Kiell. New York: International University
    Presses, 1983.

31. Hall, Peter. *Peter Hall's Diaries*. Ed. by John Goodwin.
    New York: Harper and Row, 1984.
    The diaries cover the period March
    1972-January 1980, the first eight years of Hall's
    tenure as Director of the National Theatre (and
    of the theatre's existence in its new location on
    the South Bank near Waterloo Station). Hall, who
    in 1970 had directed *The Battle of Shrivings*,
    continued a professional relationship with Shaffer
    during this later period, the most significant
    feature of which was his collaboration as director
    of the original London and New York productions
    of *Amadeus*. Hall's notes on this subject are
    densest in the final section of the book, beginning
    on page 410 with the diary entry for January 25,
    1979, when he first receives a play entitled
    "Salieri." In addition to descriptions of the
    Amadeus re-writing and rehearsal processes,
    there are brief, but fascinating, impressions of
    both Shaffer the artist and Shaffer the man. For
    example, on July 11, 1973 (page 49) Hall sees a
    run-through of *Equus* and notes: "[John] Dexter
    has done a wonderful job in cutting out the
    over-writing which Peter Shaffer is prone to, and
    which I signally failed to do on . . . *The Battle
    of Shrivings*." On June 15 (page 103), after a
    long lunch-swim-and-talk session with the
    playwright, Hall writes: "I know no one less
    restful than Peter. He talks compulsively all the
    time. But I enjoy it." On January 25, 1979 (pages
    410-411), having examined Shaffer's latest
    Amadeus re-writes, Hall remarks: "Peter's script

is tougher, more precise, and more personal than
anything he has done before. In one way, he is
writing about how he sees himself and his
uncertainties compared to, say, Sam Beckett." The
index to Hall's *Diaries* includes Shaffer-related
entries on approximately 50 pages.

32. Hayman, Ronald. *The First Thrust*. London: Davis-
    Poynter, 1975.
    Comments on Shaffer and his works through *Equus*
    appear on pages 88-92 and 106-108.

33. Hinchliffe, Arnold P. *British Theatre 1950-70*. Totowa,
    NJ: Rowman & Littlefield, 1974.
    Contains a brief mention of the Shaffer
    brothers, page 149.

34. Kauffmann, Stanley. *Persons of the Drama*. New York:
    Harper and Row, 1976.
    Kauffmann's remarks on Shaffer and his
    works through *Equus* on pages 248-251.

35. Kerensky, Oleg. *The New British Drama: Fourteen
    Playwrights Since Osborne and Pinter*. New
    York: Taplinger Publishing Co., 1977.
    The chapter devoted to Shaffer, on pages
    55-58, provides an excellent brief introduction to
    the dramatist and his works (through *Equus*). It
    begins with a capsule biography, goes on to supply
    a play-by-play analysis of Shaffer's career, and
    concludes with a description of the playwright's
    working methods and ambitions (gleaned from an
    interview conducted by the author). Kerensky
    sums up by observing, "It is very unusual to find a
    writer so concerned with ideas and psychological
    relationships who is also so skillful at creating
    visual and theatrical effects."

36. Lewis, Allan. *The Contemporary Theatre: The Significant Playwrights of Our Time.* Rev. ed. New York: Crown, 1971.
    A section on Shaffer's works through *The Battle of Shrivings* is to be found on pages 326-329. Lewis comments at length on *The Royal Hunt of the Sun*, which is hailed as "a symbolic drama of grandeur and scope."

37. Lumley, Frederick. *New Trends in Twentieth Century Drama: A Survey Since Ibsen and Shaw.* 4th ed. New York: Oxford University Press, 1972.
    Contains a section on Shaffer's career through *The Battle of Shrivings*, pages 283-288. As might be expected considering the last play covered, the author reaches a lukewarm conclusion: "Shaffer at least continues his experiments . . . [hc] is a peripatetic professional."

38. Marowitz, Charles. *Confessions of a Counterfeit Critic.* London: Eyre Methuen, 1973.
    Section on Shaffer, pages 88-90.

39. Salem, Daniel. *La Revolution teatrale actuelle en Angleterre.* Paris: Denoel, 1969.
    Remarks on *Five Finger Exercise, Royal Hunt,* and *Black Comedy,* pages 132-135.

40. Taylor, John Russell. *Anger and After: A Guide to the New British Drama.* London: Methuen, 1969.
    Taylor's influential survey of England's new dramatists, first published in 1962, damns Shaffer with faint praise (pages 272-278). *Five Finger Exercise* and the *Private Ear/Public Eye* duo are described as clever and literate but far closer in craft and tone to Pinero than to Osborne and his fellow "new" dramatists.

41. Taylor, John Russell. "Art and Commerce: The New
    Drama in the West End Marketplace." In
    Contemporary English Drama. New York:
    Holmes & Meier, 1981.

42. Taylor, John Russell. *The Second Wave: British Drama
    for the Seventies.* New York: Hill & Wang,
    1971.
    Mentions Shaffer, page 11.

43. Weise, Wolf-Dietrich. *Die 'Neuen' englishen
    Dramatiker in ihrem Verhaltuis zu Brecht.*
    Vol. 3. Bad Homberg: Frankfurter Beitrage zur
    Anglistik und Amerikanistik, 1969.
    Chapter 7 contains remarks on Shaffer.

44. Wellworth, George. *The Theater of Protest and
    Paradox: Developments in the Avant-Garde
    Drama.* 3rd Printing. New York: New York
    University Press, 1967.
    The third printing includes brief comments on
    Shaffer's works, page 254.

REVIEWS OF TWO OR MORE PLAYS

45. Anon. Book review: "The Collected Plays of Peter Shaffer."
    School Library Journal 29 (Apr. 1983): 134.

46. Barnes, Clive. "Peter Shaffer Writes for All Seasons." *New
    York Post* 19 Feb. 1983: 11-12.
    In a lengthy feature story, Barnes conjectures
    that Shaffer is so outstanding a playwright
    because of his "craftsmanship" and his ability to
    write "great parts for great [actors]." An
    explanation is also given for the volume of

negative criticism heaped on the playwright: he is
"too glib to be attractive to his critics."

47. Buckroyd, P. "British Drama 1975-1985." *Rocky
Mountain Review of Language and
Literature* 40.1 (1986): 49-66.
Mentions briefly *Amadeus* and *Yonadab*.

48. Hayman, Ronald. "Like a Woman They Keep Going Back
To." *Drama* 98 (Autumn 1970): 57-62.
Hayman comments on four contemporary
British playwrights, including Shaffer, who "have
never belonged to the avant garde [but] have not
been content to go on as naturalistically as they
began." Shaffer's career through *The Battle of
Shrivings* is briefly assessed. The verdict is a
mixed one. For example, though the construction
of *Royal Hunt* is praised, its language is faulted
for failing to produce a sense of 16th century
speech (in contrast to Bolt's in *A Man for All
Seasons*). Among other points of interest is
Hayman's contention that much of the plot of
Five Finger Exercise is derived from
Turgenev's *A Month in the Country*.

SCHOLARLY ESSAYS ON TWO OR MORE PLAYS

49. Dean, Joan F. "Peter Shaffer's Recurrent Character Type."
Modern Drama 21.3 (Sept. 1978): 297-305.
The recurrent type referred to in the title is
the "middle-aged man in a crisis of faith." The
examples studied are Pizarro (and Martin Ruiz) in
The Royal Hunt of the Sun, Mark in *The
Battle of Shrivings*, and Dysart in *Equus*.
Dean maintains that the conflicts of these central

figures reflect recurrent themes in Shaffer's
works: man's need for faith, his fear of mortality,
his estrangement from his western culture.

50. Gianakaris, C.J. "Drama into Film: The Shaffer Situation."
    Modern Drama 28.1 (Mar. 1985): 83- 98.
    Gianakaris examines Shaffer's three attempts
    to translate his stage works into screenplays. The
    bulk of the article deals with *Amadeus* (the
    most recent, and most successful, of the
    attempts), in which, Gianakaris claims, Shaffer
    was able to "develop even further than in the play"
    certain of his ideas. The question of whether the
    film *Amadeus* is an improvement or a
    debasement of the stage version is left open.

51. Glenn, Jules. "Anthony and Peter Shaffer's Plays: The
    Influence of Twinship on Creativity." *American
    Imago* 31 (1974): 270-292.
    In a follow-up to his earlier articles on the
    implications of "twinship" in Shaffer's works,
    Glenn begins by demonstrating that the two
    leading characters in *Equus* interact like twins.
    He then offers a similar analysis of the *White
    Lies/White Liars* story. Finally, Glenn states
    four hypotheses which could explain why
    audiences take special, unconscious enjoyment in
    beholding behavior characteristic of twins.

52. Glenn, Jules. "Twins in Disguise. II. Content, Form and
    Style in Plays by Anthony and Peter Shaffer."
    International Review of Psycho-Analysis 1.3
    (1974): 373-381.
    Glenn continues his discussion of "twinship"
    revealed in *Black Comedy*, *White Lies
    (Liars)*, and *The Public Eye*. [For "Part I" of
    this essay, on *Royal Hunt*, see #357.]

53. Hinden, M. "When Playwrights Talk to God: Peter Shaffer and the Legacy of O'Neill." *Comparative Drama* 16.1 (1982): 49-63.

     The author of this article views Shaffer (in his "epic" works) as an inheritor of the "O'Neill tradition" (mythic themes, theological preoccupations, anti-realistic devices such as soliloquies, etc.). The usefulness of this particular comparative study is perhaps questionable, and the author does not help matters by stating that he sees a possible "common source" for both playwrights in Nietzsche's *Birth of Tragedy*.

54. Hinden, M. "Trying to Like Shaffer." *Comparative Drama* 19.1 (Spring 1985): 14-29.

     The author reflects on the full range of Shaffer's career though *Amadeus* in an attempt to settle the issue of whether he should be considered a first-rate or mediocre playwright. Many examples of Shaffer's dialogue are cited as instances of calculated and mechanical writing, devoid of "spontaneity." On the other hand, the dramatist is praised for his "wide ranging" interests and "beautifully orchestrated" effects.

55. Jensen, Marvin D. "Peter Shaffer's Plays as Case Studies in Transactional Analysis." *Transactional Analysis Journal* 13.1 (Jan. 1983): 55-57.

56. Klein, Dennis A. "Breaking Masculine Stereotypes: The Theatre of Peter Shaffer." *University of Dayton Review* 18.2 (Winter-Spring 1986-87): 49-55.

     This article consists, for the most part, of plot condensations of five Shaffer plays, designed to establish their relevance to the theme of un-stereotypical males. Klein concludes that it is to the playwright's credit that he is willing to

depict men as sensitive, indecisive, and envious,
and women as forceful and reasonable.

57. Lounsberry, Barbara. "'God-Hunting': The Chaos of
Worship in Peter Shaffer's *Equus* and *Royal
Hunt of the Sun*." *Modern Drama* 21.1 (Mar.
1978): 13- 28.
    Shaffer's use of rituals and religious,
mythical, and mystical symbolism is discussed.
Lounsberry maintains that each of the plays "is
really an exploration of man's search for gods,
what he does when he seems to find them, and
how they ultimately elude him." [For Lounsberry's
analysis of other Shaffer works, see #58 below.]

58. Lounsberry, Barbara. "Peter Shaffer's *Amadeus* and
Shrivings: God-Hunting Continued." *Theatre
Annual XXXIX* (1984): 15-33.
    Having dissected *Royal Hunt* and *Equus*
[see #57 above], the writer probes the
"God-Hunting" theme in two more Shaffer plays.

59. Pennel, Charles A. "The Plays of Peter Shaffer:
Experiment in Convention." *Kansas Quarterly*
3.2 (Spring 1971): 100-109.
    Pennel suggests that analysts of Shaffer's
plays should take seriously the playwright's
contention (first stated in reference to *Five
Finger Exercise*) that he "makes conventional
theatrical devices serve his unconventional
theatrical purposes." Pennel sees in each Shaffer
play a single pattern: (1) a familiar scene or
character-group arouses the expectations
audiences have developed from past theatre
experiences; (2) the expectations are exploded and
the underlying truth of the situation revealed.
This pattern is identified as it occurs in four of

Shaffer's plays, with special treatment being given
to *Five Finger Exercise* and *Royal Hunt.*

60. Podol, Peter L. "Dramatizations of the Conquest of Peru:
Peter Shaffer's *The Royal Hunt of the Sun*
and Claude Demarigny's *Cajamarca.*" *Hispanic
Journal* 6.1 (Fall 1984): 121-129.

61. Rosten, N. "Culture Inside and Outside: Random Thoughts
on Our Situation (Advice to Young Playwrights)."
Michigan Quarterly Review 21.1 (1982): 57-65.
Mentions Shaffer.

62. Stacy, James R. "The Sun and the Horse: Peter Shaffer's
Search for Worship." *Educational Theatre
Journal* 28.3 (Oct. 1976): 325-335.
Stacy discusses *Royal Hunt* and *Equus* as
works which use mythic materials and formal
devices to produce "total ritualistic involvement of
the senses, the mind, and the spirit."

63. Winegarten, Renee. "The Anglo-Jewish Dramatist in
Search of His Soul." *Midstream* 12 (Oct. 1966):
40-52.
Winegarten wonders why Shaffer and Pinter
have not dealt with Jewish themes. She believes
that *Five Finger Exercise,* for example, would
have been enriched by the choice of a Jewish
family. Nevertheless, she postulates that Shaffer,
throughout his career, is "subconsciously drawing
on a vein of feeling . . . which is in part peculiar
to [his] Anglo-Jewish experience."

DISSERTATIONS AND THESES

64. Lawson, Wayne P. "The Dramatic Hunt: A Critical Evaluation of Peter Shaffer's Plays." Ph.D. Dissertation, Ohio State University, 1973. (DAI 34:7374A-75A)

65. Plunka, Gene Alan. "The Existential Ritual in the Plays of Jean Genet, Peter Shaffer, and Edward Albee." Ph.D. Dissertation, University of Maryland, 1978. (DAI 39:7342A-43A)

66. Simard, Rodney Joe. "Postmodern Anglo-American Dramatic Theory." Ph.D. Dissertation, University of Alabama, 1982. (DAI 43:2990)
    With other playwrights, Shaffer is discussed.

67. Troxel, Patricia Margaret. "Theater of Adultery: Studies in Modern Drama from Ibsen to Stoppard." Ph.D. Dissertation, Princeton University, 1986. (DAI 47:2805)
    Chapter Four mentions Shaffer.

68. Watson, John Clair. "The Ritual Plays of Peter Shaffer." Ph.D. Dissertation, University of Oregon, 1987. (DAI 48:1587)
    On *Royal Hunt, Equus,* and *Amadeus.*

Chapter Two

Interviews and Other

"Shaffer on Shaffer" Materials

The materials cited in this chapter are arranged chronologically by date of publication. This practice has been adopted to make it possible for readers to follow in consecutive order the basic pattern of "Shaffer's story in his own words." To facilitate the process of locating works dealing with a particular phase in Shaffer's career, the citations have been further broken down, arbitrarily, into five-year segments.

A. "SHAFFER ON SHAFFER," 1958-1962

69. [Shaffer, Peter.] "Peter Shaffer Calls for Magic and Mystery." *Stage and Television Today* (London) 31 July 1958: 8.

   R.B. Marriott interviews Shaffer a fortnight after the successful London opening of *Five*

Finger Exercise. On the threshold of his own
career as a dramatist, Shaffer names Terence
Rattigan ("a brilliant technician") and John
Osborne ("a brilliant rhetorician and polemicist")
as active British playwrights whom he admires.
He hints that he may be setting his sights on
amalgamating their talents: "With a combination
of the two you would have a really wonderful
play." He also supplies a critique of other, young
(anonymous) contemporaries, censuring them for
being "self-absorbed . . . contemptuous of
technique . . . resentful of audiences." It becomes
clear during this interview that Shaffer has
already written *The Royal Hunt of the Sun.*
In fact, the bulk of his conversation relates, not
to his immediate success with *Exercise* nor to
what would prove to be his next successfully
produced work—the double bill of *Private Ear*
and *Public Eye*—but to *Royal Hunt* and its
successors in the vein of "total theatre" (*Equus*
and *Amadeus*). The ambitions expressed are
epic in scale: "The theatre should . . . [be] a place
where truth and passion in all their diversity and
splendour are revealed . . . [In *Royal Hunt*] I
aim for the immediacy of effect, combined with
the high theatricality, of a Bach Passion."

70. [Shaffer, Peter.] "Committed to Nothing But the Theatre."
   Manchester Guardian 27 Aug. 1959: 4.
   As *Five Finger Exercise* completes the first
   year of its London run and prepares for a
   transplantation to American soil, W.L. Webb
   reports on his interview with Shaffer (who is
   described as being committed to no particular
   movement or style, but only to the theatre itself).
   The playwright explains that "he was encouraged
   to start writing by seeing so many good ideas
   wasted or obscured by what seemed to be

obvious and avoidable technical mistakes."
Shaffer mentions that he hopes to find a
production for a completed first draft "of a play
about the conquest of the Aztecs."

71. [Shaffer, Peter.] "Playwright's Moral Exercise." *New York Times* 29 Nov. 1959: section 2; 1, 3.
    In an interview conducted by Joseph A. Loftus during the Washington tryout of *Five Finger Exercise*, script revisions for the U.S. production are discussed. A point of some interest is Shaffer's revelation that, when he writes, he speaks every word aloud "many times."

72. [Shaffer, Peter.] "Briton Wrote New Scene to Open His Play in New York." *New York Herald Tribune* 8 Dec. 1959: 21.
    During an interview conducted by Stuart W. Little shortly after the New York opening of *Five Finger Exercise*, Shaffer discusses the rewrites he has made. In addition to attempting to clarify phrasing for American audiences, the playwright has "worked out" (with director Gielgud) an entirely new opening scene in an effort to "to get more directly into the . . . family conflicts" and to establish a more credible ("less farcical") tone than that which characterized the London production.

73. [Shaffer, Peter.] "Peter Shaffer Is an Enemy of Togetherness." *New York Herald Tribune* 3 Jan. 1960: section 4; 3.
    In an interview by Don Ross following the successful New York opening of *Five Finger Exercise*, Shaffer explains that he has made use of the "stock properties" of English drawing room plays only to reassure audiences that they are on familiar ground. His intention, however, has been

to treat the "family play" differently: more in the
style of America's "great plays of divided
families" by O'Neill, Miller, and Williams. [For a
scholarly discussion of Shaffer's "experimental"
uses of conventional materials, see #59.]

74. Shaffer, Peter. "Labels Aren't for Playwrights." *Theatre
    Arts* Feb. 1960: 20-21.
    In a brief but fascinating self-assessment,
    Shaffer discusses the very themes that will come
    to preoccupy his critics for the next 30 years. He
    insists that he does not wish to be assigned to a
    particular category (especially not that of an
    effete Tory playwright who will lead British
    drama back to the drawing room) and that he
    intends to work in many different theatrical
    conventions. In what seems to be an effort to
    blunt in advance the attacks of his harshest
    critics, he adds that "progress is the falsest of all
    the gods . . . [and] 'contemporary' is the most
    meaningless of all criteria."

75. [Shaffer, Peter.] "A Playwright's Twisty Road Toward
    Success." *Life* 21 Mar. 1960: 97.
    A short piece, presented by an anonymous
    interviewer, relating some biographical
    information on "an amiable but crusty young
    man."

76. Shaffer, Peter. "The Cannibal Theatre." *Atlantic* 206.4
    (Oct. 1960): 48-50.
    Shaffer reflects on his encounters with actors,
    contending that there is "a deep, grave
    antagonism between" playwrights and performers.
    The actor, he says, tends to disparage the
    importance of the dramatist and, if given his way,
    will alter text and stage directions mercilessly,
    bending them in the direction of "performance

values." For Shaffer, the playwright is the
proverbial "baker," and the actor the "hungry
boy." Though he confesses to having been
appalled by the spectacle of his works being
cannibalized by their interpreters, Shaffer admits
that he relies on the actors for his ultimate
success and considers it a playwright's duty "to
write good parts."

B. "SHAFFER ON SHAFFER," 1963-1967

77. [Shaffer, Peter.] "The Brains Behind the 'Eye' and 'Ear.'"
    Boston Sunday Herald 29 Sept. 1963: section
    4; 3.
        In an interview conducted by Elinor Hughes
    during the pre-Broadway tryout of *Private Ear/
    Public Eye* in Boston, Shaffer discusses re-
    writes made for the U.S. production. Some have
    been devised to "get the laughs" from American
    audiences, others have evolved in response to
    cast changes.

78. [Shaffer, Peter.] "Peter Shaffer Interviewed by Barry Pree."
    Transatlantic Review 14 (Autumn 1963):
    62-66.
        Although this interview took place shortly
    before the transferral of *Private Ear/Public
    Eye* from London to Broadway, generalities and
    future projects, rather than the double bill,
    dominate the discussions. Shaffer describes his
    working habits (four months to write a script,
    with "lots and lots" of drafts). He admits to
    lacking a strong, individualized personality
    ("something of a chameleon . . . I haven't a
    specific personality") and comments briefly on

other playwrights (Osborne ruined his career by
allowing the "Angry Young Man" label to stick,
Beckett is admirable, Ionesco's works are "all
slight, repetitious"). Another item of interest, and
in retrospect a surprising one (considering the
future success of his three highly theatrical
works), is Shaffer's remark, "I've no visual
imagination." In the final paragraph of the
interview, he announces a new project, a play
"based on the Goethe Faust legend . . . called
Om [which] uses a Brechtian technique." [This
work has apparently never been completed, at
least not in a form satisfying to the author.]

79. [Shaffer, Peter.] "Peter Shaffer's Personal 'Dialogue.'"
    New York Times 6 Oct. 1963: section 2; 1, 3.
       This piece was submitted as an alternative to
    the *Times'* request for an article by Shaffer on
    the occasion of the Broadway opening of
    Ear/Eye. In an editorial note, it is described as
    the outcome of the playwright's agreeing to "free
    associate to an Obliging Friend." Among other
    subjects, he discusses his preference for Mozart's
    Così Fan Tutte over *Don Giovanni* (perhaps
    giving us an early glimpse of interests which led
    to *Amadeus*); the barren morality he
    encountered in his youth among many English
    churchgoers (a thread later developed in
    Equus); and his dislike of being narrowly
    categorized as a playwright ("Writers are too
    easily dropped into labeled drawers where they
    languish, accused of sterility if they seem
    content, or of abusing their proper talent if they
    seek to escape").

80. [Shaffer, Peter.] "Shaffer Takes Up a Cause." *New York
    Morning Telegraph* 5 Nov. 1963: 2.

Jack Gaver interviews Shaffer with an
emphasis on the recently opened double bill of
Private Ear and *Public Eye*. The headline
refers to Gaver's (rather playful) suggestion that,
in *Public Eye*, Shaffer comes out "in behalf of
the cause of non-communication." The playwright
confirms that one of his "points" in the play is
that, in today's society, there is "too much talk
. . . [and] too little communication."

81. [Shaffer, Peter.] "Silence Is Playwright's Golden Rule."
   Sunday Star-Ledger (Newark) 10 Nov. 1963:
   section 2; 6.
   This interview by Jack Gaver is essentially the
   same as that printed a few days earlier in the
   New York Morning Telegraph [see #80
   above].

82. [Shaffer, Peter.] "Shaffer and the Incas." *Plays and
   Players* Apr. 1964: 12-13.
   Prior to the Chichester opening of *Royal
   Hunt*, John Russell Taylor interviews Shaffer,
   who discusses his new play, his previous works
   and his future plans. He explains that *Royal
   Hunt* is "about two men: one of them is an
   atheist, and the other is a god," and confirms the
   rumor that it will have an unusually large cast
   ("I'm quite Victorian in my taste for theatrical
   spectacle"). Later in the interview, Shaffer
   mentions that he is at work adapting *The Public
   Eye* for the screen and "rather enjoying it." The
   "horrors" of the film version of *Five Finger
   Exercise* convinced him that "next time I'd
   better write the script myself."

83. [Shaffer, Peter, et al.] "Artaud for Artaud's Sake." *Encore*
   11 (May-June 1964): 20-31.

This is the edited transcript of a discussion
among Peter Shaffer, Peter Hall, Peter Brook,
and Michel St.-Denis, moderated by Charles
Marowitz. The discussion followed a public
reading from Artaud's works, as part of the
"Theatre of Cruelty" program at the London
Academy of Music and Dramatic Art. Shaffer's
remarks (on the eve of the opening of *Royal
Hunt*) place him in the camp of those who find
Artaud's writings stimulating but who
passionately disagree with certain of his opinions.
He argues, for example, "When [Artaud] says the
psychological drama is dead, this seems to me to
be absolutely rubbish—it has hardly begun." Later
in the proceedings, Shaffer expresses a concern
for the future of mid-20th century playwriting.
He concedes, on the one hand, that "the modern
theater . . . has elaborated the most stunning
techniques, certainly verbally—Pinter is the
obvious example of this extraordinary
musicianship in writing." But he fears that, with
each technical advance, "the scale becomes more
and more miniature, more and more private,
there's a kind of retreat into fetish and sex-games
with your wife . . . " Shaffer characterizes such
tendencies as "merely a matter of history." In
another fifteen years, he predicts, there will be
an entirely different trend for playwrights to
follow or explode.

84. [Shaffer, Peter, with anonymous interviewer.] "London
    Diary." *Evening Standard* (London) 8 July
    1964: 6.
       Shaffer comments on his motives for writing
    The Royal Hunt of the Sun (to restore
    spectacle to the theatre; to enrich it with spiritual
    significance and intellectual challenge).

85. Shaffer, Peter. "In Search of a God." *Plays and Players* Oct. 1964: 22.
    This is a shortened version of the interview with John Russell Taylor which first appeared in the April issue [see #82 above]. It is reprinted here as a preface to the text of *The Royal Hunt of the Sun* [Act One appears in the October issue; Act Two, in the November issue].

86. Shaffer, Peter. "To See the Soul of a Man. " *New York Times* 24 Oct. 1965: section 2; 3.
    This piece was written by Shaffer to coincide with the Broadway opening of *Royal Hunt*. He clarifies his concept of "total theatre" from the perspective of the playwright: "I mean . . . a theater that is gestural as well as verbal, hallucinatory as well as cerebral magical, if that word isn't now too debased to use." Shaffer uses as the title of his piece the beginning of a phrase from Genet, which he quotes in the final paragraph: "To see the soul of a man is to be blinded by the sun."

87. [Shaffer, Peter.] "A Playwright's Critique." *Newsday* (Long Island, NY) 6 Nov. 1965: 37W.
    In an interview conducted by George Oppenheimer shortly after the Broadway opening of *The Royal Hunt of the Sun*, Shaffer discourses on a variety of topics: his attitude toward reviewers (he thinks they have "an animus against story" and "a certain contempt for the well-made play"); the staggering economics of the Broadway theater (he vows he will never open a new play in New York as the cost is prohibitive); and the nature of the American audience ("fails to make up its own mind . . . waits for the critics"). Shaffer draws a comparison between London and New York as theatre capitals: London is the heart of 20th century theater (in terms of drama), and New York is the heart of 20th century theater (in terms of technical wizardry), but

each lags a century behind the other in the opposite
sphere.

88. [Shaffer, Peter.] "A Playwright in a Hurry." *Louisville
Courier-Journal* 7 Nov. 1965: page no. not available.
A brief interview conducted (in New York) by
Phyllis Funke, prior to the opening of *The Public Eye*
at the Actors Theatre of Louisville. Perhaps most
interesting is a statement of Shaffer's values: "The
things that count in life are the ability to rise above the
limits of your birth, your breadth of view, your refusal
to be cowed by authority . . . and kindness and taste."

89. [Shaffer, Peter, interviewed by Barbara Gelb.] " . . . And
Its Author." *New York Times* 14 Nov. 1965: section 2;
1, 2, 4.
This companion piece to Taubman's review ["About
A Royal Hunt," see #340] is one of the most
informative and entertaining profiles of Shaffer in print.
Gelb not only details the progress of the playwright's
life and career in considerable detail, she also paints a
vivid picture of the man himself, pacing and smoking
restlessly throughout the interview, addressing his
interviewer as "Luv" and "Dahling," and repeatedly
referring to this-and-that as being "mahvelous." During
the course of the session Shaffer remarks, "I deeply
resent all churches . . . I despise them. No church or
shrine or synagogue has ever failed to misuse its
power." He also characterizes New York as a place he
"would enjoy living in" but which, as a playwright, he
finds "impossible . . . strangely indifferent to theatrical
experience . . . a theatrical sepulcher."

90. [Shaffer, Peter.] "English Playwright Finds New York Is
His Real Home." *Boston Herald* 11 Jan. 1967: C33.
An interview with Samuel Hirsh during *Black
Comedy*'s Boston tryout features some of Shaffer's
thoughts on writing farces and his attitudes toward

audiences (his impulse is always, he says, "toward giving an audience a good time").

C. "SHAFFER ON SHAFFER," 1968-1972

91. [Shaffer, Peter.] "Shaffer's Ambitions." *Times* (London) 21 Feb. 1968: 10.
    In a conversation with an unidentified interviewer on the eve of the London re-opening of *Black Comedy* (paired for the first time in that city with *The White Liars*), Shaffer rather frivolously divulges three "secret ambitions": to direct, to write a musical, and to become, once again, a music critic.

92. [Shaffer, Peter.] "What the Riots Did to Peter Shaffer." *Evening Standard* (London) 9 Jan. 1970: 20-21.
    In this interview conducted by Edward Sydney prior to the opening of *The Battle of Shrivings*, Shaffer reveals that his experiences in America during the 1960s (presumably while working on one or more Broadway productions of his earlier plays) contributed to the philosophical duel that is the basis of *The Battle of Shrivings*. A major starting-point of the play, he explains, was his having observed at first hand "the riots at Columbia University." Shaffer also mentions plans to begin writing a screenplay for *White Liars*. Unhappy with previous film treatments of his works, he now resolves "to be involved."

93. [Shaffer, Peter and Anthony.] "News in the Arts." *Sunday Times* (London) 1 Feb. 1970: 51.
    A brief news story, based in part on Kenneth Pearson's interview with both Shaffer twins, on the upcoming West End openings, one week apart, of *The Battle of Shrivings* and (Anthony Shaffer's) *Sleuth*.

Mention is made of the Shaffers' early collaborations on mystery novels ("Tony provided the plot, Peter did the words").

94. [Shaffer, Peter.] "Barry Pree Interviews Peter Shaffer." In *Behind the Scenes: Theater and Film Interviews from the Transatlantic Review.* Ed. by Joseph F. McCrindle. New York: Holt, Rinehart & Winston, 1971. Pree's *Transatlantic Review* interview [see #78] is reprinted on pages 205-210.

95. [Shaffer, Peter and Anthony.] "Which Twin Has the Tony?: Broadway Greets Twin Playwrights Peter and Tony Shaffer." *After Dark* Apr. 1971: 21-23.
    An interview with Peter and Anthony Shaffer, conducted in New York by Glenn Loney, not long after the successful Broadway opening of Anthony's *Sleuth* (and while Peter was "between projects," his most recent play having been the sadly disappointing *The Battle of Shrivings*). Peter discusses:
    (a) his attitude toward puzzle-solving and game-playing (unlike Anthony, he dislikes both)
    (b) the cancellation by CBS of a teleplay he had written ("too expensive to produce")
    (c) his experiments with LSD in the early 1960s (he would like to write a play "about the Faustian bargain, using lysergic technique to express . . . expanded consciousness")
    (d) the basic idea behind *The Battle of Shrivings* ("a debate on the perfectibility of man")
    (e) his hope that "Merrick will do [*The Battle of Shrivings*]" next season in New York
    (f) his growing conviction that "the profoundest questions cannot be stated in the form of a dialectic"
    (g) his belief that Freud "has had the most disastrous influence on the theatre."

D. "SHAFFER ON SHAFFER," 1973-1977

96. [Shaffer, Peter.] "Philip Oaks Talks to Peter Shaffer."
    Sunday Times (London) 29 July 1973: 33.
        Shaffer is interviewed a week after the triumphant
    London opening of *Equus*. He admits that receiving
    "the worst notices of his career" for *The Battle of
    Shrivings* "was like driving into a brick wall at a
    hundred miles an hour" but that eventually he pulled
    himself together and decided to "get on with the next
    one." The playwright reveals the genesis of *Equus* as a
    story told him by his friend, the late James Mossman;
    he also admits that he "doesn't even know if the story
    was true." During the course of this interview, Shaffer
    mentions two items that he has rarely discussed in
    print:
    (1) He believes that "farce has been destroyed by
        [our] permissive society . . . [relying as it does
        on] people whose conventional standards are
        being assaulted by some awful embarrassment."
    (2) He has written a [yet unproduced] script for
        CBS-TV based on his own experiences in taking
        LSD "some years back"; he describes "the last
        hour of the play" as a depiction of an
        hallucinatory trip: "the professor goes back into
        . . . the history of the world, in which he
        becomes ape and wolf and ends by experiencing
        a kind of rebirth."

97. Shaffer, Peter [interviewed by Christopher Ford]. "High
    Horse." *Manchester Guardian* 6 Aug. 1973: 8.
        The interviewer's focus is on the recently opened
    Equus ("enjoying a major success at the National").
    Shaffer deplores the "second-rate, dreary, passionless"
    nature of most current British theatre and says, given
    the tepid stage fare, he'd "rather go to the pictures." He
    expresses admiration for theatricality on a grand scale:

"If it's a farce, let it be a big, screaming farce. If it's an
epic, let it be big . . . " These principles are embodied in
the style and staging of his latest play. He also offers
interesting insight into the theme of *Equus*: "People's
private glories are so often related to their private
miseries . . . if you take away one, you may take away
the other."

98. Shaffer, Peter. "What We Owe Britten." *Sunday Times*
    (London) 18 Nov. 1973: 35.
    Shaffer's tribute to composer Benjamin Britten is
    based on two personal anecdotes. The first is a
    description of the impact made on him when, as a
    young man, he "accidentally" tuned in a radio
    performance of Britten's opera *Peter Grimes* and
    discovered a work so compelling that "nothing . . . in
    the spoken theatre has" ever affected him "more
    powerfully." The second tells of a chance meeting with
    Britten. It might be said that Shaffer reveals a good
    deal about himself in the course of his "appreciation."
    He says, for example: "Britten has always been a show-
    off. I adore him for that. I love the dazzle of his
    technical solutions . . . the truth is, you can never be
    clever enough."

99. [Shaffer, Peter.] "Equus: Not for the Horsey Set."
    Women's Wear Daily 10 Sept. 1974: 44.
    Howard Kissel interviews the playwright over lunch
    at Sardi's. Much of Shaffer's talk is devoted to the
    unusual staging techniques used in *Equus* and director
    John Dexter's contributions to them (the bare stage, the
    treatment of the "horses," the masks, and the onstage
    seating of the audience). In a more general vein, he
    goes on to say: "A lot of people . . . think a serious play
    has a specific message. But if a play has a message that
    can be abstracted to a single formula, it's not very good
    . . . A serious play . . . must in some area be about

conjuring the gods." [This interview was published
under a different title ten days later. See #100 below.]

100. [Shaffer, Peter.] "Horse Sense." *Women's Wear Daily*
20 Sept. 1974: page no. not available.
A reprint, under a different title, of Kissel's earlier
interview [listed as #99 above].

101. [Shaffer, Peter, interviewed by Mel Gussow.] "Shaffer
Details a Mind's Journey in Equus." *New York Times*
24 Oct. 1974: 50.
In an interview on the eve of the Broadway opening
of his new play, Shaffer discourses at length on the
nature of *Equus* ("a 'whydunit' . . . [but] it's intended
to be much more than that"). He traces the process of
writing it, from its genesis, through consultations with
an eminent, unnamed child psychiatrist, through re-
writes ("I'm a very obsessive tearer-upper, relentless"),
to the opening in New York. He addresses the
complaints of certain critics who claim that, in *Equus*,
he legitimizes all forms of excess in the name of holy
ecstasy: "I'm not giving a blanket endorsement of
passion . . . if 'your own thing' is destructive and
appalling, it has to be stopped." Shaffer also mentions
some writing projects which have not, to the present
date, found their way to fruition: "a political play . . . a
double bill . . . a pure comedy [entitled] 'The Syllabub
Saloon.'"

102. [Shaffer, Peter.] "A Playwright's Role." *New York Post*
12 Dec. 1974: 45.
In the course of this interview conducted by Jerry
Tallmer, Shaffer provides information on his early life,
his family, and various aspects of his career, including
the incidents which inspired the writing of *Royal
Hunt* and *Equus*. Of interest is the playwright's
admission, "I still have very little self-confidence."

103. Shaffer, Peter. Comments on Equus. *Vogue* Feb. 1975: 136-137, 192.

 Shaffer makes a connection between his play and Jung's ideas about archetypes and the collective unconscious. He affirms that, for him, the theatre must provide "an alarming and ecstatic" experience. "And," he adds, "a beautiful one."

104. [Shaffer, Peter.] "'Write Me,' Said the Play to Peter Shaffer." *New York Times Magazine* 13 Apr. 1975: 20-21, 25-26, 28, 30, 32, 34, 37-38, 40.

 This is the lengthy report of an interview conducted by Tom Buckley. Though Shaffer discusses in some detail relations with his family, especially with his twin brother Anthony, most of his remarks concern the recently opened *Equus*. He expresses anger over the attack made on *Equus* by Dr. Sanford Gifford [see #588]. He also admits having experimented with LSD on three occasions in the 1960s. One such experiment resulted in an exhilarating, imaginary journey through time to the Bronze Age and earlier—an experience he considers partly responsible for the genesis of Equus (presumably the play's "Dionysiac" element).

105. [Shaffer, Peter.] "Peter Shaffer on Faith, Farce and Masks." *Listener* (London) 96.2479 (14 Oct. 1976): 476-477.

 In this transcript of a BBC-2 interview conducted by Peter Adam, Shaffer responds to questions provoked by the recent success of *Equus*, including a wide range of topics relating to his writing in general. He confesses that he is often unaware of what critics later see as the "themes" of his work until after he has read what others have to say about it. He states that the art of story-telling in the theatre is one he prizes and which is currently under-valued. Finally, he touches briefly on his working methods (saying that he re-writes a script 20-30 times) and his fondness for non-naturalistic devices such as masks.

106. Shaffer, Peter. "A Note on *Equus*." A United Artists press release, circulated as "Preliminary Production Notes," for promotion of the film; undated (presumably 1976 or 1977); 2 pages (photocopy in Clippings file, Billy Rose Theatre Collection, Lincoln Center branch, New York Public Library).
   Shaffer divulges how he first heard about the actual "alarming crime" which inspired the play. Also of interest is his revelation that, while writing the stage version, he "enjoyed the advice and expert comment of a distinguished child psychologist," through whose assistance he "tried to keep things real in a more naturalistic sense."

107. [Shaffer, Peter.] "Equus—From Play to Film." *New York Post* 15 Oct. 1977: 31.
   Tom Topor interviews Shaffer (and, briefly, *Equus* actor Peter Firth) around the time of the film's opening. Shaffer comments on the transition to a new medium, or "how a highly artificial piece of theater became (more or less) a naturalistic film." He hints that he is not entirely pleased with Lumet's decision "not to ritualize things" (for which he believes there are cinematic precedents in the work of Eisenstein and others). The use of real horses constitutes the principal difference between the two versions of his work, he says. The masks used in the stage play had to be discarded to obey the screen's intrinsic demand for naturalism: "There's something about the lens of a camera that seems to cut off the vibrations emitted by masks." In elaborating on this point, he describes the potential power of ritualistic devices in the live theatre: " . . . to me [masks] are like radar screens—they bounce back at the audience the imaginative vibrations the audience itself is emitting."

E. "SHAFFER ON SHAFFER," 1978-1982

108. Shaffer, Peter. "Figure of Death." *Observer* (London) 4
     Nov. 1979: 37.
     Shaffer comments on images that haunted him and
     became the bases for three plays: the Incas watching
     through the night in search of their resurrected sun
     god, a boy stabbing at the eyes of a multitude of
     horses, and Mozart surrounded by three shadowy
     personages, including a "messenger of death," the
     messenger's assistant, and Mozart's wife.

109. [Shaffer, Peter.] "Psychic Energy." *Plays and Players*
     27.5 (Feb. 1980): 11-13.
     In this interview with Colin Chambers, Shaffer
     discusses his work on *Amadeus*. He also imparts
     considerable information about his early life and the
     entire progress of his career as a dramatist. Chambers
     concludes (crossing the line of "polite objectivity"
     which his U.S. counterparts seem to hold sacred) by
     attempting to account for the source of Shaffer's
     immense popularity despite what the interviewer
     considers his easily recognized deficiencies. "His
     melodrama," he writes, "captures a mood of despair
     and says 'do not worry.'" Chambers finally confesses
     that he does not understand Shaffer's success (and
     here he sounds rather like the playwright's most
     prominent American detractors, John Simon and
     Robert Brustein): "The amazing thing is that [Shaffer]
     gets so many people to applaud not the recognition of
     a common, resilient humanity, but of a shared,
     accepting mediocrity."

110. Shaffer, Peter. "Scripts in Trans-Atlantic Crossings May
     Suffer Two Kinds of Changes." *Dramatists Guild
     Quarterly* Spring 1980: 29-33.

An edited transcription of an informal talk
delivered by Shaffer at the annual (U.S.) Dramatists
Guild meeting held on February 26, 1980. Shaffer
describes two types of script changes: (1) those that
"audiences themselves make simply by watching plays,"
and (2) those that playwrights create in "trying to make
their work understandable or acceptable to new
audiences." His remarks, though occasioned by his
preparing *Amadeus* for Broadway, cover the entire
span of his career, beginning with the transporting of
Five Finger Exercise in 1959. (Among DG members
contributing questions or comments are Peter Stone,
Garson Kanin, Howard Richardson, Terence McNally,
and David Mamet.)

111. Shaffer, Peter. "Amadeus: A New Version " *Playbill*
June 1981: 6-10.
The playwright contributes a brief article on the
methods by which he arrived at script revisions for the
Broadway production of *Amadeus*. He expresses
gratitude for the contributions made by director Peter
Hall and leading actors Ian McKellen and Tim Curry,
especially during the tryout period in Washington, D.C.

112. [Shaffer, Peter.] "Shaffer: Why I Changed *Amadeus*."
New Standard (London) 12 June 1981: 29.
Based on a chat with an anonymous interviewer, this
is a brief report on the impending London re-opening
of Amadeus, with its post-Broadway revisions. Shaffer
identifies three goals: (1) to soften some of Mozart's
foul language, (2) to strengthen Salieri's plotting
against Mozart, and (3) to build a more powerful final
confrontation between the two principals. He also
mentions that an idea for a new play has been
suggested by his work on *Amadeus*. It would concern
a great man's widow who is left in charge of preserving
her husband's reputation.

113. [Shaffer, Peter.] Interview with Shaffer, John Wood and
     Mark Hamill. *Drama-Logue* (Hollywood) 16 Dec.
     1982: 1, 12.
         An anonymous interviewer reports on a
     conversation with the author and with the stars of the
     touring company of *Amadeus*. Shaffer mentions that
     there are two qualities in his work which he is "pleased
     to have noticed . . . a touch of symbolism and a
     resoundingly symphonic musical sense."

F. "SHAFFER ON SHAFFER," 1983-1990

114. [Shaffer, Peter and Anthony.] "Double Vision." *Sunday
     Telegraph* (London) 6 Jan. 1984: magazine section;
     26-29.
         The twin playwrights are interviewed by P.J.
     Kavanagh. They reminisce on their early lives (both,
     for instance, were "Bevin Boys," conscripted into
     World War II service in the mines). Peter Shaffer also
     comments on his most painful failure (*The Battle of
     Shrivings*, in which, he concedes, "perhaps argument
     preceded character") and his most valued success
     (*Equus*, which he calls his "private play").

115. [Shaffer, Peter.] "Mostly *Amadeus*." *Horizon* 27.7
     (Sept. 1984): 49-52.
         During the filming of *Amadeus* in Prague, Ronald
     Gelatt conducts an interview that supplies much
     interesting information. Shaffer expresses unhappiness
     with all previous film versions of his plays. Among
     other things, he expounds on his relativist
     philosophical stance: "It seems to me a near-
     impossibility to take a final position on anything that
     really matters." He also modestly commits himself to

the ongoing goal of writing "a really good play one day."

116. Shaffer, Peter. "Mostly Mozart: Making the Screen Speak." *Film Comment* 20.5 (1984): 50.
    Shaffer discusses basic differences in writing for stage and film. He also describes the collaborative processes he and director Milos Forman used in refashioning *Amadeus* for the screen.

117. Shaffer, Peter. "A Note on Writing the Film of *Amadeus*." Circulated as a press release from the Saul Zaentz Company for promotion of the film; undated (presumably 1984); 3 pages (photocopy in Clippings file, Billy Rose Theatre Collection, Lincoln Center branch, New York Public Library).
    Shaffer recounts the story of the four months ("five days a week, twelve hours a day") he spent sequestered in a Connecticut farmhouse, working out a shooting script with director Milos Forman. The premise on which they operated was one suggested by Forman: "A film based on a play is actually a new work." Shaffer writes that he intends the motion picture version, even less than the play, to be "a biography of the composer." It is to be, rather, "a fantasia on themes from Mozart's life."

118. [Shaffer, Peter, interviewed by John Higgins.] "The Challenge of Jumping into the Unknown." *Times* (London) 28 Nov. 1985: 15.
    A week prior to the opening of *Yonadab*, Shaffer describes finding the basic material for the drama in Dan Jacobson's novel, *The Rape of Tamar*, and discusses his own aims in adapting it. He suggests that a play is built to a great extent on the foundation of the playwright's past experiences: " . . . what you have learnt, what you like." He also admits that, in contrast to his approach to *Amadeus*, he conducted scant

research on the historical period and persons depicted in *Yonadab*.

119. [Shaffer, Peter.] "From *Amadeus* to King David."
    Women's Wear Daily 27 Dec. 1985: 16.
        An interview conducted by James Fallon shortly
    after the opening of *Yonadab*. Shaffer discusses the
    processes of conceiving, writing and revising the new
    script. He refers to his earlier works and his
    commitment to extending the theatre's vocabulary in
    the areas of both themes and stagecraft: "As a
    playwright, my obligation is to expand the element in
    which plays exist, through the design, the sound of it,
    the music . . ."

120. [Shaffer, Peter.] "Out to Lunch." *Vanity Fair* May 1986:
    136.
        In this luncheon interview with Peter Buckley,
    Shaffer speaks of his currently running work *Yonadab*
    (and refers to the title role as "one of my outside
    figures"). He also predicts that, despite the great
    success of *Amadeus*, he has no real future in the
    movie world. Writing directly for the screen doesn't
    interest him, he says, because he is "continually baffled
    by the literal."

121. Shaffer, Peter. "Mozart: Just When You Felt You Were
    Sure" [Letter to the Editor]. *Sunday Times* (London)
    14 Sept. 1986: 35.
        Shaffer corrects a remark made by reviewer Patrick
    Stoddart in reference to a recent BBC-TV program,
    "The Mozart Inquest." Shaffer writes: "If . . . Stoddart
    had ever seen or read [*Amadeus*], he would know
    that I declared in it most emphatically that Salieri did
    not kill Mozart." The playwright further states that he
    does "not believe that Mozart was killed at all."

122. [Shaffer, Peter.] "Quest for Perfection." *Drama* 159 (Winter 1986): 11-15.

The focus of this interview with Clare Colvin is the recently opened *Yonadab*. Shaffer discusses why and how he wrote the play, his extensive re-writes, and his functioning during rehearsals. In the final paragraphs, Shaffer expresses his fondness for "big plays" and explains why, in his opinion, audiences share that fondness: "People . . . go to the theatre to be surprised, to watch the colour and effect, to have their imaginative muscle worked . . . I think it is one of our jobs as playwrights to exercise that muscle."

123. [Shaffer, Peter.] "Shaffer's Pen." *Plays and Players* no. 410 (Nov. 1987): 6-8.

The occasion of Claire Armistead's interview is the impending London premiere of *Lettice and Lovage*. Shaffer says that he "wrote the play as a present to . . . [actress] Maggie Smith" (with whom he had not worked since *Private Ear/Public Eye* in the early 1960s) and "presented it to her over tea one afternoon." Later in the interview, he comments on his early aspirations and unexpected successes. He also predicts— incorrectly, as he did 15 years earlier in the case of *The Battle of Shrivings* [see entry #95]—that *Yonadab* will be staged on Broadway "next season."

124. [Shaffer, Peter, interviewed by Peter Lewis.] "And Finally, Another Rewrite." *Times* (London) 22 Oct. 1988: 32.

This interview focuses on re-writes Shaffer has introduced for cast replacements in *Lettice and Lovage* in London. Although he breaks no new ground, a wide range of topics is covered: his interest in improving his scripts, even if they have been judged critical and popular successes; his preference for the boldly theatrical epic over realistic drama; and the progress of his career from early collaborations with

his twin brother Anthony to his major successes *Five
Finger Exercise, The Royal Hunt of the Sun,
Black Comedy, Equus,* and *Amadeus* [no
mention being made of *The Private Ear, The
Public Eye, White Liars, The Battle of
Shrivings,* or *Yonadab*].

125. [Shaffer, Peter.] "Peter's Principles." *Vanity Fair* April
1990: 110-114.
     John Heilpern interviews Shaffer in London, prior
to the Broadway opening of *Lettice and Lovage.*
Included are comments by several of Shaffer's
colleagues and friends—John Gielgud, Maggie Smith,
Simon Callow—and an account of "an elegant dinner
party in Manhattan a while ago," during which Shaffer
vigorously disputed New York Shakespeare Festival
Director Joe Papp's contention that English
Shakespearean acting was artificial and unsuited to
American productions of the Bard's works. The
information supplied by Heilpern is not specifically
related to *Lettice.* It is, rather, biographical.
Although several amusing anecdotes are related, the
material is scanty and not especially revealing. We
learn, for instance, that Shaffer is "one of the
[wealthiest] dramatists of our time" and collects "solid
eighteenth-century English oak, Ruskin watercolors, a
few antique prints." We also get a brief review of
events which have been recounted elsewhere. These
include Shaffer's service during World War II as a
conscripted "Bevin Boy" in the mines, his early mystery
novel collaborations with his twin brother Anthony,
and his succession of jobs prior to the success of *Five
Finger Exercise.* The article does little to remedy its
own contention: "For so famous a man . . . little has
really been known about [Peter Shaffer]."

Chapter Three

Early Works—Novels, Radio and Television Plays, Pantomime

The materials grouped in this chapter are "minor works." Several are unpublished. One has been "lost."

MYSTERY NOVELS

126. Anthony, Peter [pseudonym for Peter Shaffer]. *The Woman in the Wardrobe.* London: Evans, 1951.

127. Anthony, Peter [pseudonym for collaborators Peter and Anthony Shaffer]. *How Doth the Little Crocodile?* London: Evans, 1952; New York: Macmillan, 1957.

128. Shaffer, A[nthony] and P[eter]. *Withered Murder.* London: Gollancz, 1955; New York: Macmillan, 1958.

WORKS FOR TELEVISION

129. Shaffer, Peter. *The Salt Land*. First broadcast on ITV (London), 8 Nov. 1955. Unpublished.

130. Shaffer, Peter. *Balance of Terror*. First broadcast on BBC-TV (London), 21 Nov. 1957. Script lost.

131. Shaffer, Peter. "But My Dear" and "The President of France." In *That Was the Week That Was*. Ed. by David Frost and Ned Sherrin. London: W.H. Allen, 1963.

WORK FOR RADIO

132. Shaffer, Peter. *The Prodigal Father*. First broadcast on BBC-Radio (London), 14 Sept. 1957. Unpublished.

A CHISTMAS ENTERTAINMENT WITH MUSIC

133. "The Merry Roosters' Panto." Songs by Stanley Myers. First Produced at Wyndham's Theatre, 19 Dec. 1963. Directed by Joan Littlewood. Performed at matinees by the cast of *Oh, What a Lovely War*. Unpublished.

REVIEWS OF THE MYSTERY NOVELS

134. Boucher, Anthony. Review of *Withered Murder*. *New York Times* 11 March 1956: 26-27.
       This is a review of the first published effort of "A. and P. Shaffer," which is described as an "attempt [at] a formal detective story in the classic Grand Manner . . . [with] a flamboyantly eccentric Great Detective." The reviewer does not judge the attempt successful: "Unfortunately, the wit of Mr. Fathom . . . is more rude than penetrating, his detection more lucky than astute; and the trick solution is both banal and preposterous." However, Boucher concedes that "the writing is often literally [sic] amusing."

135. Boucher, Anthony. Review of *How Doth the Little Crocodile? New York Times* 3 March 1957: 31.
       Boucher finds *Little Crocodile* "far better" than *Withered Murder*. A noteworthy improvement is "[the] truly distinguished puzzle-plot . . . with an ingenious virtuosity . . . which suggests Christie or Queen."

REVIEW OF TELEPLAY

136. Parser, Philip. "A Tale of the Treble Bluff Among the Spies." *Daily Chronicle* (London) 22 Nov. 1957: page no. not available.
       This brief review describes Shaffer's *A Balance of Terror* as "up to the minute in theme but old-fashioned in flavor."

REVIEWS OF THE PANTOMIME

137. Anon. "Pantomime by Stealth . . . 'The Merry Roosters'
     Panto.'" *Times* (London) 20 Dec. 1963: 5.
       For those interested in collecting obscure bits of
     Shaffer trivia, this review may prove to be of interest.
     It lists the principal roles (Cinderella, the Duchess of
     Margate, and A Television Set, among others) in this
     outlandish version of a familiar tale, and the actors
     who assayed them (the best known probably being
     Victor Spinetti as Eartha, one of Cinderella's "ugly
     sisters"). Also identified are the composer and lyricist
     (Stanley Myers and Steven Vinaver). The reviewer
     complains that the evening "suffers from too many
     private jokes . . . and a short-windedness of
     invention." He finds, on the other hand, that,
     "although many ideas are allowed to expire before
     they have established themselves theatrically, the
     ideas themselves are often brilliant."

138. Anon. Review of "The Merry Roosters' Panto." *Observer*
     (London) 22 Dec. 1963: 14.
       A generally favorable report accompanied by a
     caveat: "Private and progressive jokes may deter some
     parents, but plenty of audience participation for non-
     political children."

139. Darlington, W.A. Review of "The Merry Roosters' Panto."
     Daily Telegraph (London) 20 Dec. 1963: 13.
       Darlington finds the show "very acceptable" for
     children.

140. Hope-Wallace, Philip. "Joan Littlewood's Panto."
     Manchester Guardian 20 Dec. 1963: 7.
       Hope-Wallace approves of the Littlewood version
     of the Cinderella story, which he describes as "very
     different from the nostalgic early Victoriana" of the

other Christmas season pantomimes on view in London. He particularly appreciates the fact that it "happily avoids sentimentality and whimsicality: bane of the season." Shaffer's contribution to the proceedings is not mentioned.

141. Kretzmer, Herbert. Review of "The Merry Roosters' Panto." *Daily Express* (London) 20 Dec. 1963: 4.
A favorable appraisal.

142. Shulman, Milton. Review of "The Merry Roosters' Panto." *Evening Standard* (London) 20 Dec. 1963: 4.
Shulman enjoys the pantomime, which he speculates is more likely to please adults than children.

143 Worsley, T.C. Review of "The Merry Roosters' Panto." *Financial Times* (London) 20 Dec. 1963: 18.
Worsley finds the pantomime a total failure. Shaffer's name is not mentioned.

Chapter Four

Five Finger Exercise

THE TEXT

144. *The Collected Plays of Peter Shaffer.* New York: Harmony Books, 1982.

Contains the texts of each of Shaffer's plays through *Amadeus.* (*White Liars,* the third version of the work originally titled *White Lies* and the playwright's preferred rendering, is printed here). Shaffer has provided a twelve-page preface, in which he comments on various aspects of his career and the individual plays. Also included is a reprint of the playwright's preface to the published edition of *Shrivings.*

145. Shaffer, Peter. "Five Finger Exercise." *Theatre Arts* Feb. 1961: 27-56.

The complete text of the play, preceded by a brief note about the playwright.

146. Shaffer, Peter. *Five Finger Exercise*. New York: Harcourt, Brace & Co., 1959.
     The preface to this edition is written by the co-producer of the U.S. production, Frederick Brisson [see #199 below].

PLAY REVIEWS

A. Reviews: Original London Production. The Comedy Theatre, July 16, 1958.

147. Anon. "Children vs. Parents: Subtle Play at the Comedy." *Times* (London) 17 July 1958: 4.
     Shaffer's writing is given high marks for the most part ("dialogue of a lightly rippling subtlety"). The reviewer contends, however, that the characters of the two parents prove unsatisfactory, especially the father, who is thought "too stupid to be plausible."

148. Anon. "Dinner with the Family." *Times Literary Supplement* (London) 2 Jan. 1959: page no. not available.
     The reviewer defends the playwright against those who may think his work too glibly contrived: "Mr. Shaffer cares very much about all his characters, and he convinces us that they are worth our sympathies." The script, beyond the "splendid" production it has received, is judged "a work of art in its own right."

149. Anon. "Five Finger Exercise: Re-Interpretation of a Fine Play." *Times* (London) 22 Sept. 1959: 13.
     The forthcoming U.S. production having necessitated a complete change of guard in the London cast, the piece is re-reviewed and found to be "a fine play . . . [which] stands up well."

150. Brien, Alan. Review of *Five Finger Exercise*.
     Spectator (London) 25 July 1958: 133-134.
     A largely favorable report, praising Shaffer for his
     objectivity and keen observation, as well as for the
     pace and "bite" of his dialogue.

151. Clurman, Harold. Review of *Five Finger Exercise*.
     Nation 16 May 1959: 461-463.
     Clurman maintains that the play "combines the new
     material of the English theatre (a reference to the
     socially conscious young British playwrights, such as
     Shelagh Delaney, whose *A Taste of Honey* he has
     also seen on this visit) with an old mode of statement."
     The "old mode" is described as the British version of
     the "well-made play," as perfected by Terence
     Rattigan. Clurman finds Shaffer's work in *Exercise*
     too glibly crafted: "The inner turbulence of the young
     generation is made somehow to echo the complacent
     moderation of the old." He reminds his readers that
     "[it was] just so [that] Pinero years ago domesticated
     Ibsen for the English."

152. Dash, Thomas R. "*Five Finger Exercise* in London."
     Women's Wear Daily 14 Aug. 1959: 21.
     Dash sees minor flaws but considers the play
     "perceptive . . . frequently affecting, drama."

153. Gibbs, Patrick. Review of *Five Finger Exercise*. *Daily
     Telegraph* (London) 17 July 1958: 10.
     A favorable reception. Shaffer is welcomed as "a
     new English playwright of undeniable and very
     individual quality, working not in the avant-garde
     idiom but in traditional style."

154. Hope-Wallace, Philip. Review of *Five Finger Exercise*.
     Manchester Guardian 17 July 1958: 5.
     Hope-Wallace calls Shaffer's play "unusually
     competent . . . [reminiscent] of Turgenev's *A Month*

in the Country [and] Mauriac's *Asmodee*." He
adds, however, that the thought uppermost in his mind
as he left the theatre was, "How hard it is to make a
play." He suggests that what is lacking in *Five Finger
Exercise* is "the ability to create sympathy." Because
of that failing, and despite its keen character analyses,
the play fails "to catch [us] up into emotional
surrender or belief."

155. Keown, Eric. Review of *Five Finger Exercise*. *Punch*
23 July 1958: 118-119.
　　　Keown applauds Shaffer's skillful writing and his
"message" but claims that the play has been
overpraised by his fellow critics.

156. M., A. "Compelling Sincerity of *Five Finger Exercise*."
Stage and Television Today (London) 24 July
1958: 9.
　　　While the reviewer expresses disappointment in the
inconclusive ending, he holds that "the only blemishes
are minor ones" and goes on to declare *Exercise* "the
best written . . . play seen in the West End for a long
time."

157. Panter-Downes, Mollie. Brief review of *Five Finger
Exercise*. *New Yorker* 6 Sept. 1958: 121.
　　　In her report on the London opening, Panter-
Downes suggests that one of Shaffer's scenes seems to
have been inspired by Noel Coward's *The Vortex*.

158. Pope, W. MacQueen. "A Promising New Dramatist Who's
Not an Angry Young Man." *Morning Telegraph*
(New York) 29 July 1958: page no. not available.
　　　Pope gives *Five Finger Exercise* a "very good"
rating and announces that "Mr. Shaffer appears to have
the makings of a really good dramatist."

159. Rich, Frank. Review of *Five Finger Exercise*. *Variety* 23 July 1958: 58.
    A mixed verdict. Shaffer is judged a playwright "of undoubted potential," and the play is deemed to be, in many respects, effective. However, Rich finds the writing uneven in tone, as if Shaffer were not sure whether he "is attempting a psychological drama or a slick comedy."

160. Shulman, Milton. Review of *Five Finger Exercise*. *Evening Standard* (London) 17 July 1958: 10.
    A largely favorable response. Shulman considers "the mercurial emotional shifts" of the characters unconvincing but applauds Shaffer for writing "with telling perception of this over-refined strata of the middle class."

161. Trewin, J.C. Review of *Five Finger Exercise*. *Illustrated London News* 2 Aug. 1958: 200.
    Trewin holds that Shaffer's felicity of language is matched by "few recent playwrights."

162. Tynan, Kenneth. Review of *Five Finger Exercise*. *Observer* (London) 20 July 1958: 13.
    Tynan claims that, despite the elegance of Shaffer's writing, his characters are "drawing-room figures in the reality of whose desperation I found it impossible to believe." The critic even maintains that, ironically, it is the playwright's "good lines . . . that make us most conscious of the surrounding falseness."

163. Walsh, Michael. Review of *Five Finger Exercise*. *Daily Express* (London) 17 July 1958: 5.
    A rave, proclaiming Shaffer a new "great" of the British theatre.

164. Worsley, T.C. "Give Me a Good Play." *New Statesman* 56 (26 July 1958): 112-113.

Shaffer's theatrical and storytelling skills are compared favorably to those of J.B. Priestly. Referring to the title of his review, Worsley explains, "I am using 'a good play' in the vulgarest sense, as Aunt Edna would use it." For this critic, who maintains, "I do not go to the theatre to be educated or to be alienated," *Exercise* proves to be satisfying fare.

165. Worsley, T.C. Review of *Five Finger Exercise*. *Financial Times* (London) 17 July 1958: 13.
   Worsley describes *Exercise* as a "good play" but one which offers nothing especially new in the way of character, setting, or theme. The drama's success is attributed to Shaffer's skills as a craftsman.

B. Reviews: New York Production.
The Music Box Theatre, December 2, 1959.

166. Anon. "Family Portrait." *Newsday* (Long Island, NY) 9 December 1959: 7C.
   A very favorable appraisal of the play, coupled with the prediction that Shaffer will "go on to writing even better [plays]."

167. Anon. Review of *Five Finger Exercise*. *Time* 74 (14 Dec. 1959): 77.
   The reviewer praises Shaffer's ability to "write sharp dialogue that is also characterizing" and commends his power to "cunningly create atmosphere and character." The play is criticized, however, for its "contrived moments and false notes." (The role of the tutor, for example, is thought to serve too many functions to be convincing.)

168. Aston, Frank. "*Five Finger Exercise* Subtle and Substantial." *World-Telegram and Sun* (New York) 3 Dec. 1959: 37.

The play is praised for its elegance and
craftsmanship and is summed up as "a good, tough
show . . . smashing." Aston includes a few notes about
Shaffer's structure: "Each character is given a turn at
making a long speech of exposition, analysis and
comment. Rather surprisingly, these recitals are of
gripping interest and lead to a climax . . . " [This item
is reprinted, along with six other reviews, in *New
York Theatre Critics' Reviews*, for which see #189
below.]

169. Atkinson, Brooks. "*Five Finger Exercise*: Music Box
Presents a Study of Britons." *New York Times* 3
Dec. 1959: 45.
The keynote of this review is high praise for
Shaffer as one who "under-writes" skillfully: "The prose
is precise . . . no gaudy phrases . . . characterizations
are subtle . . . avoids bravura scenes." He sums up the
quality of the script (and production) by avouching
that it is "not so much written as lived." [This item is
reprinted, along with six other reviews, in *New York
Theatre Critics' Reviews*, for which see #189
below.]

170. Atkinson, Brooks. "Family Affairs: Peter Shaffer's *Five
Finger Exercise* Has Been Staged by John Gielgud."
New York Times 13 Dec. 1959: section 2; 3.
In a follow-up to his opening night review, Atkinson
writes a glowing assessment of Shaffer's work in
Exercise: " . . . immaculate writing . . . a gem of
civilized theatre . . . one of [England's] most admirable
theatre works."

171. Balch, Jack. Review of *Five Finger Exercise*. *Theatre
Arts* Feb. 1960: 14-16.
In an enthusiastic endorsement of the play, Balch
describes it as "a haunting dissection of evil" with a
dramatic force that is very great.

172. Beaufort, John. Review of *Five Finger Exercise*.
     Christian Science Monitor 5 Dec. 1959: 14.
     Beaufort's opinion is favorable: " . . . an expert
     piece of dramatic craftsmanship."

173. Bolton, Whitney. "Engrossing, Adult British Import."
     Morning Telegraph (New York) 4 Dec. 1959: 2.
     An approving review, describing *Five Finger
     Exercise* as "painstaking and engrossing."

174. Chapman, John. "*Five Finger Exercise* a Doodle."
     New York Daily News 3 Dec. 1959: 79.
     Chapman, unlike the majority of New York
     reviewers, is not captivated by the subtleties of *Five
     Finger Exercise*. While he admires the intelligence
     and deftness of the writing, he uses the term "doodle"
     to describe what he considers its essential
     pointlessness. He complains that, as the scenes
     progressed, he discovered that he "wasn't giving a
     particular damn about anybody." His verdict:
     unsatisfying because "it fails to strike a major chord."
     [This item is reprinted, along with six other reviews, in
     New York Theatre Critics' Reviews, for which see
     #189 below.]

175. Clurman, Harold. Review of *Five Finger Exercise*.
     Nation 19 Dec. 1959: 475-476.
     After seeing the Broadway production, Clurman
     admits that his judgment of the original London
     version [see #151 above] may have been "too severe."
     He now commends Shaffer's work: "The writing is neat
     . . . and the sentiment honorable." He qualifies his
     praise, however, by adding that, in *Exercise*, "there
     still seems to me to be something forced and false in
     every one of the crucial plot turns—contrived either to
     make effective curtains or to drive home the play's
     'points.'" The prognosis for the fledgling playwright's
     career is nonetheless bright: "[He] will grow in stature

when he has freed himself from the symmetry of
conventional English theatrical forms and feelings."

176. Coleman, Robert. "*Five Finger Exercise* Thrilling."
     Daily Mirror (New York) 3 Dec. 1959: page no. not
     available.
     Coleman is enthusiastic in his praise for Shaffer's
     "hypnotic and fascinating . . . study of an unhappy
     family." He stresses the playwright's skillful
     craftsmanship ("the precision of a fugue") and raves
     about the direction and performances, remarking that
     "less than perfect casting could have been fatal." In
     passing, Coleman provides a piece of information
     seldom mentioned elsewhere: the person responsible
     for the play's being optioned for a New York
     production was Rosalind Russell, who no doubt saw in
     it a possible film vehicle for herself (and later turned
     the vision into reality). [This item is reprinted, along
     with six other reviews, in *New York Theatre Critics'
     Reviews*, for which see #189 below.]

177. Cooke, Richard P. "Family Drama." *Wall Street Journal*
     4 Dec. 1959: 12.
     A favorable report, referring to the work as "tightly
     and interestingly written . . . a well-made play
     [without] the somewhat glib neatness of the genre."

178. Dash, Thomas R. "*Five Finger Exercise* an Impressive
     British Import." *Women's Wear Daily* 3 Dec. 1959:
     60.
     Warmer in tone than Dash's earlier report on the
     London production [see #152]. Despite "venial faults,"
     Exercise is declared a "sterling play."

179. Driver, Tom F. "Drama Wanted: Fresh Air." *Christian
     Century* 77.1 (6 Jan. 1960): 15-16.
     In a column which also includes a review of *A
     Loss of Roses*, Driver writes that he finds Shaffer's

work superior to Inge's in both its construction and its credibility. Nevertheless, he criticizes Shaffer for not writing about important ideas as well as for failing to provide a true plot. He contends that whatever impact the play has "can be exploded forever if the spectator [only asks]: 'So what?'"

180. Field, Rowland. *"Five Finger Exercise* Is Triumphant Performance." *Newark Evening News* 3 Dec. 1959: 58.
    Field's notice is a rave: " . . . a simply wonderful play of extraordinary lucidity."

181. Hayes, Richard. Review of *Five Finger Exercise. Commonweal* 71.12 (1 Jan. 1960): 395.
    This reviewer begins on a harsh note, referring to Shaffer's work as "the queerest divertissement of serious assumption on the Broadway scene." In the end, however, Hayes concedes that the play offers points of considerable interest "to the ear and the attention, if not quite the mind."

182. Hewes, Henry. "Oedipus Wreaks." *Saturday Review* 19 Dec. 1959: 24.
    Hewes admires Shaffer's "virtuosity" but complains that the play is "seldom gripping" and "lacks a sense of inevitability."

183. Hipp, Edward Sothern. Review of *Five Finger Exercise. Newark Sunday News* 6 Dec. 1959: section 3, E6.
    A favorable review. Hipp notes that, while the play's characters all "talk and talk and talk," he finds the talk "absorbing." Exercise, he claims, lends "a touch of distinction" to the New York theater scene.

184. Kerr, Walter. Review of *Five Finger Exercise. New York Herald Tribune* 3 Dec. 1959: 18.

Kerr expresses appreciation for Shaffer's skills. He begins by revealing a personal inclination for theatrical characters who are either highly intelligent or violently passionate; but here, for the first time, he found himself "fascinated by a stageful of people who were . . . withdrawn and . . . obtuse." Kerr particularly admires the way in which the subtlety and "spareness" of Shaffer's writing lead to climaxes which "have tension, surprise and sting." [This item is reprinted, along with six other reviews, in *New York Theatre Critics' Reviews*, for which see #189 below.]

185. Lewis, Emory. Review of *Five Finger Exercise*. *Cue* 12 Dec. 1959: 9.

While he regards the play as "slight" and "not very satisfying," Lewis recognizes that Shaffer demonstrates considerable promise. Furthermore, he admits that his lack of enthusiasm may be attributable to the fact that he has grown "weary of the small, well-made play."

186. Lewis, Theophilus. Review of *Five Finger Exercise*. *America* 102 (9 Jan. 1960): 428.

A brief, favorable review, praising Shaffer for handling his "fetid material" with tasteful circumspection.

187. McClain, John. "Top-Draw Import with Sterling Cast." *New York Journal American* 3 Dec. 1959: 19.

McClain, who enthuses over Shaffer's gift for dialogue, finds many of the scenes "riveting" and the entire evening "great theatre." His view of the play's theme: " . . . the inability of people to unburden themselves honestly to one another." [This item is reprinted, along with six other reviews, in *New York Theatre Critics' Reviews*, for which see #189 below.]

188. Morrison, Hobe. Review of *Five Finger Exercise*.
    Variety 9 Dec. 1959: 70.
        Morrison's report is highly favorable. He considers
    the New York production superior to its London
    predecessor, though he finds it "hard to be sure why."

189. *New York Theatre Critics' Reviews* 20.23 (Week of 7
    Dec. 1959): 207-210.
        Contains reviews listed here as entries #187, #194,
    #168, #174, #184, #176, and #169.

190. Prideaux, Tom. "One Family Split Four Ways." *Life* 21
    Mar. 1960: 93-94.
        A synopsis and brief review of *Five Finger
    Exercise*, with several production photos. Shaffer is
    greeted as "a young playwright of disciplined and
    durable talent" whose play, unlike others currently on
    view in New York, is "built as solidly as a cement
    corncrib."

191. Tynan, Kenneth. Review of *Five Finger Exercise*. *New
    Yorker* 12 Dec. 1959: 100-102.
        Tynan's attitude toward the play has changed little
    since the time of his review of the London production
    for the *Observer* five months earlier [see #162]. He
    praises Shaffer's skill at construction ("seeking
    comparisons, one's mind turns to Swiss watches or
    chess problems"). But he again finds that the writing
    has about it "a curious bloodlessness;" and he warns
    the audience, "You may be mesmerized, but you are
    not likely to be moved." He sums up with a dubious
    tribute: "Despite these objections, *Five Finger
    Exercise* is the most accomplished new play
    Broadway has seen this wretched season."

192. Tynan, Kenneth. *Curtains: Selections from the
    Drama Criticism and Related Writings*. New
    York: Atheneum, 1961.

Includes a reprint, pages 335-337, of the review of
Five Finger Exercise which originally appeared in
New Yorker [see #191 above].

193. Vidal, Gore. "Strangers at Breakfast." *Reporter* 22 (7
Jan. 1960): 36-37.
Vidal declares that Shaffer has worked unpromising
materials (familiar drawing-room, domestic drama)
into a play of quality. The critic suggests that the
playwright has not recognized his own "very great"
theme, the corruption of the modern family, and goes
so far as to describe *Exercise* as the first successful
anti-family play since Strindberg.

194. Watts, Richard, Jr. "A Powerful New Play from England."
New York Post 3 Dec. 1959: 55.
A rave, lauding Shaffer for his dialogue, his
characterizations, and the penetrating nature of his
psychological observations. Watts particularly admires
the author's attitude toward his characters ("merciless
but compassionate"). His capsule assessment: " . . .
powerful and absorbing . . . a notable new play." [This
item is reprinted, along with six other reviews, in *New
York Theatre Critics' Reviews*, for which see #189
above.]

195. Watts, Richard, Jr. "The Power of *Five Finger
Exercise*." *New York Post* 13 Dec. 1959: 13.
In a Sunday follow-up to his opening night review,
Watts appraises Shaffer: "[He] seems to me the most
talented and interesting new dramatist to emerge from
the English theater since John Osborne."

196. Whittaker, Herbert. "Direction Defeats an Old Cliche."
Globe and Mail (Toronto) 2 Jan. 1960: 10.
A generally favorable review, though, as the
headline suggests, more approving of Gielgud's staging
than of Shaffer's text.

NEWS REPORTS AND FEATURE STORIES

197. Anon. *"Five Finger Exercise." The Theatre* Jan. 1960: 18-19.
      A news report on "Broadway's new smash hit" with eight production photos. The brief commentary describes *Exercise* as "England's most meaningful play for Americans in many a year."

198. Anon. "Sir John Gielgud to Produce a First Play." *Times* (London) 10 June 1958: 5.
      A news story announcing the July opening of *Five Finger Exercise.*

199. Brisson, Frederick. "Importing Foreign Drama: *Five Finger Exercise* Crosses the Atlantic." *The Theatre* Dec. 1959: 24-25.
      Brisson, co-producer of the American production (and husband of Rosalind Russell, who later starred in the film), discusses his first encounter with Shaffer's play in London and the process of arranging for the new production on Broadway. He refers to *Five Finger Exercise* as:
      " . . . variations on the theme of . . . one's powerlessness to communicate his emotional needs to another . . . It's like a Bach piano piece: seemingly simple, yet interwoven, enormously complicated . . . "

200. Brisson, Frederick. Preface to Published Edition of *Five Finger Exercise.* New York: Harcourt, Brace & Co., 1959 [pages 5-7].
      Brisson describes the process through which he became the co-producer (along with Roger L. Stevens and Hugh Beaumont) of the New York production of *Exercise.* Upon first seeing Shaffer's drama in London, he recognized it as "a great woman's play." As for Shaffer's career, Brisson's forecast has proved

prophetic: "[Shaffer] is articulate, meticulously honest, endowed with a fine theatrical awareness. He has a definite future in the theatre of the United States as well as his native land."

201. Darlington, W.A. "London Letter: New Author Heartens West End Reviewers." *New York Times* 17 Aug. 1958: section 2; 1.
    A brief report on the London critics' response to the recently opened *Five Finger Exercise*: "Praise without a dissenting voice." Darlington places Shaffer among a welcome, new group of British playwrights who "have no avant garde theories to work out, and no anger against society to get off their chests . . . [but have] an eye for human nature and an ear for human speech, and write good plays."

202. Reuter. "Critics Choose *Five Finger Exercise*." *Times* (London) 21 Apr. 1960: 16.
    A brief note stating that Shaffer's debut piece has been named "the best foreign play of the year by the New York critics."

203. Reuter. "N.Y. Welcome for London Play." *Times* (London) 4 Dec. 1959: 15.
    A report on the "generally favorable welcome" given by the New York critics to *Five Finger Exercise*.

SCHOLARLY ESSAYS

204. Lambert, J.W. Introduction to *Five Finger Exercise*. In *New English Dramatists*, Vol. 4. Ed. by Tom Machsler. Harmondsworth, England: Penguin Books, 1962, pages 9-10.

205. Taylor, John Russell. *The Rise and Fall of the Well-Made Play.* New York: Hill & Wang, 1967.
     Taylor's comments on *Five Finger Exercise* may be found on page 162.

THE FILM

206. Mann, Daniel, dir. *Five Finger Exercise* [film: "Screenplay by Frances Goodrich and Albert Hackett, based on the play by Peter Shaffer"] with Rosalind Russell, Jack Hawkins, and Maximilian Schell, Columbia Pictures, 1962.

FILM REVIEWS

207. Beckley, Paul V. Review of film version of *Five Finger Exercise. New York Herald Tribune* 20 Apr. 1962: 9.
     The reviewer finds much that is admirable in the film, but he complains that the script has been insufficiently adapted to its new medium: "It remains a good play without becoming an exceptional movie—which it might have been, had the transition from stage to screen been complete."

208. Crowther, Bosley. Review of film version of *Five Finger Exercise. New York Times* 20 Apr. 1962: 20.
     Crowther is disappointed in the film. Although uncertain as to the precise problem, he insists that "something vital and essential to the dramatic quality [of Shaffer's play] has been lost, mislaid or stolen in the translation of it to the screen."

209. Winsten, Archer. Review of film version of *Five Finger
Exercise*. *New York Post* 20 April 1962: page no.
not available.
   The reviewer is less than enthusiastic. He complains
that "when the picture is good and honest, it is also
treading ground that has been beaten pretty flat . . .
[and] when it tries to strike out on some new path, it
doesn't go anywhere."

Chapter Five

The Private Ear/The Public Eye

THE TEXT

The complete texts of *The Private Ear* and *The Public Eye* are included in *The Collected Plays of Peter Shaffer* [see #144] and in other publications, including the one listed below.

210. *"The Private Ear" and "The Public Eye"*. New York: Stein and Day, 1964.

PLAY REVIEWS

A. Reviews: Original London Production.
Opened at the Globe Theatre on May 10, 1962.

211. Anon. "Variations on a Triangle." *Times* (London) 11 May 1962: 12.

The double bill is described as "an unexacting evening of skilled entertainment." The reviewer complains that Shaffer's dialogue suffers from "the frivolity of revue [writing]" and that his work seems, on the whole, self-conscious: " . . . a playwright enjoying his own virtuosity." A major disappointment, says the critic, is the fact that "neither of the two plays is anchored to the kind of compact social background which enabled us to become deeply involved in *Five Finger Exercise*."

212. Anon. "New Cast Alter [sic] Emphasis . . . *The Private Ear* and *The Public Eye*." *Times* (London) 10 Sept. 1963: 13.

The *Times* critic takes another look [for the first, see #211] at the plays. The result of cast changes (replacements Geraldine McEwan and Barry Foster), he reports, is that the evening's "subtleties are frequently lost in conventional histrionics." Though he finds that the "rather more expansive treatment" does no great harm to *The Private Ear*, he thinks it a disaster when applied to the "fantastic and demanding labyrinths of evasion and revelation in *The Public Eye*."

213. Clurman, Harold. Review of *The Private Ear* and *The Public Eye*. *Nation* 2 June 1962: 501-502.

Having recently seen Shaffer's double bill and Ustinov's *Photo Finish*, Clurman is prompted to say, "How much smoother talent is than genius." He appreciates the craft demonstrated by both playwrights but finds little else to admire. Shaffer's short plays, he allows, are enjoyable; moreover, their triviality should not necessarily be taken as a hallmark of the author, who is "still a novice."

214. Darlington, W.A. "Making Up Lost Time." *Daily Telegraph* (London) 11 May 1962: 16.

Applause for both plays. *The Public Eye* is considered "clever and very funny," *The Private Ear* even better: " . . . will live in one's mind as an exquisite little gem of writing . . . "

215. Gascoigne, Bamber. "Touched by Pleasure." *Spectator* no. 6986 (18 May 1962): 653.

In spite of the critic's reservations about certain shortcomings in the writing ("weaknesses for . . . humorous misunderstandings . . . and coy literary phrases"), this is a heartily favorable review. *Ear* is declared successful but "slight." *Eye* is upheld as a more ambitious work, one which marks Shaffer as a "master of serious fantasy" in the manner of Giraudoux.

216. Gellert, Roger. "Encircling Gloom." *New Statesman* 63.1627 (18 May 1962): 732.

A mixture of faults and virtues are seen in both plays. The reviewer especially objects to certain speeches which he refers to as "poetic-philosophic." In the end, however, he suggests that Shaffer may be the heir to "the master's mantle" which once belonged to Noel Coward.

217. Hobson, Harold. Review of *The Private Ear* and *The Public Eye*. *Christian Science Monitor* 12 May 1962: 4.

Hobson distinguishes Shaffer as the only one of the new British dramatists "who speaks with the old accent of educated and tolerant sophistication." He describes *Private Ear* as "an essay in that most difficult of genres, the polished middle-class or suburban comedy." *Public Ear* is called a "drama . . . [whose] situation trembles on the edge of farce." In both plays Shaffer's work is judged "cunning and charming."

218. Keown, Eric. Review of *The Private Ear* and *The Public Eye*. *Punch* 16 May 1962: 768.
An extremely favorable review, which labels Shaffer "one of England's major playwrights."

219. Kretzmer, Herbert. Review of *The Private Ear* and *The Public Eye*. *Daily Express* (London) 12 May 1962: 7.
Kretzmer reports enthusiastically on both plays but expresses a slight preference for *The Public Eye*, which he considers the more significant work.

220. Shulman, Milton. Review of *The Private Ear* and *The Public Eye*. *Evening Standard* (London) 11 May 1962: 21.
Shulman is in the critical minority in maintaining that *The Public Eye* is less successful than its companion piece due to its uncertainty of tone, which falls midway between fantasy and realism.

221. Trewin, J.C. Review of *The Private Ear* and *The Public Eye*. *Illustrated London News* 26 May 1962: 860.
Trewin likes both plays but expresses a slight preference for *The Private Ear*.

222. Tynan, Kenneth. "London Can Keep It." *Observer* (London) 13 May 1962: 25.
Tynan draws a sharp (class) distinction between the two halves of the double bill. He considers *Private Ear* a complete failure, especially in its depiction of a lower-class character, toward whom Shaffer's attitude is described as "sickeningly condescending." *Public Eye*, in which the playwright deals with "his own class," is declared more successful: " . . . a free flow of linguistic fantasy that recalls the very best of John Mortimer."

223. Worsley, T.C. Review of *The Private Ear* and *The Public Eye*. *Financial Times* (London) 11 May 1962: 26.

   Worsley turns thumbs down. While admitting that the audience seemed to enjoy the evening's fare, he complains that both plays lack form and coherence, and that their characters are mere puppets contrived by the playwright to produce his effects.

B. Reviews: New York Production.
Opened at the Morosco Theatre on October 9, 1963.

224. Anon. Review of *The Private Ear* and *The Public Eye*. *Newsweek* 21 Oct. 1963: 104.

   A brief, unfavorable report on both ends of the double bill. The reviewer particularly deplores the fact that, in *Public Eye*, Shaffer contradicts his theme ("people understand each other . . . through silence, not words") by "cranking out words unendingly."

225. Anon. "Love Antic and Frantic." *Time* 18 Oct. 1963: 76, 78.

   The critic acknowledges that the challenging promise of light entertainment has been "entrancingly met." Both plays are applauded, although *Public Eye* receives particular kudos for its "freshness and invention."

226. Bolton, Whitney. "*Private Ear* and *The Public Eye* Enchanting, Superbly Cast." *New York Morning Telegraph* 11 Oct. 1963: 2.

   A warmly favorable opinion of both plays. Shaffer's writing is judged "heavenly, smooth and persuasive," and the double bill is hailed as "the first blockbuster of the . . . season."

227. Chapman, John. "*Private Ear* and *The Public Eye*
     Are Irresistible English Comedies." *New York Daily
     News* 10 Oct. 1963: 94.
          This review congratulates Shaffer on the creation
     of two "ingenious" works. Chapman sees something
     unusual in both plots, a peculiarity that he attempts to
     identify by pointing to the program, which refers to the
     works not as "plays" but as "stories." His summation of
     the proceedings: " . . . silky-smooth, literate, witty and
     irresistibly humorous." [This item is reprinted, along
     with six other reviews, in *New York Theatre Critics'
     Reviews*, for which see #247 below.]

228. Christiansen, Richard. Review of *The Private Ear* and
     The Public Eye. *Chicago Daily News* 11 Dec.
     1963: 79.
          The reviewer likes both halves of the double bill:
     " . . . a happy combination of substance and style."

229. Clurman, Harold. Review of *The Private Ear* and *The
     Public Eye*. *Nation* 9 Nov. 1963: 305-306.
          Clurman has little to say on the occasion of the
     New York opening, referring readers to his earlier
     appraisal of the London production [see #213 above].
     While he approves of both plays, which he describes as
     "engaging comedies of good sense," he advises that
     they "ought not to be taken as more than bright,
     literate, well-bred entertainment."

230. Colby, Ethel. "Two One-Act Plays Latest Fine Import
     from Britain." *Journal of Commerce* 10 Oct. 1963:
     6.
          A rave for both halves of the double bill.

231. Coleman, Robert. "*Eye-Ear* Delightful Imports." *Daily
     Mirror* (New York) 10 Oct. 1963: page no. not
     available.

Avid approval for both plays. Coleman describes the evening as a "remarkable tour de force" and Shaffer as having "the skill of a magician." [This item is reprinted, along with six other reviews, in *New York Theatre Critics' Reviews*, for which see #247 below.]

232. Cooke, Richard P. "Winning Pair." *Wall Street Journal* 11 Oct. 1963: 12.
 The verdict is favorable: "Mr. Shaffer's ear for speech and eye for comedy are first-rate."

233. Dash, Tom. Review of *The Private Ear* and *The Public Eye. Show Business* 2 Feb. 1963: 2.
 A favorable report on both *Ear* and *Eye.*

234. Gassner, John. "Broadway in Review." *Educational Theatre Journal* 15.4 (Dec. 1963): 358-362.
 While Gassner is favorably impressed with the construction and dialogue of both plays, he criticizes them as superficial and lacking incisiveness or profundity of observation. He places Shaffer's current work "midway between the 'angry' new drama . . . and Britain's trusty old drawing-room comedy."

235. Gottfried, Martin. Review of *The Private Ear* and *The Public Eye. Women's Wear Daily* 10 Oct. 1963: 36.
 Gottfried likes *The Private Ear* but finds *The Public Eye* "very talky, very static . . . "

236. Hewes, Henry. Review of *The Private Ear* and *The Public Eye. Saturday Review* 26 Oct. 1963: 32.
 This is a favorable review which includes a mild rebuke to the playwright. Hewes finds the plays "entertaining and delightful" but also "somewhat slight, frivolous and contrived." Shaffer receives a (back-

handed) compliment for being "a playwright who knows his depth."

237. Hipp, Edward Sothern. "Shaffer Serves Double Treat." *Newark Evening News* 10 Oct. 1963: 70.
A vote of approval for both plays.

238. Kerr, Walter. Review of *The Private Ear* and *The Public Eye. New York Herald Tribune* 10 Oct. 1963: 16.
Shaffer is praised as one "who doesn't care what chances he takes." This compliment is based not only on the free-wheeling fantasy elements in the two new plays but also on their sharp divergence in aim and tone from *Five Finger Exercise.* Though he likes both halves of the double-bill, Kerr expresses a slight preference for *Private Ear.* His assessment of the program: " . . . slight inventions, deftly contrived, cheerfully entertaining." [This item is reprinted, along with six other reviews, in *New York Theatre Critics' Reviews,* for which see #247 below.]

239. Kerr, Walter. Review of *The Private Ear* and *The Public Eye. New York Herald Tribune* 27 Oct. 1963: 25.
Kerr hands in another favorable report in this follow-up article but qualifies his praise by stressing the fact that both plays are intended as light entertainment.

240. Lewis, Allan. Review of *The Private Ear* and *The Public Eye. Sunday Herald* 27 Oct. 1963: 18.
An unqualified rave.

241. Lewis, Emory. Review of *The Private Ear* and *The Public Eye. Cue* 19 Oct. 1963: 28.

A rave for both "meticulously observed and subtly orchestrated vignettes." The writing, says Lewis, "beautifully blends wit and pathos."

242. Lewis, Theophilus. Review of *The Private Ear* and *The Public Eye. America* 109 (7 Dec. 1963): 752-753.
    In this approving capsule review, Shaffer's dialogue is said to range in quality from "brilliant to incandescent."

243. McCarten, John. Review of *The Private Ear* and *The Public Eye. New Yorker* 19 Oct. 1963: 99-100.
    McCarten's response is lukewarm-to-chilly. He concedes that *Public Eye* "has a quota of wit" and is "jolly enough." On the other hand, he finds *Private Ear* "actively bothersome."

244. McClain, John. "An Import—But Why?" *New York Journal American* 10 Oct. 1963: 17.
    Despite the querulous headline, this is essentially a favorable report. McClain praises Shaffer's dialogue and admires the playwright's "fine sense of the ridiculous." The theme of the review, however, questions the trend toward producing so many British "hits" on Broadway. The critic's conclusion: Shaffer's double bill is "amiable" but did not demand to be imported. [This item is reprinted, along with six other reviews, in *New York Theatre Critics' Reviews*, for which see #247 below.]

245. Morrison, Hobe. Review of *The Private Ear* and *The Public Eye. Variety* 16 Oct. 1963: 54.
    Morrison declares both playlets "brilliantly written." He predicts that Shaffer's double bill will disprove "the Broadway truism that one-acter plays aren't box-office."

246. Nadel, Norman. "Emotions Gently Laid Bare in Shaffer's *Eye* and *Ear*." *New York World-Telegram and Sun* 10 Oct. 1963: 19.
     Nadel likes both plays but prefers *The Public Eye*. He extends an unusually vigorous compliment to Shaffer on his psychological acumen, referring to him as one "who has uncontested access to the intimate feelings of the people he observes." Nadel goes on to praise both the dramatist's "skill at construction" and his "wisdom, sensitivity and compassion." [This item is reprinted, along with six other reviews, in *New York Theatre Critics' Reviews*, for which see #247 below.]

247. *New York Theatre Critics' Reviews* 24.13 (Week of 14 Oct. 1963): 248-251.
     Contains reviews listed here as #231, #246, #227, #238, #244, #251, and #252.

248. Oppenheimer, George. "1-Acter Plus 1-Acter May Add Up to Long Run." *Newsday* (Long Island, NY) 10 Oct. 1963: 2C.
     Oppenheimer enjoys both plays but is "especially taken with" *The Private Ear*. He predicts a long run for the double bill.

249. Pryce-Jones, Alan. Review of *The Private Ear* and *The Public Eye*. *Theatre Arts* Jan. 1964: 65-66.
     Pryce-Jones considers neither play "a total success" but claims that both demonstrate Shaffer's "expanding talent." Comparing the two, he finds *Private Ear* to be "on a higher level of farce, and a lower level of real interest."

250. Smith, Michael. Review of *The Private Ear* and *The Public Eye*. *Village Voice* 17 Oct. 1963: 10, 14.
     A mixed report card is delivered. Smith declares *The Private Ear* to be largely a failure. He finds

The Public Eye admirably amusing but too static to be completely satisfactory as a play.

251. Taubman, Howard. "*The Private Ear* and *The Public Eye* Open." *New York Times* 10 Oct. 1963: 51.

Taubman enthuses over *Public Eye* ("gay, sophisticated and wise") and bluntly dismisses *Private Ear* ("a trifling anecdote"). [This item is reprinted, along with six other reviews, in *New York Theatre Critics' Reviews*, for which see #247 above.]

252. Watts, Richard, Jr. "Two Delightful London Comedies." *New York Post* 10 Oct. 1963: 45.

In a favorable review for both plays, Watts expresses a slight preference for *Public Eye*. He joins the ranks of those who see these works as successful ventures into the domain of Noel Coward, praising the author's "gift for witty urbanity." [This item is reprinted, along with six other reviews, in *New York Theatre Critics' Reviews*, for which see #247 above.]

NEWS REPORTS AND FEATURE STORIES

253. Anon. "Mr. Peter Shaffer's Two Stories." *Times* (London) 15 Feb. 1962: 8.

An announcement that a new double bill entitled "Two Stories" (a composite label for *The Private Ear* and *The Public Eye*) is to be premiered at Cambridge on April 9. [Note: the title of the first half of the bill here receives an unfortunate typographical error: "The Private BAR."]

254. Devlin, Diana. "Plays in Print." *Drama* No. 141 (Summer 1981): 51-52.

In a brief report on recently reprinted play scripts, Devlin suggests that Shaffer's *Private Ear* and *Public Eye* "paved the way for Ayckbourne's comedies."

255. Lapole, Nick. "S-Men Try for Another Broadway Hit." *New York Journal American* 6 Oct. 1963: 231.
    A news story on the impending opening of *Private Ear/Public Eye*. The "S-Men" of the headline are Shaffer and producer Roger L. Stevens.

256. Prideaux, Tom. "Best and Brightest Season in a Decade." *Life* 22 Nov. 1963: 38.
    An illustrated retrospective on the 1963 Broadway season, focusing on more than a dozen plays considered to be of particularly high quality. *Private Ear* and *Public Eye*, according to Prideaux, "represent the most polished high comedy writing in many years."

SCHOLARLY ESSAY

257. Lewis, Allen. *American Plays and Playwrights of the Contemporary Theatre*. New York: Crown, 1965.
    Comments briefly on *The Private Ear* and *The Public Eye*, page 258.

THE FILMS

258. Hutton, Brian G., dir. *The Pad (And How to Use It)*, [Film: "Screenplay by Thomas C. Ryan and Ben Starr, based on the play *The Private Ear* by Peter Shaffer"]

with Brian Bedford, Julie Sommars, and James
Farentino, Universal Pictures, 1966.

259. Reed, Carol, dir. *The Public Eye* [Film: "Screenplay by
Peter Shaffer, based on his play of the same title;
released in England under the title *Follow Me*"] with
Mia Farrow and Chaim Topol, Universal Pictures,
1972.

FILM REVIEWS:
THE PAD (AND HOW TO USE IT)
[BASED ON *THE PRIVATE EAR*]

260. Carroll, Kathleen. "*The Pad* Presents New Faces." *New
York Daily News* 18 Aug. 1966: page no. not
available.
   Carroll assigns the film a near-perfect rating of
three-and-a-half stars. She applauds director Brian
Hutton for giving Shaffer's work "the Rock Hudson-
Sandra Dee treatment" while retaining the "poignancy
and humor of the play."

261. Crowther, Bosley. Review of *The Pad (And How to
Use It)*. *New York Times* 18 Aug. 1966: 27.
   Crowther expresses disappointment in the film
treatment, complaining that it lacks the play's "special
humor, whimsy, poignancy and charm." He reserves
particular disdain for the screen writer's adaptation
(which relocates the action to a rooming-house garret
in Los Angeles) and calls the whole enterprise "[a]
downright sappy excuse for a movie."

262. Winsten, Archer. Review of *The Pad (And How to Use
It)*. *New York Post* 18 Aug. 1966: page no. not
available.

A pan. Winsten remarks that "the author of the
play . . . must have had a very different story to tell."

FILM REVIEWS: *THE PUBLIC EYE*
[RELEASED IN ENGLAND UNDER THE TITLE
FOLLOW ME]

263. Canby, Vincent. Review of film version of *The Public
     Eye*. *New York Times* 19 July 1972: 22.
     A thumbs-down for the movie, which Canby
     condemns for "pretending to be in favor of all of life's
     good things . . . and [succeeding] in making them seem
     . . . unbearably boring."

264. Carroll, Kathleen. "*Public Eye* Light and Frothy." *New
     York Daily News* 19 July 1972: 82.
     The headline of this review may mislead; it is
     intended to parody the press releases circulated by the
     film's producers. In fact, Carroll finds the movie
     "about as light as an overcooked pancake; about as
     frothy as quicksand." She describes Shaffer's
     screenplay as "strangely lifeless." Despite her
     overwhelmingly negative tone, the critic assigns the
     film a rating of two-and-a-half stars.

265. Cocks, Jay. "Obtuse Triangle." *Time* 11 Sept. 1972: 78.
     Cocks' opinion of the work in question could
     hardly be lower: "The film would be a laughable
     travesty were it not directed by Carol Reed . . . that
     makes it a sad travesty."

266. Gilliatt, Penelope. Review of film version of *The Public
     Eye*. *New Yorker* 29 July 1972: page number not
     available.

Gilliatt briefly dismisses *The Public Eye* as "a thoroughly dubious film."

267. Kissel, Howard. Review of film version of *The Public Eye* [under the title used for its release in England: *Follow Me*]. *Women's Wear Daily* 19 July 1972: 22.
Kissel complains that the script "suffers in cinematic transition" and that the dialogue has "a brittle cleverness that one relishes in the theatre . . . but that grows tiresome . . . in a movie."

268. Knight, Arthur. Review of film version of *The Public Eye*. *Saturday Review* 19 Aug. 1972: 69.
Knight's view is negative. He finds the film overlong due to the attempt to expand a one act play by adding "what is essentially travelogue footage."

269. Mallett, Richard. Review of film version of *The Public Eye* [under the title used for its release in England: *Follow Me*]. *Punch* 10 May 1972: 662.
Mallett refers to the film as "an agreeable surprise." He praises Shaffer's screenplay for being "full of entertaining lines" and applauds Carol Reed's direction as "one of the best things he's done for some time."

270. Melly, George. Review of film version of *The Public Eye* [under the title used for its release in England: *Follow Me*]. *Observer* (London) 7 May 1972: 36.
A pan. Melly complains, "What possessed Peter Shaffer to recast his nice little play into this sloppy gooey yuk remains as unsolved as the song the sirens sang."

271. Sterritt, David. Review of film version of *The Public Eye*. *Christian Science Monitor* 19 Aug. 1972: 7.

Sterritt says that the screenplay is "unabashedly talky, unashamedly epigrammatic" and tries "too hard for its witty salvos and neat turns of event."

Chapter Six

The Royal Hunt of the Sun

THE TEXT

The complete text of *The Royal Hunt of the Sun* is included in *The Collected Plays of Peter Shaffer* [see #144] and in many other single editions and anthologies, two of which are listed below.

272. Macdonald, John W., and John C. Saxton, eds. *The Royal Hunt of the Sun.* Introduction by A.W. England. 6th edition. London: Longman Group, 1976.
A historical note and an analysis of the play's themes are included.

273. Richards, Stanley, ed. *Best Plays of the Sixties.* Garden City, NY: Doubleday, 1970.
The text of *The Royal Hunt of the Sun* and a biographical note on Shaffer are on pages 523-624.

PLAY REVIEWS

**A. Reviews: Original Chichester Production.
Opened at the Chichester Festival Theatre on
July 6, 1964.**

274. Anon. "Glittering Epic of Spanish Conquest." *Times*
(London) 8 July 1964: 7.
    The reviewer suggests that the term 'epic' has come
to carry "the alternate meaning of a lavish spectacle
and of a play which requires audiences to think for
themselves." On the first count *Royal Hunt* is
declared an "undoubted success"; on the latter, it
"hardly impinges on the spectator." This judgment is
rephrased for the concluding paragraph: " . . . if the
play seems hollow at the centre, its externals are
magnificent."

275. Barker, Felix. "A Young Man's Dazzling Success."
Evening News (London) 12 Sept. 1964: page no. not
available.
    This brief review, looking forward to the opening of
the play at the Old Vic, is a rave. Barker asks, "Has
any other spectacle achieved such visual excitement
and, by avoiding any hint of the bogus, so touched the
historical imagination?" The critic answers: "No."

276. Bryden, Ronald. "Ruin and Gold." *New Statesman* 17
July 1964: 95.
    Bryden states that, though many of his critical
colleagues have found *Royal Hunt* "the greatest play
of our generation," he feels obliged to dissent. The
work is, he claims, "a good, conventional chronicle play
. . . distinguished by some heartfelt flights of historical
imagination, a stunning production, and [splendid]
acting."

277. Gascoigne, Bamber. "All the Riches of the Incas."
      Observer (London) 12 July 1964: 24.
      Unreserved enthusiasm for the Chichester
      production: "I haven't found such pleasure in the sheer
      weight and colour of language in any new play since
      John Whiting's *The Devils*."

278. Kingston, Jeremy. Review of *The Royal Hunt of the
      Sun. Punch* 15 July 1964: 99.
      Kingston gives *Royal Hunt* a strong vote of
      approval: "I cannot think of any other modern play to
      compare with it for unusual beauty and excitement." In
      his single criticism, he complains that "two of the
      dialectical arguments are overlong."

279. Lambert, J.W. Review of *The Royal Hunt of the Sun.*
      Christian Science Monitor 11 July 1964: 6.
      Lambert describes the Chichester premiere as
      "Total Theatre to a degree never yet attempted in the
      British theatre." Although his first impression is
      favorable, he warns, "Only time will tell . . . whether
      its quality is equal to the spectacle."

280. M., E. C. "Rhetoric but Ordinary Philosophical Content."
      Stage and Television Today (London) 9 July 1964:
      23.
      This reviewer expresses the hope that Shaffer has
      gotten the urge to write an epic on a grandiose theme
      "out of his system" and will "revert to his wonderfully
      observed comedies." The major complaint: the central
      conflict, Pizarro's struggle of conscience, lacks
      dramatic force.

281. Nightingale, Benedict. Review of *The Royal Hunt of
      the Sun. Manchester Guardian* 8 July 1964: 7.
      Although Nightingale concedes that Shaffer's play is
      "mightily ambitious" and that the production is "often
      good to look at," this report is utterly negative.

"Shaffer's shoulders are . . . too slim," he charges, for the great themes he has chosen. Not only is the play marred by "blotches of tedium, digressions, repetition, and a general feeling of muddle," Shaffer is accused of having "no particular originality" in his ideas and "no particular feeling" for his characters. Finally, Nightingale dissents from his fellow critics who have so admired *Royal Hunt*'s spectacular staging: "The marching Spaniards look as if they are doing a soft-shoe shuffle; a slaughter of Indians reminds me of a display . . . I once saw in a pseudo-Indian camp at Disneyland."

282. Roberts, Peter. "After the Fanfare." *Plays and Players* Sept. 1964: 26-28.

   Roberts suggests that *Royal Hunt* has been eagerly awaited by audiences and critics as a test of whether Shaffer can successfully shatter his previous reputation as "a brilliant miniaturist." He concludes that the dramatist has passed the test by constructing a "complex and rivetting" [sic] play.

283. Rutherford, Malcolm. "The Christ that Died." *Spectator* no. 7099 (17 July 1964): 82, 84.

   In this brief review, one of the few dissents from the generally approving London press, the play is described as a "terrible disappointment." Rutherford complains that it "lacks both characters and a language of its own."

284. Shorter, Eric. Review of *The Royal Hunt of the Sun. Daily Telegraph* (London) 8 July 1964: 16.

   Shorter maintains that the documentary drama concerning the conquest of Peru and the philosophical reflections on man's immortal longings do not always easily co-exist in Shaffer's work.

285. Shulman, Milton. Review of *The Royal Hunt of the Sun*. *Evening Standard* (London) 8 July 1964: 4.
     A favorable report, which nevertheless complains that at least 20 minutes of playing time should be cut from the script.

286. Trewin, J.C. Review of *The Royal Hunt of the Sun*. *Illustrated London News* 8 Aug. 1964: 208.
     Although he praises Shaffer's ambitious theme and his technical skills, Trewin finds the language of the play inadequate and longs for a Christopher Marlowe treatment of the material to achieve the requisite heroic tone.

287. Watts, Richard, Jr. "Peter Shaffer's Historical Drama." *New York Post* 9 Aug. 1964: 18.
     Upon seeing the Chichester opening, Watts reports (not quite correctly) that the response of the London critics has been "unanimously ecstatic." He finds it "brilliant and powerful" but less successful as historical drama than Bolt's *A Man for All Seasons*.

288. Young, B.A. "Chichester Views New Shaffer Play." *New York Times* 8 July 1964: 40.
     Young asserts that, "as a spectacle," *Royal Hunt* is "superb." He adds that "what it lacks is depth, though not importance, of argument."

289. Young, B.A. Review of *The Royal Hunt of the Sun*. *Financial Times* (London) 8 July 1964: 24.
     In a second review [see #288 above], Young applauds Shaffer's inventiveness and theatrical boldness. He finds in the play moments of "genius" but reports that the drama's ideas are not profound and that its language lacks beauty.

B. Reviews: London Production.
Opened at the Old Vic on December 8, 1964.

290. Anon. "Stage Challenge to Production . . . *The Royal Hunt of the Sun.*" *Times* (London) 9 Dec. 1964: 9.
The critic complains that the attempt to keep the original (Chichester Festival, thrust-stage) version of the play "as nearly as possible as it was," has not been successful, at least from the viewpoint of "the stalls" (the orchestra level seating) at the Old Vic. In his only comment on the quality of the script, he claims that "the merits of the show reside largely in its management of physical action and very little in its more reflective scenes of character development and theological disputation."

291. Benedictus, David. Review of *The Royal Hunt of the Sun. Plays and Players* Feb. 1967: 22.
A re-review of the play on the occasion of a cast change (Paul Curran taking over as Pizarro from Colin Blakely). Benedictus notes that there are those who consider *Royal Hunt* "a masterpiece" and those who denounce it as "a pretentious, overwritten pantomime." His position: "the former are right."

292. Brien, Alan. "Silent Epic—with Words." *Sunday Telegraph* (London) 13 Dec. 1964: 12.
The critic catalogues *Royal Hunt*'s themes ("theology, sociology, psychology, history, politics, morals . . . it would make an operatic subject to daunt even Wagner") and remarks that Shaffer's language seems to have been "flattened under the load." He points out that the two scenes which have already become famous—the first appearance of Atahuallpa and the final tableau—are both devoid of dialogue. He also complains that the language suffers from "a continual ambiguity of tone . . . as though [Shaffer] is

never quite certain whether he is competing against
Rider Haggard or Christopher Fry."

293. Brien, Alan. "In London: Peter Shaffer's *The Royal
    Hunt of the Sun* . . ." *Vogue* 146 (1 Aug. 1965): 49.
    This "preview" of a coming Broadway attraction is a
    re-shaped reprise of Brien's earlier review for the
    Sunday Telegraph [see #292 above]. While
    promising spectacular delights for New York
    audiences, Brien warns them that the play's language is
    not up to its mighty theme. He describes *Royal Hunt*
    as "an epic for eggheads . . . a blend of *Ben Hur*,
    The King and I, and *The Devils*."

294. Bryden, Ronald. "Firebird." *New Statesman* 18 Dec.
    1964: 972.
    Bryden maintains that *Royal Hunt* suffers more
    than most plays from second viewing." He complains
    that the first act is nothing more than "an enormously
    protracted overture." The drama is saved from
    stagnation, he adds, by Robert Stephens' performance
    as Atahuallpa, which is lauded for being "as unique,
    self-generating and memorable [as] that vanished
    masterpiece, Fonteyn's *Firebird*."

295. Crosby, John. "Huge, Tragic Canvas." *New York
    Herald-Tribune* 18 Dec. 1964: 1.
    In this brief review, Crosby hails Shaffer's work as
    a welcome return to theatrical "first principles" after
    "the bare stages of Ionesco and Beckett." The Old Vic
    production is called "superb," but the playwright is
    criticized for having "failed most honorably" at the
    difficult task of making truly dramatic Pizarro's
    conquest of Peru.

296. Darlington, W.A. Review of *The Royal Hunt of the
    Sun*. *Daily Telegraph* (London) 9 Dec. 1964: 18.

Although Darlington offers a favorable review, he
notes that the effectiveness of the staging helps to
compensate for weaknesses in the script.

297. Esslin, Martin. "All in the Text." *Plays and Players*
   Feb. 1965: 34.
   Having missed the Chichester production, Esslin
   gets his first look at *Royal Hunt* in London. He
   disputes those who have emphasized the purely
   theatrical qualities of the play, maintaining that it is
   "above all a first rate text: witty, wise and well
   written." Nevertheless, he complains about "a certain
   paleness in the characterisation of Pizarro's men . . .
   even . . . the narrator remains somewhat schematic."

298. Esslin, Martin. *Reflections: Essays on Modern
   Theatre*. Garden City, NY: Doubleday & Co., 1969.
   Esslin remarks briefly on *Royal Hunt* on page 85.
   His comments are in line with the views he expressed
   earlier in his *Plays and Players* review [see #297
   above].

299. Gilliatt, Penelope. "A Huge Stride Backwards—with the
   Inca." *Observer* (London) 13 Dec. 1964: 24.
   Gilliatt joins a second wave of London
   critics—those opposing their colleagues who greeted
   Royal Hunt so favorably at its Chichester premiere.
   She detects in the play "little content intellectually"
   and contends that Shaffer's writing reduces the drama
   "to the level of a pageant play."

300. Hewes, Henry. "Unsentimental Journeys." *Saturday
   Review* 29 May 1965: 31.
   In this brief review of the London production,
   Hewes reaffirms his earlier opinion of the play,
   lauding Shaffer for having written his play "with
   penetrating insight rather than showy grandiosity."

301. Hobson, Harold. "In Search of Bliss." *Sunday Times* (London) 13 Dec. 1964: 25.

Hobson comments on the adaptation required in transferring the play from Chichester's thrust stage to the Old Vic's proscenium arrangement. He concludes that "the spectacular aspects . . . are still magnificent . . . but at the Old Vic they do not, as they tended to do at Chichester, overwhelm the text." His opinion of the script is unchanged: " . . . a very fine play."

302. Hobson, Harold. "*Royal Hunt of the Sun* Acclaimed." *Christian Science Monitor* 15 Dec. 1964: 5.

Hobson's piece for the *Monitor* restates his earlier position, outlined in the *Sunday Times* [see #301 above]. He regards *Royal Hunt* as "a play of quality" and holds that the Old Vic version, as compared to the original production at Chichester, offers "less pantomime but more thought."

303. Levin, Bernard. "Thank You Mr. S for the Greatest Play in My Lifetime." *Daily Mail* (London) 9 Dec. 1964: page no. not available.

As the headline indicates, this is perhaps the most enthusiastic review Shaffer (or any other playwright) has ever received. Levin's praise is unqualified. He describes the theme of *Royal Hunt* as "a humanist hymn, an agnostic affirmation . . . [that] it is man's honour that conquers, not God's." Shaffer's language, Levin adds, "clothes his theme in majesty."

304. Marowitz, Charles. Review of *The Royal Hunt of the Sun*. *Encore* 12 (Mar.-Apr. 1965): 44-45.

A provocative review, not so much for its insights into the play as for its frank discussion of a seldom broached topic: the internal politics of drama criticism, with special relevance to Shaffer's career. Marowitz acknowledges the existence of what he calls an "intellectual underground" which dismisses *The Royal*

Hunt of the Sun as "an overrated blunderbuss." He
claims that this enclave of intellectual critics often
forms its views in response to the more conservative
"popular press," rather than arriving at them
"naturally." According to Marowitz, these critics ask
themselves, "If Levin and Kretzmer like it, how can
we?" Finally, Marowitz outlines his own reactions to
Royal Hunt: (1) he admires it more than he
"expected to"; (2) it is Shaffer's best play; and (3) the
production is not, as the "intellectual underground"
would have it, overblown and needlessly showy, but is
"what the play demands." This review might be taken
as a fascinating demonstration of the lengths to which
a member of the "underground" feels he must go when
dissenting from his fellows.

305. Marowitz, Charles. *Confessions of a Counterfeit
     Critic: A London Theatre Notebook, 1958-1971.*
     London: Eyre Methuen, 1973.
         Contains a reprint, on pages 88-89, of Marowitz's
     review of *Royal Hunt* which first appeared in
     Encore [see #304 above].

306. Myro. Review of *The Royal Hunt of the Sun. Variety*
     16 Dec. 1964: 64.
         A rave, calling the play "one of the great theatrical
     contributions of our time." Shaffer's "majestic
     command of language" is said to match the quality of
     the spectacle.

307. Rutherford, Malcolm. "Sun Worship." *Spectator*
     (London) 18 Dec. 1964: 844.
         Rutherford finds the Old Vic production "less
     pretentious" than the original at Chichester [for his
     review of the earlier production, see #283 above]. He
     continues to insist, however, that the play lacks
     genuine dramatic content and that the language is
     inadequate for its great theme. He sums up by

describing a notable "gap between intention and achievement."

308. Shulman, Milton. Review of *The Royal Hunt of the Sun*. *Evening Standard* (London) 9 Dec. 1964: 14. A favorable review which nevertheless mentions reservations about the historical pageant aspect of the proceedings ("always trembles on the verge of sounding like a dramatization of a novel by Fenimore Cooper"). The final verdict: "But the intensity, maturity and intelligence of Shaffer's writing gives these ultraromantic events an extraordinary urgency and relevance."

C. Reviews: New York Production.
Opened at the ANTA Theatre on October 26, 1965.

309. Anon. "Hunting Heaven." *Newsweek* 8 Nov. 1965: 96. A mixed-yet-favorable review: "The evening [is] vigorous, uncertain, exciting, disappointing, lucid and confusing, ending finally on the side of the angels by a fair margin." Among the reviewer's complaints are the play's occasional descents into "pure pageantry" and its "attempt to wrap up every historical, psychological and moral issue."

310. Anon. "Tiny Alice in Inca Land." *Time* 86 (5 Nov. 1965): 77. The judgment is mixed. The critic reports that *Royal Hunt* "dazzles the eye as a spectacle." As a drama, however, it is deemed "mechanical, preachy, largely unaffecting, and sometimes silly."

311. Bolton, Whitney. "*Royal Hunt* Is a Play of Beauty and Spectacle." *New York Morning Telegraph* 28 Oct. 1965: 3. A rave. The headline sums up the content.

312. Brustein, Robert. "Familiar Peru, Exotic Brooklyn." *New Republic* 153 (27 Nov. 1965): 45-46.
    Brustein's keynote is that, beyond the production's spectacular theatricality, "the play amounts to very little . . . it may be total theatre, but it is strictly fractional drama." He finds the theme pretentious, the characters conventional, and the dialogue "poetastrical." Like John Simon, Brustein considers Shaffer not merely an affront to his own high intelligence, but a splendid springboard for japes on the order of: " . . . being exposed to Peter Shaffer's meditations on religion, love, life and death for three solid hours is like being trapped in a particularly active wind tunnel with no hope of egress."

313. Brustein, Robert. *The Third Theatre*. New York: Alfred A. Knopf, 1969.
    Contains, on pages 114-116, a revision of Brustein's review of *The Royal Hunt of the Sun*, originally printed in *New Republic* [see #312].

314. Chapin, Louis. Review of *The Royal Hunt of the Sun*. *Christian Science Monitor* 30 Nov. 1965: 4.
    A favorable review. Chapin expresses some dissatisfaction with the show's "slow start" but reports that the total effect is that of a "beautifully written play."

315. Chapman, John. "*The Royal Hunt of the Sun* Fills the ANTA Theatre with Beauty." *New York Daily News* 27 Oct. 1965: 96.
    An unqualified rave. *Royal Hunt* is judged a beautiful work, filled with superb spectacle. Shaffer is praised for his "command of language." [This item is reprinted, along with three other reviews, in *New York Theatre Critics' Reviews*, for which see #337 below.]

316. Chapman, John. "*Royal Hunt of the Sun* a Lovely Play." *New York Sunday News* 7 Nov. 1965: section 2; 2.

As in his earlier piece for the *Daily News* [see #315 above], Chapman awards *Royal Hunt* an unqualified rave: "Shaffer's most impressive play . . . theatrical writing at its beautiful best."

317. Clurman, Harold. "Marking Time ." *Nation* 22 Nov. 1965: 397-398.

After damning *Royal Hunt* with what proves to be faint praise, calling it "the best offering [of the season] thus far," Clurman issues an overwhelmingly negative assessment. He laments that this work should have been "mistaken for a good play, even a 'masterpiece' . . . " He admits that Shaffer has hit on a splendid "idea" (Pizarro's growing sympathy toward the Incas and his inability to extricate himself from the corruption of his own civilization). However, he charges that the idea "is set forth in scenes dramatically commonplace, in language without individual savor or edge." Shaffer's prose, in fact, is likened to what "any deft English university fellow might [write]."

318. Cohen, Marshall. "Theatre 66." *Partisan Review* 33.2 (Spring 1966): 269-276.

A mixed review which finally concludes that Shaffer's stature among current British playwrights remains an open question.

319. Cohen, Nathan. "Mortal Messengers on Broadway." *National Review* 18.2 (11 Jan. 1966): 37-38.

The play is dismissed as "vulgarized nonsense," and the interest and acclaim it has received is the subject of further complaint. Cohen speculates that the highbrow tone of the work, with its "superficial

ruminations" has gained it "respect out of all
proportions to its content."

320. Cooke, Richard P. Review of *The Royal Hunt of the
Sun. Wall Street Journal* 28 Oct. 1965: 16. Cooke
charges that Shaffer's writing in *Royal Hunt* suffers
from "stiffness" in the early sections, but on the whole
he finds the production "superb" and the drama itself
"worthy of respect."

321. Gassner, John. "Broadway in Review." *Educational
Theatre Journal* 18.1 (Mar. 1966): 55-58.
   An unfavorable verdict is rendered. Gassner sees as
a major flaw the (perhaps historically accurate)
passiveness of Atahuallpa and his fellow Incas, which
inevitably leads to an almost action-less play. He joins
those critics who find Shaffer's writing "impersonal,"
lacking a genuinely passionate involvement with
characters or events.

322. Gassner, John. Review of *The Royal Hunt of the Sun.*
In *Dramatic Soundings: Evaluations and
Retractions Culled from Thirty Years of
Dramatic Criticism.* Ed. by Glenn Loney. New
York: Crown, 1968.
   On pages 609-611 Gassner's earlier review for the
Educational Theatre Journal is reprinted [see
#321 above].

323. Gaver, Jack. *Season In, Season Out: 1965-1966.*
New York: Hawthorne Books, 1966.
   Gaver's rave review of *Royal Hunt* appears on
pages 60-64. The play is hailed as "the finest piece of
stage writing in the historical area since . . . *Saint
Joan* of forty-five years ago," and Shaffer is
acclaimed "the most versatile playwright using the
English language today." Gaver's theme for this piece
is the disparity between the play's worth and its box-

office failure. [The Broadway run resulted in losses of
$90,000 on the $120,000 put up by investors. In fact,
these losses were recovered during the lengthy national
tour which followed.] He concludes: "[It is] pathetic
. . . that *Royal Hunt* . . . is done in a sudden death
commercial atmosphere instead of by a prominent
repertory group that is not under the economic
pressure prevailing on Broadway."

324. Gottfried, Martin. Review of *The Royal Hunt of the
Sun*. *Women's Wear Daily* 27 Oct. 1965: 55.
    This is one of the few completely negative New
York reviews of the play, calling it "a very spectacular
bore."

325. Hering, Doris. Review of *The Royal Hunt of the Sun*.
Dance Magazine 39.12 (Dec. 1965): 138-139.
    Hering's view of the proceedings is enthusiastic.
She is especially struck by the form of the play
("grandly structured") and its choreographed
movement, about which she remarks that it is hard to
see "where the director . . . left off and the mime
staged by Madame Claude Chagrin took over."

326. Hewes, Henry. "Inca Doings." *Saturday Review* 48 (13
Nov. 1965): 71.
    A hugely approving review. The playwright is
applauded for "[using] theatre as a resonant
instrument." Hewes calls *Royal Hunt* "the season's
most thrilling, most imaginative, and most beautiful
event."

327. Hipp, Edward Sothern. "New Version of Conquest."
Newark Evening News 27 Oct. 1965: 48.
    Although he warns that the play is "palpably
imperfect" (some scenes being static, others
overwritten), Hipp's message is that he finds *Royal
Hunt* "an exhilarating experience."

328. Hipp, Edward Sothern. "A Conquest Missed by
Historians." *Newark Sunday News* 7 Nov. 1965: E1,
E6.
This is an even warmer endorsement of the play
than Hipp issued in his opening night review [see #327
above]: " . . . a vibrant entertainment written with
consummate skill."

329. Kerr, Walter. Review of *The Royal Hunt of the Sun*.
New York Herald Tribune 27 Oct. 1965: 17.
While he admires the ambitious scope of the play,
Kerr's verdict is negative. His most severe complaints
concern the structure ("the first half is without
momentum . . . not a drama but a stately, studied
oratorio") and the language (not "vivid" enough,
"faintly sententious").

330. Lewis, Emory. Review of *The Royal Hunt of the Sun*.
Cue 6 Nov. 1965: 13.
High praise for the play, especially for its power to
influence Broadway in the exciting new direction of
"total theatre." Lewis' applause, however, is tempered
by a qualification: " . . . not as good as it should be . . .
[because] Shaffer offers hollow rhetoric all too often."

331. Lewis, Theophilus. "*The Royal Hunt of the Sun*."
America 113 (20 Nov. 1965): 648-649.
A rave which not only calls *Royal Hunt* the best
play of the season but also predicts that it will claim "a
place among the significant works of world drama."

332. McCarten, John. "Gods Against God." *New Yorker* 6
Nov. 1965: 115-116.
A favorable report, congratulating Shaffer on his
"probity, wit, skill, and imagination." It also includes a
modest rebuke to the playwright: life among the Incas,
as depicted in this drama, is "almost too idyllic to be
plausible."

333. McClain, John. "Size, Style and Talent." *New York Journal American* 27 Oct. 1965: 20.

A mildly approving review. Although McClain praises the play as "an effort of vast thought and consideration," he reports that it is "a long evening and at times a tedious one."

334. Morrison, Hobe. Review of *The Royal Hunt of the Sun. Variety* 3 Nov. 1965: 60.

A generally favorable appraisal. While seeing in the play "serious flaws," Morrison finds it "one of the more interesting dramas of recent years" and predicts a lengthy run.

335. Nadel, Norman. "*Royal Hunt* a Shimmering Sunburst of Talent." *New York World-Telegram and Sun* 27 Oct. 1965: 25.

Again Nadel champions Shaffer. "No other Englishman in this century, save Shaw and Christopher Fry," writes Nadel, "has achieved such sensible beauty with words, such noble clarity of ideas." He goes on to state that he thinks *Royal Hunt* "might well be a masterpiece." [This item is reprinted, along with three other reviews, in *New York Theatre Critics' Reviews*, for which see #337 below.]

336. Nadel, Norman. "*Royal Hunt* Still Shining." *New York World-Telegram and Sun* 9 Apr. 1966: 23.

Reviewing a cast replacement (Robert Burr relieving Christopher Plummer), Nadel takes the opportunity to address what he feels is a mistaken impression of the play promulgated by many critics. Too much attention has been given, he writes, to *Royal Hunt* "as visual theater, and not sufficient appreciation of its remarkable intelligence as a play . . . its prose has the soaring flight of poetry and, at times, the grandeur of scripture."

337. *New York Theatre Critics' Reviews* 26.12 (Week of 8
     Nov. 1965: 294-296.
     Contains reviews listed here as entries #335, #344,
     #315, and #342.

338. Oppenheimer, George. Review of *The Royal Hunt of
     the Sun*. *Newsday* (Long Island, NY) 27 Oct. 1965:
     3C.
     A rave: " . . . poetry, drama, compassion, intellect
     . . . the theatre is touched by magic."

339. Sheed, Wilfred. Review of *The Royal Hunt of the Sun*.
     Commonweal 83.7 (19 Nov. 1965): 215-216.
     Sheed maintains that the production suffers from
     "familiar spectacle problems" (unauthentic, stylized
     renditions of exotic locales and customs). Most of the
     review is devoted to the premise that "less production
     would have meant a better play." Shaffer is criticized
     for placing so much thematic weight on the shoulders
     of a single character (Pizarro). Little else is directly
     said of the dramatist's contribution except that his
     dialogue is "literate."

340. Simon, John. Review of *The Royal Hunt of the Sun*.
     Hudson Review 18.4 (Winter 1966): 571-574.
     Simon compares his impressions of the play in two
     productions, the original one at Chichester (" . . . on
     an open stage . . . [it] looked like an adequate, though
     undistinguished, text for a superlative production") and
     the later Broadway version (" . . . looks pretentious
     and sounds hollow"). He does, however, congratulate
     Shaffer on "making the theatre visual again."

341. Smith, Michael. Review of *The Royal Hunt of the Sun*.
     Village Voice 4 Nov. 1965: 19-20.
     Smith cannot decide why he doesn't like *Royal
     Hunt* as much as he feels he should. He is
     disappointed, despite "brilliant performances . . .

language of unusual literacy and flexibility, and a
subject of extraordinary interest." He finally concludes
that the play is too narrowly personal in its concerns:
"Shaffer tries to write about the struggle in everyman's
soul, but ends up writing about himself."

342. Taubman, Howard. "Pizarro, Gold and Ruin." *New York
Times* 27 Oct. 1965: 36.
Taubman maintains that he is willing to forgive
certain weaknesses in the writing ("affectations . . . and
theatrical hocus-pocus") because he admires Shaffer's
brave attempt to "expand the narrow horizons of [our]
theatre." He claims that even a partial success in such
a difficult endeavor is "more commendable than
victory in a routine venture." [This item is reprinted,
along with three other reviews, in *New York Theatre
Critics' Reviews*, for which see #337 above.]

343. Taubman, Howard. "About a *Royal Hunt* . . . " *New
York Times* 14 Nov. 1965: section 2; 1.
Taubman debates which of his fellow critics are
correct, those who regard Shaffer's play as "a modern
masterpiece" or those who consider it "a showy fraud."
He decides that "the truth lies somewhere between
these extreme judgments."

344. Watts, Richard, Jr. "With Pizarro in Inca Peru." *New
York Post* 27 Oct. 1965: 83.
A generally favorable review. Watts commends the
writing as "dignified, thoughtful and distinguished" and
applauds the play as a "fascinating synthesis of the arts
of the theatre." He complains, however, that "Mr.
Shaffer actually never goes very deeply into the
conflict of men and civilizations." [This item is
reprinted, along with three other reviews, in *New
York Theatre Critics' Reviews*, for which see #337
above.]

345. Watts, Richard, Jr. "The Conqueror and the Conquered."
New York Post 14 Nov. 1965: 20.
     In re-reviewing the play, Watts retracts certain
     negative comments made in his opening night review.
     He no longer finds Shaffer's work "pretentious" or
     "superficial." On the contrary, he now concedes that
     Royal Hunt may be accepted, without qualification,
     as a drama of "noble proportions and high distinction."

NEWS REPORTS AND FEATURE STORIES

346. Anon. "British Plays Modified for Broadway." *Times*
(London) 31 Dec. 1965: 13.
     The *Times*'s anonymous "New York drama critic"
     examines the ways in which several recent British
     imports (including plays by John Osborne, Joe Orton,
     and John Whiting) have been "reinterpreted to suit
     American preferences." A case in point is Shaffer's
     Royal Hunt, which is deemed "more fortunate in its
     Broadway version" [than Whiting's *The Devils*],
     thanks to John Dexter's staging and the author's
     "probably beneficial" trimming of the philosophical
     debates between Pizarro and Atahuallpa.

347. Bolton, Whitney. "Grand Opera Techniques in 2 Plays."
New York Morning Telegraph 1 Nov. 1965: 3.
     A feature story on *Royal Hunt* and the Lincoln
     Center production of *Danton's Death*. The common
     thread linking them, according to Bolton's theory, is
     that both are instances of "grand opera without a
     score."

348. Chagrin, Claude. "French Dressing: Claude Chagrin Talks
to Sheridan Morley about Mime and Movement."
Plays and Players Mar. 1969: 52-53.

Chagrin, who staged mime and movement for *The Royal Hunt of the Sun* (and would later handle a similar assignment for *Equus*), explains the process by which a movement concept for the Incas was worked out in collaboration with director John Dexter, designer Michael Annals and Shaffer. [While the first name would indicate otherwise, Chagrin is female. She worked for several years during the mid-1960s as a teacher of mime and movement at the National Theater.]

349. Hewes, Henry. Report on Atlanta Production of *The Royal Hunt of the Sun*. *Saturday Review* 49 (19 Nov. 1966): 72.

Hewes provides not so much a review of the play or its production as a commentary on the emergence of Theatre Atlanta as a regional theatre company of promise.

350. Knussen, Oliver. Review of Iain Hamilton's operatic version of *The Royal Hunt of the Sun*. *New Statesman* 93 (11 Feb. 1977): 200.

351. Lapole, Nick. "Pizarro Invades Broadway." *New York Journal-American* 24 Oct. 1965: 23L.

A pre-opening news story which describes *The Royal Hunt of the Sun* as "a historical drama of stunning strength."

352. Prideaux, Tom. "The Royal Hunt of Virtue." *Life* 10 Dec. 1965: 134-138.

A plot summary of the play and a description, with photographs, of its production. *Royal Hunt* is related to Broadway successes of the past: historical plays dealing with moral convictions (*A Man for All Seasons*, *Becket*, *Luther*, *The Crucible*) and works depicting a clash of cultures (*South Pacific*, *The King and I*, *A Majority of One*).

353. Rissik, Andrew. Review of television production of *The Royal Hunt of the Sun*. *New Statesman* 110 (5 July 1985): 35.

354. Terry, Walter. "Grandma and the Incas." *New York Herald Tribune* 23 Jan. 1966: magazine section; 27.

SCHOLARLY ESSAYS

355. Cohn, Ruby. *Currents in Contemporary Drama*. Bloomington: Indiana University Press, 1969. Contains comments on *The Royal Hunt of the Sun*, pages 124-125.

356. Garstenauer, Maria. *A Selective Study of English History Plays in the Period Between 1960 and 1977*. Salzburg: Inst. fur Anglistik & Amerikanistik, University of Salzburg, 1985.

357. Glenn, Jules. "Twins in Disguise: A Psychoanalytic Essay on *Sleuth* and *The Royal Hunt of the Sun*." *Psychoanalytic Quarterly* 43.2 (1974): 288-302.
     Here analyst Glenn is primarily interested in the ways in which the experience of twinship is embodied, in disguised forms, in creative works by twins Anthony and Peter Shaffer. He notes that both plays deal with pairs of male protagonists who display traits common to twin relationships: ambivalent feelings towards each other ranging from intense rivalry to profound affection, mutual identification, frequent role reversal, and a desire to "keep the score even." He also speculates that these traits are fascinating on stage, at least in part, because many audience members have undergone a childhood phase of fantasizing about having a twin. [Glenn has written extensively on the

implications of twinship in the Shaffers' works. See also entries #30, #51, and #52.]

358. Hammerschmidt, Hildegard. *Das historische Drama in England (1956-1971): Erscheinungsformen und Entwicklungstendenzen.* Wiesbaden and Frankfurt, 1972.

359. Kernodle, George R. *Invitation to the Theatre.* New York: Harcourt, Brace & World, 1967.
     Comments on *The Royal Hunt of the Sun* are to be found on pages 53 and 227.

360. Kernodle, George, and Portia Kernodle. *Invitation to the Theatre: Brief Edition.* New York: Harcourt Brace Jovanovich, 1971.
     Reprints from the complete edition [see #360] include Kernodle's comments on *Royal Hunt*, on pages 55 and 140-141.

361. Knapp, Bettina L. *Antonin Artaud: Man of Vision.* New York: David Lewis, 1969.
     The author maintains, on page 202, that a major source of *The Royal Hunt of the Sun* is to be found in Artaud's *The Conquest of Mexico.*

362. Osorio de Negret, Betty. "La sintaxis basica del teatro: Ensayo comparativo de dos tradiciones dramaticas sobre la prision y muerte de Atahuallpa." *Lexis* (Lima, Peru) 8.1 (1984): 113-129.

363. Plunka, Gene A. "Roles, Rites, and Rituals: Peter Shaffer's *The Royal Hunt of the Sun.*" *Ball State University Forum* 27.3 (Summer 1986): 71-79.

364. Podol, P.L. "Contradictions and Dualities in Artaud and Artaudian Theatre." *Modern Drama* 26.4 (Dec. 1983): 518-527.

Podol contrasts the "Artaudian" techniques utilized in productions of Shaffer's *The Royal Hunt of the Sun* (Broadway version) and Claude Demarigny's *Cajamarca* (as staged by Francisco Javier in Buenos Aires). The latter is thought to be more faithful to Artaud's ideals.

365. Schultz, Dieter. "Peter Shaffer: *The Royal Hunt of the Sun*." In *Das englische Drama der Gegenwart: Interpretationen*. Ed. by Oppel Horst. Berlin: Erich Schmidt, 1976.
     Schultz's analysis of the play is on pages 107-119.

366. Trussler, Simon. "Peter Shaffer: *The Royal Hunt of the Sun*." *Notes on Literature* 142 (British Council, 1973).
     An excellent brief introduction to the play.

367. Westarp, K.H. "Myth in Peter Shaffer's *The Royal Hunt of the Sun* and in Arthur Kopit's *Indians*." *English Studies* 65.2 (April 1984): 120-128.
     This essay sets out to demonstrate that, while dealing with mythic elements, Kopit and Shaffer are essentially "de-mythologizers" rather than "mythmakers." To this end, the plots of the plays in question are summarized at length.

THE FILM

368. Lerner, Irving, dir. *Royal Hunt of the Sun* [film: "Screenplay by Philip Yordan, based on Peter Shaffer's play *The Royal Hunt of the Sun*] with Robert Shaw and Christopher Plummer, Rank Organization, 1969.

Shaw and Christopher Plummer, Rank Organization,
1969.

FILM REVIEWS

369. Anon. Review of film version of *The Royal Hunt of
the Sun*. *America* 121 (18 Oct. 1969): 340.
   An unfavorable assessment, which lays the burden
of blame at the doorstep of screenwriter Philip Yordan
for taking too literal an approach in adapting Shaffer's
play. The review complains that the film does not
capture "the terrible reality of the Inca society" and
that it "illustrates the booby traps involved in
transferring a play to the screen."

370. Canby, Vincent. "Pizarro Conquers Peru." *New York
Times* 7 Oct. 1969: 41.
   After seeing the movie, Canby theorizes that the
original stage version "looked a great deal more
impressive than it really was." The film gets a mixed
notice. It is "entertaining . . . because of its excesses
. . . and because of its moments of dark intelligence
that can't be hidden behind overblown prose."

371. Carroll, Kathleen. "Sun Shines in Just Last Quarter of
Film." *New York Daily News* 7 Oct. 1969: 61.
   Carroll finds all but the final section of the film
version "weak" and "ineffectual." She assigns blame, in
about equal portions, to the direction ("stagey and old-
fashioned") and to the screenplay ("like the play, it is
essentially cerebral").

372. Kael, Pauline. Review of film version of *The Royal
Hunt of the Sun*. *New Yorker* 45.35 (18 Oct.
1969): 196.

Kael has nothing good to say about the film,
denouncing it as "solemn, pretentious, [and]
unconvincing." She condemns Plummer's performance
as Atahuallpa for its "absurd overacting" and expresses
equal disdain for Philip Yordan's screenplay. Her
summary judgment is that the motion picture version
of Shaffer's play could become "a classic of the hooting
variety."

373. Rich, Frank. Review of film version of *The Royal Hunt
of the Sun. Variety* 1 Oct. 1969: 61.
    Rich regards the film as "striking in many ways" but
"talky" and prone to "moralizing a lot." He predicts that
it "should have a big following in art houses" but that
elsewhere it "may find the going a bit rough."

374. Zimmerman, Paul D. Review of film version of *The
Royal Hunt of the Sun. Newsweek* 74 (13 Oct.
1969): 117.
    The reviewer begins by speculating that *Royal
Hunt* would seem to be an ideal candidate for
conversion to film. He concludes, however, that
director Irving Lerner "has turned Shaffer's fine,
dramatic pageant into a hopelessly dated, clumsy,
slow-moving vehicle" which resembles "every
Hollywood epic in memory."

Chapter Seven

Black Comedy and White Lies

(The White Liars/White Liars)

THE TEXT

The complete texts of *Black Comedy* and *White Liars* (the third and final revision of the play) are included in *The Collected Plays of Peter Shaffer* [see #144]. *Black Comedy* and the original version of *White Lies* have been published in many single editions and anthologies, two of which are listed below.

375. Richards, Stanley, ed. *Modern Short Comedies from Broadway and London.* New York: Random House, 1969.
    Includes the text of *Black Comedy* and biographical notes on Shaffer, pages 7-69.

376. *"Black Comedy," Including "White Lies".* New York: Stein and Day, 1967.

PLAY REVIEWS

A. Reviews: *Black Comedy*,
Original Chichester Production.
Opened at Chichester Festival Theatre on July 27, 1965.

377. Anon. "Total Darkness Lit by Brilliant Gags." *Times*
(London) 28 July 1965: 14.
Briefly hails *Comedy* as "a very funny play."

378. Barker, Felix. Review of *Black Comedy*. *Evening
News* (London) 28 July 1965: page no. not available.
A favorable report of the Chichester production.

379. Benjamin, Philip. "Chichester Views Play by Shaffer."
New York Times 29 July 1965: 19.
Reporting from England for the benefit of New
York readers, Benjamin explains the Peking Opera
roots of *Black Comedy* and awards it a brief rave:
" . . . the possibilities are galactic . . . and Mr. Shaffer
generally makes the most of them."

380. Bryden, Ronald. Review of *Black Comedy*. *New
Statesman* 70.1795 (6 Aug. 1965): 194-195.
Here is perhaps the clearest "position paper" to be
put forward by the intellectual critics who can usually
be counted on to oppose Shaffer. In attempting to
explain his own biases toward Shaffer's works, Bryden
cites Robert Brustein's opinion in The Theatre of
Revolt: the great modern dramatists, such as Ibsen,
Strindberg, Chekhov, Shaw, and O'Neill, were
essentially asking their audiences to reject their own,
and their society's, corrupt way of life. To Bryden as
well as to Brustein, it is this "revolutionary nay-saying"
which is the hallmark of serious contemporary writing
for the theatre. In such a context, *Black Comedy* is
reviewed alongside (and compared unfavorably to) the

play with which it was coupled, both at Chichester and
in its London premiere, Strindberg's *Miss Julie*.

381. Curt. Review of *Black Comedy* [and *Miss Julie*].
Variety 15 Sept. 1965: page no. not available.
Approbation for *Black Comedy* : " . . . an
exercise in farce."

382. Darlington, W.A. Review of *Black Comedy*. *Daily
Telegraph* (London) 28 July 1965: 16.
Darlington's review is favorable.

383. Frost, David. Review of *Black Comedy*. *Punch* 4 Aug.
1965: 174-175.
Frost approves of Shaffer's "lightest work to date."

384. Gilliatt, Penelope. "Power-Cut Laughter." *Observer*
(London) 1 Aug. 1965: 19.
The play is said to contain "a blinding idea, not
very boldly pursued." Gilliatt complains that "the
characters very seldom do anything arrestingly human
in the dark."

385. Gilliatt, Penelope. *Unholy Fools. Wits, Comics,
Disturbers of Peace: Film and Theater.* New
York: Viking, 1973.
Includes a reprint of her "Power-Cut Laughter"
review of *Black Comedy* [see #384 above], pages
190-192.

386. Hobson, Harold. "Riot of Laughter." *Christian Science
Monitor* 4 Aug. 1965: 4.
An enthusiastic response to *Black Comedy*: " . . .
a side-splitting farce."

387. Hope-Wallace, Philip. Review of *Black Comedy*.
Manchester Guardian 28 July 1965: 7.

Praise for the Chichester premiere: " . . . an uproarious piece of slapstick-vaudeville."

388. Kretzmer, Herbert. "In the Dark, But They Can See the Light." *Daily Express* (London) 28 July 1965: page no. not available.
    The Chichester premiere of *Black Comedy* is commended as ingenious and effective farce.

389. Levin, Bernard. "Out of the Darkness a Blind Farce." *Daily Mail* (London) 28 July 1965: page no. not available.
    Levin (one of the most outspoken admirers of *Royal Hunt*) praises Shaffer's versatility. He describes *Black Comedy* as the author's "most elaborate departure yet" and judges it (though a bit too long) "an uproarious farce." He goes on to say that the play demonstrates qualities beyond the demands of farce: " . . . wit, elegance, and sophistication."

390. Marriott, R.B. "Death in the Morning and a Comedy in the Dark." *Stage and Television Today* (London) 29 July 1965: 13.
    Marriott offers a favorable review of *Black Comedy*, calling the idea for the play "brilliant." His single reservation: "fifteen minutes or so before the end . . . Shaffer's invention weakens." (The "Death in the Morning" of the headline refers to Strindberg's *Miss Julie*, with which *Black Comedy* was paired both at Chichester and for its first London production at the Old Vic.)

391. Shulman, Milton. "It's a Mad, Mad Romp." *Evening Standard* (London) 28 July 1965: 4.
    A laudatory report on *Black Comedy* in its original incarnation at Chichester.

392. Trewin, J.C. Review of *Black Comedy. Illustrated
    London News* 7 Aug. 1965: 36.
       Trewin finds much in *Black Comedy* that is
    appealing but suggests that cutting would improve the
    second half of the play.

393. Young, B.A. Review of *Black Comedy. Financial
    Times* (London) 28 July 1965: 22.
       A favorable, but unenthusiastic, report.

**B. Reviews: *Black Comedy*, First London Production.
Opened at the Old Vic on March 8, 1966.**

394. Anon. "Double Bill Delights." *Times* (London) 9 Mar.
    1966: 76.
       A review of the Old Vic production of
    (Strindberg's *Miss Julie* and) *Black Comedy*,
    calling Shaffer's play "a dazzlingly unassuming farce."

395. Hobson, Harold. Review of *Black Comedy* [and *Miss
    Julie*]. *Sunday Times* (London) 13 Mar. 1966: page
    no. not available.
       Another bravo from Hobson: "Mr. Shaffer's
    brilliant comic charade."

396. Hobson, Harold. "Hero of the National Theater."
    Christian Science Monitor 21 Mar. 1966: 4.
       In a combined news article-and-review for U.S.
    readers, Hobson reports that the Old Vic staging of
    Black Comedy is "a huge success."

397. Marowitz, Charles. Review of *Black Comedy. Village
    Voice* 14 July 1966: page no. not available.
       Reporting from London for the benefit of New
    Yorkers, Marowitz hands in a lukewarm-to-negative
    review. He finds *Black Comedy* too obviously
    "mechanical."

398. Shulman, Milton. "In the Dark—One Brilliant Joke."
     Evening Standard (London) 9 Mar. 1966: page no.
     not available.
         The London opening at the Old Vic is given a
     brief and favorable review: " . . . a hilarious one-act
     play."

399. Spurling, Hilary. "Mad Craze." *Spectator* (London) 18
     Mar. 1966: 327.
         In a review of three London openings, Spurling
     devotes only one sentence to the Shaffer play: " . . .
     don't miss *Black Comedy*. "

     C. Reviews: *Black Comedy* and *White Lies*
     (premiere), New York Production.
     Opened at the Ethel Barrymore Theatre
     on February 12, 1967.

400. Anon. "Dancing in the Dark." *Time* 17 Feb. 1967: 70.
         While *Black Comedy* is hailed as "an
     unflaggingly funny drawing-room farce," *White Lies*
     is condemned for its failed attempt "to be wise rather
     than clever."

401. Barnes, Clive. "Amiable *Black Comedy* Succeeds in Its
     Aim of Providing Simple Entertainment." *New York
     Times* 19 Oct. 1967: 58.
         Barnes, who has previously seen both plays, takes
     another look at the double bill as the major roles
     change hands. While he continues to find *White Lies*
     disappointing ("a rather labored piece"), his opinion of
     Black Comedy has risen: " . . . machine-made, but
     skillful . . . a theatrical tour de force . . . far more
     successful than . . . *The Royal Hunt of the Sun*,"
     which he describes as "that Verdi opera without Verdi
     music."

402. Bolton, Whitney. Redgrave in *Black Comedy*. *New York Morning Telegraph* 14 Feb. 1967: 3.

This is primarily a public love-letter to Lynn Redgrave (with a few similarly flattering remarks about Geraldine Page). Of the plays themselves, Bolton has little to say except that he likes *White Lies* and has "vast affection" for *Black Comedy*.

403. Bunce, Alan N. Review of *Black Comedy* and *White Lies*. *Christian Science Monitor* 27 Feb. 1967: 4.

Bunce characterizes *White Lies* as an elegantly constructed depiction of "a world of self-deception and false fronts," but not "sharply dramatized." *Black Comedy* is hailed as an ingenious farce whose "every moment becomes a comedy routine."

404. Chapman, John. "Peter Shaffer's Black Comedies a Splendid Theatrical Evening." *New York Daily News* 13 Feb. 1967: 48.

A highly favorable review of both plays. *Lies* is deemed a "deft, sharply-edged [character] study"; *Comedy*, "artful slapstick." [This item is reprinted, along with five other reviews, in *New York Theatre Critics' Reviews*, for which see #420 below.]

405. Chapman, John. "Peter Shaffer's Surprises." *New York Sunday News* 19 Feb. 1967: S3.

In his enthusiastic Sunday follow-up, Chapman describes *White Lies* as "a cunningly wrought work [with] many surprises." He pronounces *Black Comedy* the funniest play of the season and goes on to praise it as more than light entertainment, delivering as it does the message that "people who talk loudly in the dark may reveal more about their inner selves because other people can't see them."

406. Clurman, Harold. Review of *Black Comedy* and *White Lies*. *Nation* 27 Feb. 1967: 285-286.

Clurman justifies, at some length, his enjoyment of
Black Comedy despite its lack of "intellectual
significance." He calls it "very good sport." *White
Lies,* on the other hand, is considered "noteworthy
only for Geraldine Page's acting" and an ending which
constitutes "a collapse of the play in platitude."

407. Cooke, Richard P. "Shaffer Strikes Again." *Wall Street
Journal* 14 Feb. 1967: page no. not available.
Cooke likes both works, judging *White Lies* "an
intriguing sort of morality melodrama" and *Black
Comedy* "a remarkably ingenious farce." The
playwright's versatility is the reviewer's major theme:
"Mr. Shaffer seems to have an inexhaustible bag of
tricks." [This item is reprinted, along with five other
reviews, in *New York Theatre Critics' Reviews,*
for which see #420 below.]

408. Gottfried, Martin. Review of *Black Comedy* and
White Lies. Women's Wear Daily 13 Feb. 1967:
page no. not available.
With reservations, Gottfried commends *Black
Comedy,* calling it "genuinely artistic . . . pure theatre
[of] invention and execution." Of *White Lies,* on the
other hand, he has little to say except that he finds it
"thin." [This item is reprinted, along with five other
reviews, in *New York Theatre Critics' Reviews,*
for which see #420 below.]

409. Gussow, Mel. "Shedding No Light." *Newsweek* 20 Feb.
1967: 102-103.
Thumbs down for both halves of the double bill.
White Lies has "too few surprises," according to
Gussow, a result of the playwright's having "run short
of ideas." The plot of *Black Comedy* is deemed so
weak that "even Chinese gimmickry cannot save it."

410. Hewes, Henry. "When You're Having More Than One."
     Saturday Review 25 Feb. 1967: 59.
       Hewes declares *Black Comedy* to be
     "shamelessly farcical" and the funniest play currently
     on Broadway. His major interest here, however, is not
     the recently opened double bill but an appraisal of the
     playwright's career to date. Overall, he assigns
     medium-high marks, calling Shaffer a dramatist with "a
     modest but very wisely directed talent to fashion a
     wide variety of theatre exercises." Shaffer is compared
     to other contemporary British dramatists: " . . . in the
     same category with Robert Bolt . . . somewhere
     slightly beneath Arden, Osborne, Pinter, and Wesker."
     At the same time, Hewes concedes that he may be
     underestimating Shaffer, pointing out that
     "distinguished intellectual critic" Bernard Levin has
     described *Royal Hunt* as "the greatest play of our
     generation."

411. Hipp, Edward Sothern. Review of *Black Comedy* and
     White Lies. *Newark Evening News* 13 Feb. 1967:
     20.
       A rave for both plays. *White Lies* is said to be a
     source of "fun . . . but also poignancy and heartbreak."
     Black Comedy is lauded as "a brilliant farce."

412. Kerr, Walter. "Vaudeville Variations on a Chinese
     Theme." *New York Times* 13 Feb. 1967: 42.
       A mixed review. While praising Shaffer's
     craftsmanship, Kerr judges him "a sort of
     manufacturer's writer [who] fabricates instead of
     feeling his way." [This item is reprinted, along with
     five other reviews, in *New York Theatre Critics'
     Reviews*, for which see #420 below.]

413. Kerr, Walter. "In Black (Comedy) and White (Lies)."
     New York Times 26 Feb. 1967: section 2; 1.

In his follow-up, Kerr reports that he finds both plays trivial "theatre pieces."

414. Lewis, Emory. Review of *Black Comedy* and *White Lies*. *Cue* 25 Feb. 1967: 8.
    The verdict is favorable. Nothing specific is said of *White Lies*, but Lewis reports that *Black Comedy* provides "an enchanted evening of loony laughter." The bill is summed up as "not profound, but . . . damnably clever."

415. Loney, Glenn. "Broadway and Off-Broadway Supplement." *Educational Theatre Journal* 19.2 (May 1967): 198- 201.
    A review of the New York version of *Black Comedy* (which Loney had seen in London) and its companion piece. The longer of the two works is praised ("still tremendously funny"). *White Lies* is mentioned only in reference to Geraldine Page's "moving and memorable" performance.

416. McCarten, John. "Chinese Kookie." *New Yorker* 25 Feb. 1967: 91.
    Though McCarten finds *White Lies* "slight" and overlong, he writes enthusiastically about *Black Comedy*, welcoming it as the "wildest bout of slapstick in some time." He also praises (in these and earlier works) Shaffer's versatility.

417. Morgan, Derek. "Mixed Bag from Britain." *Reporter* 36.5 (9 Mar. 1967): 50.
    Thumbs down. Morgan claims that audiences will like *Black Comedy* only if they are amused by pratfalls and cheap homosexual jokes. He dismisses *White Lies* as "badly acted non-theatre."

418. Morrison, Hobe. Review of *Black Comedy* and *White Lies*. *Variety* 15 Feb. 1967: 58.

A tepid reception for the double bill. Though
Morrison concedes that *Black Comedy* is "good fun,"
he finds both plays too long and calls *White Lies* "a
yawn."

419. Nadel, Norman. "Hilarity Never Stops for *Black
Comedy* ". [Also reviews *White Lies*] *New York
World Journal Tribune* 13 Feb. 1967: 16.
Modest praise is given *White Lies* ("a good little
play"), while *Black Comedy* receives an unqualified
rave. Nadel calls it "uproarious, the rediscovery of
laughter . . . by itself worth the price of admission."
[This item is reprinted, along with five other reviews,
in *New York Theatre Critics' Reviews*, for which
see #420 below.]

420. *New York Theatre Critics' Reviews* 28.4 (Week of 13
Feb. 1967): 371-374.
Contains reviews listed here as entries #408,
#404, #407, #425, #419, and #412.

421. Oppenheimer, George. "*Black Comedy* Opens on
Broadway." [Also reviews *White Lies*] *Newsday* 13
Feb. 1967: 2A.
Although Oppenheimer judges both plays "too
long," he recommends *Black Comedy* as "uproarious
. . . not to be missed."

422. Prideaux, Tom. "Things That Go Bump in the Dark." *Life*
10 Mar. 1967: 70A-70D.
A special report, with several photos, on the
Broadway production of *Black Comedy/White
Lies*. A brief review of *Comedy* is included: " . . .
the gimmick works . . . [but] drags on a bit too long."

423. Richardson, Jack. "English Imports on Broadway."
Commentary 43.6 (June 1967): 73-75.

Richardson describes *Black Comedy* as "entirely commonplace." He finds both plays, in their separate ways, "old-fashioned" and "workmanlike," serving notice that "the genteel days of English drama are not quite over."

424. Smith, Michael. Review of *Black Comedy* and *White Lies*. *Village Voice* 16 Feb. 1967: 21.
    Black Comedy is considered by Smith to be "hilarious," yet not entirely satisfactory. *White Lies*, on the other hand, is deemed an unmitigated disaster: " . . . contrived, trite, and pretentious."

425. Watts, Richard, Jr. "Comedy of Light in Darkness." *New York Post* 13 Feb. 1967: page no. not available.
    Watts likes both plays but suggests that each would have been "twice as effective if half as long." His judgment on Shaffer's stature to date: " . . . a brilliantly versatile dramatist." [This item is reprinted, along with five other reviews, in *New York Theatre Critics' Reviews*, for which see #420 above.]

426. Watts, Richard, Jr. "The Versatility of Peter Shaffer." *New York Post* 25 Feb. 1967: 20.
    In a follow-up to his opening night review, Watts explains that he is favorably disposed toward the double bill but insists that both one-acts would benefit from pruning. This piece includes a reconsideration of Shaffer's output to date.

427. Watts, Richard, Jr. "Peter Shaffer's Play Revisited." *New York Post* 14 Sept. 1967: 57.
    On taking another look at the double bill (for the purpose of reviewing cast replacements), Watts reiterates his view of *Black Comedy* as an "ingenious, farcical tour-de-force." At the same time, *White Lies* is elevated in his esteem: " . . . a perceptive and touching one-act . . . of striking merit."

428. West, Anthony. "*Black Comedy* Enormously Funny."
     Vogue 15 Mar. 1967: 54.
     While West ignores *White Lies*, he awards an
     unqualified rave to *Black Comedy*: " . . . a milestone
     in the history of comedy."

**D. Reviews: *Black Comedy* (2nd London production)
and *The White Liars* (1st London Production).
Opened at the Lyric Theatre on February 5, 1968.**

429. Bryden, Ronald. "Red-Nosed Revival." *Observer*
     (London) 25 Feb. 1968: 26.
     A negative appraisal of both halves of the double
     bill. Bryden considers *The White Liars* to be
     "imperfectly adapted to the stage." *Black Comedy*'s
     major Broadway revision is acknowledged ("shedding
     the Negro-hating diatribes of the spinster from
     upstairs"), but the sum of the re-writes is judged
     inadequate: " . . . [the play] emerging flabbier rather
     than leaner."

430. French, Philip. "Surprise, Surprise." *New Statesman*
     75.1929 (1 Mar. 1968): 279.
     French is displeased with what he considers the
     coarsening of *Black Comedy* in both script and
     performance for its Broadway incarnation. He dislikes
     The White Liars ("shallow . . . sententious").

431. Hope-Wallace, Philip. Review of *Black Comedy* and
     The White Liars. *Manchester Guardian* 22 Feb.
     1968: 6.
     A lukewarm report on both plays, including the
     "now famous *Black Comedy*."

432. Kingston, Jeremy. Review of *Black Comedy* and *The
     White Liars*. *Punch* 28 Feb. 1968: 319.
     Approval for both halves of the double bill.

433. Kretzmer, Herbert. Review of *Black Comedy* and *The White Liars*. *Daily Express* (London) 22 Feb. 1968: 3.

    While re-reviewing *Comedy* ("the brilliant basic idea . . . stands up well"), Kretzmer takes his first look at *The White Liars*, which he gives an unenthusiastic endorsement: " . . . more than a mere curtain-raiser."

434. Lewis, Peter. "Black and White Brilliance." *Daily Mail* (London) 22 Feb. 1968: page no. not available.

    Lewis approves of *The White Liars* (though he complains that, toward the end, "one becomes conscious of the contrivance"). A second viewing of *Black Comedy* convinces him that it "establishes Peter Shaffer as our most brilliant theatrical conjurer."

435. Nathan, David. "Night of Double Delight." *Sun* (London) 22 Feb. 1968: page no. not available.

    A rave for both halves of the bill, with *Black Comedy* winning particular praise: " . . . probably the best farce of this century."

436. Rich, Frank. Review of *Black Comedy* and *The White Liars* . *Variety* 13 Mar. 1968: 75.

    Rich finds *Black Comedy* over-extended but very amusing. He is less kind to *The White Liars*, terming it a "contrived anecdote."

437. Say, Rosemary. Review of *Black Comedy* and *The White Liars*. *Sunday Telegraph* (London) 25 Feb. 1968: page no. not available.

    The White Liars is judged "puzzling . . . intelligent, sensitively written, meticulously shaped, almost orchestrated, full of insight and observation, yet somehow for me a cold, unmoving, unconvincing exercise in play-making." Say maintains that *Black Comedy* "remains one of the most hilarious displays of pure comic invention ever seen on any stage."

438. Shorter, Eric. "Comedy of 'Images' Is Overstrained."
    Daily Telegraph (London) 22 Feb. 1968: 19.
    The review is devoted entirely to *The White
    Liars*. Shorter, who has seen the earlier New York
    version (*White Lies*), claims that, though revisions
    have made the play clearer, it remains "unduly
    pretentious and eager to moralize."

439. Shulman, Milton. Review of *Black Comedy*. *Evening
    Standard* (London) 22 Feb. 1968: 4.
    Shulman has nothing to add to his earlier appraisal
    of *Black Comedy* beyond finding it "still fresh." The
    White Liars receives mild praise.

440. Spurling, Hilary. "Tatty Pegs." *Spectator* (London) 1
    March 1968: 271-272.
    On her third viewing, Spurling continues to praise
    Black Comedy. Despite re-writes, however, she is
    still unable to recommend its companion piece: "*The
    White Liars* . . . has neither the taut shapely grace of
    Black Comedy nor its impeccable organisation."

441. T., J.R. Review of *Black Comedy* and *The White
    Liars*. *Times* (London) 22 Feb. 1968: 13.
    While the London premiere of *The White Liars*
    is almost ignored ("not much of a play really"), the
    revival of *Black Comedy* is heartily approved: " . . .
    Mr. Shaffer's dazzlingly adroit piece of comic plotting."

**E. Reviews: *Black Comedy* and *White Liars*
(third revision), London Revival.
Opened at the Shaw Theatre on June 28, 1976.**

442. Cushman, Robert. "Better Black Than White." *Observer*
    (London) 4 July 1976: 22.
    A revival at the Shaw Theatre is reviewed. Little is
    said of the third and last version of *White Liars*

except that its "most interesting addition, in view of
the long line of male attachments in Mr. Shaffer's
plays, is the explicit acknowledgment that this
[attachment] really is homosexual." A final verdict is
rendered on *Black Comedy*. It is described as "a
single mechanical joke," on the order of the Marx
Brothers' stateroom sequence in *A Night at the
Opera*, which is "indefinitely prolonged and becoming
more irresistible every second." Cushman maintains
that the play is "probably the only classic farce written
in England since the war."

443. Hurren, Kenneth. Review of *Black Comedy* and
White Liars. *Spectator* (London) 10 July 1976: 28.
   In reviewing four London openings, Hurren
remarks, ". . . the week's only joy was [*Black
Comedy*]." His view of the re-written *White Liars*,
however, is less generous: " . . . [it] remains an
unsatisfactory grapple with the knotty problems of
separating the realities of the human personality from
the deceptive veneers."

444. Nightingale, Benedict. Review of *Black Comedy* and
White Liars. *New Statesman* 9 July 1976: 59.
   In a brief report on the revival, Nightingale states,
"*White Liars* remains a miss; but *Black Comedy* is
a palpable hit in spite of . . . its [being] 15 or 20
minutes too long." The critic uses this opportunity to
assess the playwright's career: "If Shaffer had
continued to write as unpretentiously and
entertainingly as this, we might now claim him as a
major exponent of a minor genre, instead of a minor of
a major."

445. Wardle, Irving. "What Comes After a Smash?" *Times*
(London) 29 June 1976: 8.

Wardle assesses the re-writes for *White Liars*:
" . . . [the] revision consists more of tinkering about
than any real structural overhaul."

F. Reviews: Other Productions.

446. Carleton, Don. Review of *Black Comedy*. *Drama* 151
(Winter 1984): 38.
This is a brief note on the Bristol Old Vic
production: "a romp . . . the audience loved it . . . "

NEWS REPORTS AND FEATURE STORIES

447. Anon. "Shaffer Double Bill at the Shaw." *Times*
(London) 11 June 1976: 9.
A short news item announcing the director and
cast for a forthcoming revival of *Black Comedy* and
a revised, third version of its companion piece, now re-
titled (by dropping the definite article) *White Liars*.

448. Day, Doris M. "Theatre Bookshelf." *Drama* No. 126
(Autumn 1977): 80, 82.
In reviewing the published edition of *White
Liars*, Day suggests that the revised version is "more
effective in presenting the harsh truth than was [the]
original." She lauds Shaffer as "a master playwright,
someone who understands the medium of the theatre
and the demands of a modern, intelligent audience."

449. Lyons, Leonard. "The Lyons Den." *New York Post* 6
Mar. 1967: page no. not available.
Lyons reports that "the movie rights to Peter
Shaffer's hit *Black Comedy* were sold last week." [A
film version, however, was never made, quite likely

owing to the difficulty of solving on celluloid the
central "light for dark" convention of the play.]

Chapter Eight

The Battle of Shrivings

THE TEXT

The complete text of *The Battle of Shrivings* has not been published, but the as yet unproduced revision entitled *Shrivings* is included in *The Collected Plays of Peter Shaffer* [see #144] and in the single edition listed below.

450. Shaffer, Peter. *Shrivings*. London: Andre Deutsch, 1974.

PLAY REVIEWS

London Production.
Opened at the Lyric Theatre on February 5, 1970.

451. Anon. "Games Playwrights Play." *Time* 30 Mar. 1970: 77.

An unfavorable verdict, calling the work "a Shaw
play without Shaw."

452. Anon. "Gielgud, Hiller, Magee in Shaffer Drama." *Stage
and Television Today* (London) 29 Jan. 1970: 14.
A generally approving report which nonetheless
remarks that Shaffer "never [uses] one word where a
dozen will do."

453. Bail. Review of *The Battle of Shrivings*. *Variety* 11
Feb. 1970: 61.
A mixed review. "[Seen] as [an] expertly staged
melodrama with an intellectual vein, the play is
magnetic and occasionally profound." However, Bail
goes on to complain that the work is marred by its
"inherent incredibility."

454. Barker, Felix. "Gielgud Makes This a Night to
Remember." *Evening News* (London) 6 Feb. 1970:
page no. not available.
Not the usual "mixed" review; rather, an
apparently contradictory one: the play is "not moving,"
but the evening is one of "searing emotional fire." As
its title indicates, this is primarily an appreciation of
the actors' contributions, especially Gielgud's.

455. Bryden, Ronald. Review of *The Battle of Shrivings*.
Observer (London) 8 Feb. 1970: 31.
A pan. Bryden suggests that Kenneth Tynan's
catalogue of "Bad British Plays of Today" should be
updated for the 1970s, with *The Battle of Shrivings*
topping the list. His major complaint: the play is
unconvincing and "arbitrarily theatrical," resembling
"Iris Murdoch's philosophical court-comedies."

456. French, Philip. Review of *The Battle of Shrivings*.
Plays and Players 20.59 (Mar. 1970): 20, 59.

The playwright's work is deemed manipulated, unconvincing, pretentious, and hollow. French charges that, in *The Battle of Shrivings*, it is as if Shaffer has "imposed the ideological framework of *Royal Hunt of the Sun* on to the domestic scene of *Five Finger Exercise*."

457. Hobson, Harold. Review of *The Battle of Shrivings*. *Sunday Times* (London) 8 Feb. 1970: 53.
    The verdict is negative. Hobson admits that Shaffer "can manage the homely cliche . . . as well as anyone this side of Los Angeles." But he asks the playwright (1) to stop insisting that he is a writer of significant drama and stick to the less demanding pieces that he does so well and (2) to remember that "mediocrity of style is not improved by having a great subject to work on."

458. Hobson, Harold. "Gielgud, Shaffer, and Hall—Had a Great Fall." *Christian Science Monitor* 13 Feb. 1970: 6.
    Another unfavorable review from Hobson. He writes that the piece falls into two separate (and unsatisfactory) parts: the first is all philosophical argument; the last is all bogus melodrama. He concludes that Shaffer has tried "to seize something that is altogether beyond the reach of what proves to be his very tiny hand."

459. Hope-Wallace, Philip. Review of *The Battle of Shrivings*. *Manchester Guardian* 6 Feb. 1970: 8.
    While Hope-Wallace approaches his task with unwavering respect, describing Shaffer's latest work as "serious and honorable," he concludes that it is "too long for its own good . . . witty, but not always quite witty enough."

460. Kingston, Jeremy. Review of *The Battle of Shrivings*. *Punch* 11 Feb. 1970: 236.
    Although he complains that the evening is overlong, Kingston finds much to admire in the play.

461. Lewis, Peter. "This Truth Game Makes Us All Groggy." *Daily Mail* (London) 5 Feb. 1970: page no. not available.
    Lewis sees *The Battle of Shrivings* as a mix of "Shaw plus melodrama." He considers it odd that the defective ingredient should turn out to be the melodrama while "the Shavian part is fine."

462. Marcus, Frank. "Poet v. Philosopher." *Sunday Telegraph* (London) 8 Feb. 1970: page no. not available.
    Marcus approves of Shaffer's intentions and maintains that the writing bears the evidence of solid craftsmanship. Nonetheless, the play's ideas are deemed unworthy of close examination.

463. Marriott, R.B. "The Philosopher and the Poet Join Battle at Shrivings." *Stage and Television Today* (London) 12 Feb. 1970: 13.
    Marriott dismisses the work as unconvincing, pretentious, and boring.

464. Nightingale, Benedict. "Some Immortal Business." *New Statesman* 79.2031 (13 Feb. 1970): 227.
    Nightingale pans *The Battle of Shrivings*, and makes use of the occasion to offer a larger appraisal of Shaffer's career. He admires the earlier, less ambitious works (by a "modest, agreeable young playwright"): *Five Finger Exercise*, *Private Ear*, *Public Eye*, and *Black Comedy*. But he finds *The Battle of Shrivings*, as he did *Royal Hunt* before it, "solemn, affected, empty."

465. Pouteau, Jacques. "New Shaffer Play Analysis of Man."
     Newark Evening News 7 Feb. 1970: 6.
     In this a news report disguised as a review,
     Pouteau calls *The Battle of Shrivings* Shaffer's
     "most ambitious work," but makes no reference to the
     quality of the play.

466. Shorter, Eric. Review of *The Battle of Shrivings*.
     Daily Telegraph (London) 6 Feb. 1970: 16.
     Shorter concedes that the play's ideas are "highly
     intelligent," but he complains that the characters,
     whom he considers "mere mouthpieces," have failed to
     move him.

467. Shulman, Milton. "Arguments Without Soul." *Evening
     Standard* (London) 6 Feb. 1970: 24.
     Shulman judges *The Battle of Shrivings* a
     "brave, but flawed, event." He calls it "an interesting
     literary exercise . . . immured in the walls of its own
     rhetoric."

468. Spurling, Hilary. "Stags at Bay." *Spectator* (London) 14
     Feb. 1970: 217.
     A pan. Spurling describes Shaffer as "a problem
     playwright," but one who shares with J.M. Barrie "a
     kind of nursery tone: dire but twinkling, as though he
     feared that such big topics might prove alarming unless
     approached in tiny thoughts." She congratulates the
     actors for their professionalism, given the fact that it is
     "hard to deliver lines like these with a straight face."

469. Trewin, J.C. Review of *The Battle of Shrivings*.
     Illustrated London News 21 Feb. 1970: 26.
     The entire evening is judged to be an "artificial
     contrivance."

470. Wardle, Irving. "Philosopher of Peace." *Times* (London)
     6 Feb. 1970: 13.

Wardle begins with praise for the dramatist's
ambitious aims: "Peter Shaffer . . . belongs to the small
band of playwrights who believe that matters of
conscience and intellect can be fitly debated in a
popular form." Nevertheless, the new work falls far
short of doing "justice to its theme." Like Robert Bolt's
The Tiger and the Horse, says Wardle, *The Battle
of Shrivings* leaves one with doubts "about the
capacity of orthodox West End craftsmanship to come
to grips with such material."

471. Wardle, Irving. "Play by Shaffer Opens in London: *Battle
    of Shrivings* Tells of Philosopher's Plight." *New
    York Times* 7 Feb. 1970: 23.
        In his report to American readers, Wardle
    describes the play as "a well-made traditional
    [domestic melodrama]," but adds that it "lamentably
    fails to honor its philosophic theme."

472. Young, B.A. Review of *The Battle of Shrivings*.
    Financial Times (London) 6 Feb. 1970: 3.
        A negative opinion. Young asserts that, whatever
    merits the play possesses, they are outweighed by the
    simple fact that both plot and characters are
    incredible.

NEWS REPORTS AND FEATURE STORIES

473. Anon. Interview with John Gielgud. *Cue* 7 Nov. 1970: 9.
        During this conversation, Gielgud briefly discusses
    the difficulties which surrounded the production of
    The Battle of Shrivings (in which he starred as
    Gideon): "The management and the director were
    rather at odds over what should be cut and changed
    . . . I think [this] bewildered Shaffer, and the final

cutting was not as good for the play as it could have been."

474. Anon. "Peter Shaffer's New Battle for Olivier-Gielgud." *Variety* 9 Sept. 1969: 63.

A news report on plans for the forthcoming National Theater production of *The Battle of Shrivings* which is to star England's two most famous actors. [Olivier, originally scheduled to play Mark, withdrew from the cast for reasons of ill health and was replaced by Patrick Magee.]

475. Knox, Collie. Note on *Shrivings*. *New York Morning Telegraph* 31 Mar. 1971: 3.

In a report on the current London theatre scene, Knox writes that Shaffer has re-written *The Battle of Shrivings*, and that the new version will be "presented next season on Broadway." [This news, in the course of time, proved only half correct. The revised *Shrivings* has, to the present date, received no major professional production, either in London or the U.S.]

Chapter Nine

Equus

THE TEXT

The complete text of *Equus* is included in *The Collected Plays of Peter Shaffer* [see #144] and in many other single editions and anthologies, three of which are listed below.

476. Shaffer, Peter. *Equus*. London: Andre Deutsch, 1973.

477. Barnet, Sylvan, Morton Kerman and William Burto, eds. *Types of Dramas: Plays and Essays*. 2nd ed. Boston: Little, Brown & Co., 1977.
    Contains the text of *Equus* with a brief note on Shaffer's works, pages 250-299.

478. Guernsey, Otis L., ed. *The Best Plays of 1974-1975*. New York: Dodd, Mead & Co., 1975.
    Includes an abridged version of *Equus* and a biographical sketch of Shaffer.

PLAY REVIEWS

A. Reviews: Original London Production.
Opened at the Old Vic on July 26, 1973.

479. Barber, John. Review of *Equus*. *Daily Telegraph*
(London) 27 July 1973: 13.
Barber voices a minor complaint about the
transparently "literary" quality of some of the dialogue.
Otherwise, he finds much to praise.

480. Billington, Michael. Review of *Equus*. *Manchester*
Guardian 27 July 1973: 12.
This is an unqualified rave, with the opening
paragraph describing the play as "sensationally good."
Billington suggests that *Equus* repeats the basic
theme Shaffer previously mined in both *Royal Hunt*
and *The Battle of Shrivings*, "a direct confrontation
between passion and intellect." The new work,
however, is judged superior to its predecessors because
in it "the intellectual argument and the poetic imagery
are virtually indivisible."

481. Christie, Ian. Review of *Equus*. *Daily Express*
(London) 27 July 1973: 10.
Christie charges that the excellence of the
production obscures the fact that the script is
"pretentious, philosophical claptrap."

482. Cushman, Robert. Review of *Equus*. *Observer*
(London) 29 July 1973: 30.
Complaints about unconvincing aspects of the
script are overbalanced by enthusiasm for the
production's effectiveness: " . . . taken realistically, the
play is a dud . . . theatrically, it is a triumph."

483. Davies, Russell. Review of *Equus*. *New Statesman*
     86.2211 (3 Aug. 1973): 165-166.
     This is a mixture of lavish praise for the
     production and mild censure for Shaffer's having
     created a "worrying" script of dubious intellectual
     merit.

484. Dawson, Helen. Review of *Equus*. *Plays and Players*
     Sept. 1973: 43-45.
     Dawson's view is negative. She claims that the
     script relies on glib oversimplifications and that
     Shaffer is unable to support the grand theme
     (Dionysus vs. Apollo) with appropriate language or
     invention.

485. Gottfried, Martin. "*Equus* in London." *Women's
     Wear Daily* 16 Jan. 1974: 22.
     Gottfried, who calls the play "flashy but a fake,"
     charges that its content is "irrelevant and forgettable."

486. Hobson, Harold. Review of *Equus*. *Sunday Times*
     (London) 29 July 1973: 33.
     A rave, in which Hobson predicts that audiences
     will be "stunned and blasted away by the power of the
     play." This article is of interest as a rebuttal to those
     reviewers who found the content of the play trite and
     the author's intentions exclusively popular: "What
     Shaffer says in *Equus* is so nonconformist that a
     large proportion of his audiences . . . will go away
     pretending either that Mr. Shaffer does not believe
     what he says, or says something quite different from
     his plain and (to the present eye) unacceptable
     meaning." The nonconformist theory to which Hobson
     refers is that, without Dionysian ecstasy, "life is empty
     and cold."

487. Hobson, Harold. "A Triumph at London's National
     Theater." *Christian Science Monitor* 10 Aug. 1973:
     14.
         As in his London *Times* review a few days
     earlier [#486 above], Hobson awards the play an
     unqualified rave. He not only finds *Equus*
     "formidable . . . inspiring," but affirms its tremendous
     success with its audience: "Not even at the memorable
     first night of *Oklahoma* a quarter of a century ago
     have I heard applause so prolonged and so insistent."

488. Hughes, Catherine. "London's Stars Come Out." Review
     of London production of *Equus*. *America* 129 (8
     Dec. 1973): 443-444.
         In her brief appraisal, Hughes calls the play's
     theatricality "stunning." She places Shaffer among a
     rare group of modern playwrights: he not only "has
     something to say," but keeps his audience enthralled
     while saying it.

489. Hurren, Kenneth. Review of *Equus*. *Spectator* no.
     7571 (4 Aug. 1973): 159.
         Hurren considers the plot unconvincing and the
     theme "of dubious validity." Despite strong
     reservations, he encourages his readers to see the play
     for its extraordinary production values, which make it
     an exciting piece of theatre.

490. Kalson, Albert E. Review of *Equus*. *Educational
     Theatre Journal* 25.4 (Dec. 1973): 514-515.
         The reviewer is favorably impressed in spite of
     what he regards as the play's major flaw: the
     development of Dysart's character is necessarily less
     vivid than the incidents in Alan's story. Kalson goes on
     to express disappointment with Shaffer for failing to
     confront his audience with "current problems" (the
     play is compared unfavorably in this respect to
     Hampton's *Savages*).

491. Kerr, Walter. "A Psychiatric Detective Story of Infinite Skill." *New York Times* 2 Sept. 1973: section 2; 1, 3.
     Kerr's admiration for *Equus* is great: " . . . the closest I have seen a contemporary play come—it is powerfully close—to reanimating the spirit of mystery that makes the stage a place of breathless discovery."

492. Kingston, Jeremy. Review of *Equus*. *Punch* 8 Aug. 1973: 188.
     A warmly approving reception is given "Mr. Shaffer's distinguished play."

493. Lambert, J.W. Review of *Equus*. *Drama* 111 (Winter 1973-1974): 14-16.
     A generally favorable review, though more appreciative of the production than of the script. The theme is found effective but not so well realized in *Equus* as previously in *Royal Hunt*. Shaffer is summed up as "an honest, sometimes stiff writer."

494. Pit. Review of *Equus*. *Variety* 8 Aug. 1973: 44.
     A bravo for the London production: " . . . powerful and moving."

495. Shulman, Milton. Review of *Equus*. *Evening Standard* (London) 27 July 1973: 28-29.
     A favorable report.

496. Wardle, Irving. Review of *Equus*. *Times* (London) 27 July 1973: 15.
     A mixed opinion. Wardle appreciates "the excellence of the writing in Dysart's speeches." However, he grumbles that the play contains "very little real dialogue" (the relatively brief scenes involving two or more characters are considered to be a bit perfunctory, serving mainly to set up Dysart's next big monologue). The critic includes a general observation on Shaffer's career: "In style, one can

never predict what kind of piece he will write next; but his theme remains constant . . . a tournament between Apollo and Dionysus."

497. Watts, Richard, Jr. "The Boy Obsessed with Horses." *New York Post* 18 Aug. 1973: 16.
A brief and approving report.

498. Young, B.A. Review of *Equus*. *Financial Times* (London) 27 July 1973: 3.
Enthusiastic approval is given the play both for its thought-provoking theme and its highly original theatrical techniques.

B. Reviews: New York Production.
Opened at the Plymouth Theatre on October 24, 1974.

499. Barnes, Clive. "*Equus* a New Success on Broadway." *New York Times* 25 Oct. 1974: 26.
Barnes' opening night review is highly favorable (though perhaps less so than his several follow-ups). He judges *Equus*, "a very fine and enthralling play," and goes on to point out the dual nature of the work's appeal: " . . . a popularly intended play . . . but it has a most refreshing and mind-opening intellectualism." [This item is reprinted, along with nine other reviews, in *New York Theatre Critics' Reviews*, for which see #524 below.]

500. Barnes, Clive. "Perkins in *Equus*: Shaffer Drama Is Still Magnificent Theater." *New York Times* 17 July 1975: 19.
Re-reviewing the play as the leading roles change hands (Perkins and Hulce taking over as Dysart and Alan), Barnes affirms that it "remains an engrossing, enthralling piece of theater."

501. Barnes, Clive. "Alec McCowen in *Equus.*" *New York Times* 28 Feb. 1977: 23.

Reviewing the play yet again, as McCowen reclaims the Dysart role, Barnes looks back upon its two and a half year history on Broadway. He finds it remarkable that the "the play holds up," even with actors in the primary role as dissimilar as Richard Burton (a leading man in the romantic-heroic mold) and McCowen ("almost charismatically a failure").

502. Beaufort, John. "Brilliant British Import: Shaffer's Inventive *Equus* Hits Broadway." *Christian Science Monitor* 4 Nov. 1974: 12.

Beaufort's report is an unqualified rave. He finds Shaffer's work "powerfully moving . . . a stunning piece of inventive play-making [which] calls on all the resources of imagery, symbolism, and allusions that range from TV commercial jingles to mythical centaurs." [This item is reprinted, along with nine other reviews, in *New York Theatre Critics' Reviews,* for which see #524 below.]

503. Brukenfeld, Dick. "All That Fuss About Horses?" *Village Voice* 31 Oct. 1974: 91-92.

Brukenfeld finds the first act disappointing but the second impressive: "When Mr. Shaffer stops being crafty and evasive and lets out the stops, he is superb."

504. Clurman, Harold. Review of *Equus.* *Nation* 16 Nov. 1974: 506-507.

Equus is described as "something like a detective story with philosophic implications." Clurman praises the detective story element as "brilliantly crafted, handsomely written and unusually compelling." The play's philosophy, on the other hand, he finds "bogus . . . an echo of the new cant that the schizophrenic is closer to the truth of life than the ordinary citizen."

505. Gill, Brendan. "Unhorsed." *New Yorker* 50.37 (4 Nov. 1974): 123-124.
     Shaffer is praised, both for his ingenuity and as a "superb writer of dialogue." Gill also commends the playwright for having taken, in *Equus*, "greater chances" than ever before and for succeeding in making a stimulating inquiry into the complexities of contemporary life "in the midst of a melodrama continuously thrilling on its own terms."

506. Gottfried, Martin. "Shaffer's *Equus* at the Plymouth." *New York Post* 25 Oct. 1974: page no. not available.
     This item is of interest as an example of a rave review which nonetheless drubs the playwright. Gottfried compares his impressions of the Broadway opening with those he experienced at the London premiere some ten months earlier. In London he had considered the play trite social drama. In New York he is surprised to find it "a devastating experience." Most of the credit for this improvement is given to Anthony Hopkins (in contrast to Alec McCowen, as Dysart). Gottfried continues to denigrate the script. On Broadway, he contends, production values have outweighed "essentially trite and occasionally weird ideas." [This item is reprinted, along with nine other reviews, in *New York Theatre Critics' Reviews*, for which see #524 below.]

507. Gottfried, Martin. "*Equus*, with New Stable Mates." *New York Post* 17 July 1975: 24.
     Writing on the occasion of cast changes (Perkins and Hulce replacing Hopkins and Firth as Dysart and Alan), the reviewer reports that he was able this time to "concentrate on the script" more completely than on previous viewings. In a major critical turnaround [see #485 and #506 above], while still faulting Shaffer on minor points (some awkward dialogue and a few "trite ironies"), Gottfried now declares the play to be "in the

main extremely well written . . . [it] has a wonderful
combination of intelligence, honesty, true feeling,
poetry and a willingness to state its ideas."

508. Gottfried, Martin. "Burton's Just Horsing Around." *New
York Post* 27 Feb. 1976: 20.

Reporting on yet another cast change in *Equus*,
Gottfried adds nothing concerning the script but
complains of Burton's "implausible" overacting as
Dysart. The play is therefore not, as in the past,
"devastating."

509. Gottfried, Martin. "Alec McCowen Stifles *Equus.*" *New
York Post* 24 Feb. 1977: 18.

Gottfried's fifth report (on the occasion of
McCowen's joining the New York cast) belongs to the
small, but much-talked-of, group of reviews which
maintain that the play has a disguised homosexual
theme. The pertinent (impertinent from Shaffer's
viewpoint) section reads: "[The play's] questioning of
'normalcy' and championship of primitivism are
bourgeois, and beneath it all lies an overly familiar
justification of homosexuality, master-slave
subcategory."

510. Greer, Edward G. A note on the New York production of
Equus. *Drama* 117 (Summer 1975): 32.

Greer rates the New York version of the play "a
major success." Mention is made of letters to the
editor of the *New York Times* which complain of the
drama's portrayal of psychotherapy and
psychotherapists [see #528 and #626].

511. Hewes, Henry. "The Crime of Dispassion." Review of
Equus. *Saturday Review* 25 Jan. 1975: 34.

A favorable review which politely expresses a few
reservations, including the view that "the play's
statement is less impressive than is Shaffer's skillful

theatrical fabrication." Pointing to the clever use of
comic relief which keeps the audience involved
through the increasingly violent events of the last act,
Hewes writes that "*Equus* emerges as a surprisingly
painless modern tragedy, which accounts for both its
popularity and the reservations some serious critics
have expressed about its significance." He sums up his
impressions with the suspicion that the play "is at its
truest when it is reflecting its author's anger at his own
civilization."

512. Hughes, Catharine. Review of Broadway production of
Equus. America 131 (30 Nov. 1974): 349.
Preferring Anthony Hopkins' portrayal of Dysart
to Alec McCowen's, Hughes declares the New York
production of *Equus* superior to the London version.
Her final assessment: *Equus* is not great drama, but
great theatre.

513. Kalem, T.E. "Freudian Exorcism." *Time* 104 (4 Nov.
1974): 119.
Kalem joins the party of those who find *Equus*
excellent theatre ("a galvanizing psychological thriller")
but dispute its value as serious drama. Nevertheless,
the critic places Shaffer in distinguished company
when he lists other plays handicapped by "dubious
intellectual premises:" T.S. Eliot's *Cocktail Party*,
Archibald MacLeish's *J.B.*, and Edward Albee's
Who's Afraid of Virginia Woolf. [This item is
reprinted, along with nine other reviews, in *New York
Theatre Critics' Reviews*, for which see #524
below.]

514. Kauffmann, Stanley. Review of *Equus. New Republic*
7 Dec. 1974: 18, 33-34.
Kauffmann disparages earlier works by Shaffer
(*Five Finger Exercise, Royal Hunt of the Sun*)
as a prelude to his contention that *Equus* "does

better, but not enough." The plot is deemed "thin," and both the "mythical" elements and Dysart's envy of Alan's passion are criticized as incredible.

515. Kerr, Walter. "*Equus*: A Play That Takes Risks and Emerges Victorious." *New York Times* 3 Nov. 1974: 11.

This review is a closely reasoned and well-developed argument for the play's being granted the stature of greatness. The "risk-taking" approved in the headline refers to both the script's subject matter and its manner of presentation. Kerr concludes by saying that "*Equus* is one of the most remarkable examples of stagecraft, as well as of sustained and multifaceted sensibility, the contemporary theatre has given us."

516. Kerr, Walter. "*Sherlock* and *Equus* Revisited." *New York Times* 5 Oct. 1975: section 2; 1, 5.

Returning to the play, with replacements Anthony Perkins and Tom Hulce taking up the major roles, Kerr deals exclusively with the new actors, whose work he admires.

517. Kissel, Howard. Review of *Equus*. *Women's Wear Daily* 28 Oct. 1974: 10.

An enthusiastic reception is given the play, which is called "a theatrical event of the greatest importance." [This item is reprinted, along with nine other reviews, in *New York Theatre Critics' Reviews*, for which see #524 below.]

518. Kroll, Jack. "Horse Power." *Newsweek* 4 Nov. 1974: 60.

Kroll manages to deliver a rave while withholding his full approval. He finds *Equus* "dynamite" as theatre, a "devilishly masterful work of craftsmanship," and "not to be missed." But he is quick to point out that he considers the play "too pat in its intellectual substance."

519. Kroll, Jack. "In from the Cold." *Newsweek* 87 (8 Mar.
     1976): 70.
         Reviewing Burton as Dysart, Kroll concentrates
     exclusively on the star and says nothing of the play.
     [This item is reprinted, along with nine other reviews,
     in *New York Theatre Critics' Reviews*, for which
     see #524 below.]

520. Leonard, John. "Critic's Notebook: An Evening with Two
     Walking Anachronisms." *New York Times* 26 May
     1976: 24.
         Reviewing Broadway replacements (Anthony
     Perkins and Tom Hulce), Leonard describes *Equus*
     as "a not very good play, brilliantly staged."

521. Michener, Charles. Review of *Equus*. *Newsweek* 86
     (11 Aug. 1975): 71.
         A re-review of the play as the leading roles change
     hands. Both new stars (Anthony Perkins as Dysart,
     Tom Hulce as Alan) are warmly received. Shaffer's
     script is not reassessed.

522. Mootz, William. Review of *Equus*. *Louisville
     Courier-Journal and Times* 15 Dec. 1974: H8.
         A brief review of the New York production,
     calling it "an intriguing melodrama . . . sensational and
     oddly satisfying."

523. Morrison, Hobe. Review of *Equus*. *Variety* 30 Oct.
     1974: 88, 90.
         The play is found "fascinating and strangely
     suspenseful." Morrison prophesies "a successful
     Broadway run and road tour."

524. *New York Theatre Critics' Reviews*. 25.17 (Week of
     4 Nov. 1974): 201-207.

Contains reviews listed here as entries #541, #502, #550, #517, #499, #519, #513, #506, #529, and #535,

525. Novick, Julius. "*Equus* Rehorsed." *Village Voice* 1 Sept. 1975: 79-80.

Novick offers a second review of the New York production with its new principals, Anthony Perkins and Tom Hulce (both of whom are thought "wonderfully adroit"). Once again, the critic offers a mixed verdict on the script. He finds the play "interesting and memorable . . . but, until nearly the end, not emotionally involving."

526. Oppenheimer, George. Review of *Equus*. *Newsday* (Long Island, NY) 10 Nov. 1974: Section II; 9, 70.

A rave for the play and its author. Shaffer's "macabre imagination and his amazing versatility" are considered unmatched among contemporary playwrights. Seeing *Equus*, Oppenheimer says, is "like watching an ancient ritual."

527. Oppenheimer, George. Review of *Equus*. *Newsday* (Long Island, NY) 14 Mar. 1976: section 2; 9.

A re-review following Burton's advent as Dysart. The play is admired as "one of the few important dramas of the past decade."

528. Pacheco, Patrick. Review of *Equus*. *After Dark* Dec. 1974: page no. not available.

Although he expresses displeasure with early portions of the play, Pacheco praises *Equus*'s construction and compassion and deems it "finally beautifully moving."

529. Probst, Leonard. Review of *Equus*. NBC-TV, Channel 4, New York City, 24 Oct. 1974.

A brief critique, in which Probst finds fault with
the play's long opening act but judges the second act to
be "the best I've seen in years." The reviewer considers
Shaffer's work "more thrilling than logical" and "more
sexy . . . than sound." But clever conception and
performance, he says, produce an end result that is
"overwhelming." [This item is reprinted, along with
nine other reviews, in *New York Theatre Critics'
Reviews*, for which see #524 above.]

530. Real, Jere. "A Rocking Horse Winner." *National Review*
28.3 (31 Jan. 1975): 114-115.
   A thorough rave. The critic finds that the play's
ambiguities and "rich complexities" add up to "truly
superb theatre."

531. Reed, Rex. "*Equus*: A Bad Premise, but Good Theater."
New York Sunday News 3 Nov. 1974: leisure
section; 7.
   Reed's single, vigorous complaint about the play
concerns Dysart's final speech, in which (as Reed puts
it) he questions whether he "should have helped this
tragic child [Alan]." The reviewer admits that he has
"always loved . . . plays that ask the question: who is
really . . . insane, the acknowledged loonies, or the sick
society?" He maintains, however, that such a premise
only works "when the loonies are lovable, not when [as
in *Equus*] they are dangerous to themselves and to
society."

532. Reed, Rex. "Perkins Improves *Equus*. " *New York Daily
News* 14 Nov. 1975: 82.
   Harking back to his earlier review [see #531],
Reed notes that he was "impressed with the play's
dramatic impact and disappointed in its lack of
feeling." It was the final Dysart speech which "ruined
the play" for him. But Anthony Perkins' handling of
the speech has changed his opinion because "Perkins

makes his obsessions personal—allowing the audience
the luxury of knowing they are his alone."

533. Rich, Alan. "Of Men and Other Beasts." *New York* 9.11
(15 Mar. 1976): 75.

This is a re-review, devoted primarily to the task
of assessing the impact of Richard Burton's having
replaced Anthony Perkins in the role of Dysart. Rich's
verdict: Perkins was superior; Burton's "frigid,
oratorical tone" further distances the audience from
involvement. Rich's view of the play remains
unchanged: a "non-event."

534. Richardson, Jack. "The English Invasion." *Commentary*
59.2 (Feb. 1975): 76-78.

In the course of this emphatically negative review,
a brief appraisal of Shaffer's stature, through *Equus*,
is provided. The dramatist is described as having "very
modest talents." His most recent play is condemned for
its "schematic psychology" and "simpleminded cultural
criticisms." Richardson recounts the plot of *Equus* in
detail in order to point out "the mediocrity of insight
necessary nowadays for a play to enjoy a popular
reputation for profundity." Like many other critics
opposed to Shaffer, Richardson professes to admire
the production values and admits that the event, in
theatrical terms, is effective.

535. Sanders, Kevin. Review of *Equus*. WABC-TV, New
York City Channel 7, 30 Oct. 1974.

A favorable review. After voicing one complaint
([it] "gets a bit soupy at times"), the reviewer waxes
enthusiastic: " . . . highly literate, sophisticated, and
has great, soaring speeches." [This item is reprinted,
along with nine other reviews, in *New York Theatre
Critics' Reviews*, for which see #524 above.]

536. Simon, John. "The Blindness Is Within." *New York* 7.45 (11 Nov. 1974): 118.
    Simon begins by describing Shaffer as a dramatist "of talent and intelligence." He then proceeds, as did Benedict Nightingale in his *New Statesman* review of *The Battle of Shrivings* [see #460], to express his preference for Shaffer's earlier, "smaller and zanier" plays (*Public Eye*, *Black Comedy*, etc.) Simon concedes that *Equus* has received a splendid physical production, but he claims that the theatrical splendors mask a "hollowness within."

537. Simon, John. "Hippodrama at the Psychodrome." *Hudson Review* 28.1 (Spring 1975): 97-106.
    Simon addresses the question: what makes *Equus* virtually the only Broadway play to be succeeding without benefit of stars? First and foremost, he says, it is "pretentious, which the public likes." The critic maintains that the play "pullulates with dishonesty," and that it pampers its "affluent, bourgeois, conformist" audience members by allowing them to affirm their libertarianism and unconventionality in a very safe manner. Finally, Simon disparages the viewpoint of the play's protagonist, finding the plight of the "cured" Alan Strang a desolate one. "Clearly, if anyone needs psychiatric help," writes the reviewer, "it is Dr. Dysart."

538. Sontag, Frederick. "God's Eyes Everywhere." *Christian Century* 92.42 (17 Dec. 1975): 1162, 1164.
    Sontag maintains that the most debatable element in the play is its "theology." Shaffer is reprimanded for having oversimplified the Christian deity by dwelling on the "constantly watching us" theme without adding that the watcher looks on with "limitless compassion."

539. Stasio, Marilyn. Review of *Equus*. *Cue* 4 Nov. 1974: 23.

In a largely favorable review ("a seductive piece of writing . . . altogether compelling"), Stasio adds her voice to those who discover a hidden homosexual theme in the play: " . . . the young patient's driving urge to worship horses . . . becomes a dramatic metaphorical argument for . . . the glorification of homosexuality."

540. Tobias, Tobi. "Playing Without Words." *Dance Magazine* 49.5 (May 1975): 48-50.

This article is an unusual combination of a review and an interview (with the six actors who play the horses in the production). Tobias, who expresses great admiration for the horse-actors, begins her article by quoting one of them: " . . . we are acting the roles of the horses . . . not dancing these roles." The critic stresses that "the most vivid sequences [in the play] are [the] textless moments." Her attitude toward the highly verbal bulk of the play is far from favorable ("an old-fangled, fancy-art garble of ideas").

541. Watt, Douglas. "*Equus* Is a Smashing Psychodrama." *New York Daily News* 25 Oct. 1974: 76.

Though Watt expresses a few reservations about the play's intellectual content ("may strike you as bargain-basement psychoanalysis"), he finds it "gripping theater . . . a taut and rather flashy little thriller." [This item is reprinted, along with nine other reviews, in *New York Theatre Critics' Reviews*, for which see #524 above.]

542. Watt, Douglas. "*Equus* A Stunner Filled with Chills, Drama, Psychiatry." *New York Sunday News* 3 Nov. 1974: leisure section; 3.

In a follow-up to his opening night review, Watt discusses the play at length, referring to it as "essentially a thriller" and hailing it as "powerful, exciting theatre."

543. Watt, Douglas. "Perkins, Hulce Sit *Equus* Well." *New York Daily News* 17 July 1975: 76.

Re-reviewing as the leading roles change hands (Anthony Perkins and Tom Hulce taking over as Dysart and Alan), Watt continues to refer to the play as a "superb thriller" and praises its "devilishly clever" construction.

544. Watt, Douglas. "Dr. McCowen Is Back on the Case." *New York Daily News* 24 Feb. 1977: 64.

On his fourth viewing of the play, Watt writes that he has "enjoyed it all over again" and reports that McCowen (the original London Dysart) "is superb."

545. Watts, Richard, Jr. "A Brilliant New Drama." *New York Post* 2 Nov. 1974: 14.

Watts applauds with gusto, calling *Equus* Shaffer's "finest achievement . . . not only an exciting drama, but an important one."

546. Weales, Gerald. "Horse Choler." *Commonweal* 102.3 (25 Apr. 1975): 78-79.

Weales begins by expressing reservations about the quality of the writing but proceeds to deliver one of the most eloquently simple statements of praise ever given this work. He suggests that the core of the play is "a cry for the power of irrationality," and he claims that Shaffer's handling of the theme is more serious and timely than he is usually given credit for. Weales reports that on the night he watched, the audience burst into extended, spontaneous applause for the speech in which Dysart admits that he envies Alan's passionate devotion to an unseen reality. This, he posits, is evidence that the play has genuinely "touched a nerve in the New York audience."

547. Weightman, John. "Christ as Man and Horse." *Encounter* Mar. 1975: 44-46.

Weightman finds *Equus* "to some extent a good play," but he finds himself unable to sympathize with Dysart's ethical position. He especially objects to the psychiatrist's (and presumably the playwright's) notion that there is no hope for a happy future for Alan after his "cure."

548. Weiner, Bernard. "Does *Equus* Need Sex and Violence?" *San Francisco Chronicle* 26 Feb. 1975: 48.

The reviewer thinks the play is "fascinating" and "wonderfully theatrical," but his discomfort over the sex-and-violence issues (especially the latter) prompts him to pose the question: "Why write such a play at all?" He ends by confessing that he is still confused as to his own reactions.

549. Wetzsteon, Ross. "Burton's *Equus*: They Shoot Actors, Don't They?" *Village Voice* 8 Mar. 1976: 92.

In reviewing the cast change, Wetzsteon does not reserve all his critical bullets for Richard Burton. He also guns down the play. His article begins with a mock-definition: "*Equus*: pejorative noun . . . (circa 1976) used to describe an intellectual sham, in particular a loathsome, meretricious piece of patronizing claptrap, derived from an odious Broadway play of the period."

550. Wilson, Edwin. "Conflicting Elements in a Human Soul." *Wall Street Journal* 28 Oct. 1974: page no. not available.

An effusive tribute. Wilson believes that *Equus* works on many levels, all of which coalesce to produce "one of the most powerful and provocative theatrical experiences of our time." [This item is reprinted, along with nine other reviews, in *New York Theatre Critics' Reviews*, for which see #524 above.]

C. Reviews: Other Productions.

551. Grant, Steve. Review of *Equus*. *Plays and Players*
     June 1976: 29.
        Grant reviews a slightly revised version of John
     Dexter's staging as the play re-opens in London's
     Albery Theater (with Colin Blakely as Dysart). He
     regrets that Shaffer has not found (using Eliot's
     terminology) "a sufficient 'objective correlative'" for
     his thematic ideas and that he lacks the "verbal power
     . . . to prop up what is a fairly routine philosophy," a
     philosophy which Grant sums up as "Laingean pseudo-
     liberal manure."

552. Lennartz, K. Review of *Equus*. *Theater der Zeit* 39.1
     (1984): 4.

553. Nightingale, Benedict. "Horse Sense." *New Statesman*
     30 Apr. 1976: 583.
        Nightingale suggests that "we should be wary of
     the thinking behind *Equus*," as the play seems to him
     to be "too neatly put together, too easily untied," and
     the ideas it presents are "exceptionally suspect, and
     sentimental, too." The critic confesses that he may be
     "over-reacting to the inflated" critical reception the
     play has received.

554. Simons, Piet. "K.V.S. op toernee met *Equus.*" *Ons
     Erfdeel: Algemeen-Nederlands Tweemaandelijks
     Kultureel Tijdschrift* (Rekkem, Belgium) 19
     (1976): 449.

555. Spurling, Hilary. "Horse-Play in Hampshire." *Observer*
     (London) 25 Apr. 1976: 26.
        This review, on the re-opening of *Equus* at the
     Albery Theatre, complains of the script's simplified
     motives and predictable attitudes. Spurling feels that,
     if one ignores the "puzzle" of a plot premise (why did

the stableboy blind six horses?), "its framework is instantly recognizable as fairly standard soap opera." The critic ends by likening Shaffer to J.M. Barrie as a clever and exploitative popular playwright.

NEWS REPORTS AND FEATURE STORIES

556. Anon. "Brief on the Arts." *New York Times* 4 June 1975: 26.
    Reports that the Outer Critics Circle Award has been awarded to Shaffer for *Equus.*

557. Anon. "*Equus* Owners Plan Two Moves—One on Broadway, One for Road." *New York Times* 14 Sept. 1976: 45.

558. Anon. Success of *Equus. New York Times* 9 July 1976: C2.
    A report on the recent opening of the play in Los Angeles and its forthcoming performances in Mexico City, Paris, and Vienna.

559. Barnes, Clive. "Peter Shaffer's *Equus* Is Box-Office Success." *New York Times* 17 Aug. 1973: 11.
    A report on the current offerings at London's National Theatre. *Equus* is denied status as "an imperishable masterpiece" but is judged "enormously enjoyable" and "a very important play . . . ideally suited to an institutional repertory."

560. Bassett, Abe. "*Equus*: A Case for Censorship?" *ACA Bulletin* 56 (Apr. 1986): 53-57.
    The author describes in some detail a heated controversy which arose over a 1984 production of the play at Wright State University (where he was then

Chairman of the Theatre Department). The element
which led to many audience complaints was the
decision to produce "the play as written" with both
Alan and Jill nude for the second act seduction scene
in the stables. Special factors may have contributed to
the volume of complaints; i.e., both actors involved
were relatively young (younger, that is, than their
professional predecessors in the parts), and they were
also "locals" who resided in the Dayton area and drew
numerous family members and friends as audience.

561. Bosworth, Patricia. "Richard Burton: 'I Knew If I Didn't
    Come Back Now I Never Would.'" *New York Times*
    4 Apr. 1976: section 2; 5, 10.
    Bosworth interviews Burton as he is about to
    assume the role of Dysart in the Broadway production
    of *Equus*. Of some interest is the fact that Burton at
    first refused to read the play because he "hated the
    title . . . thought it specious." Then, when he was
    finally persuaded by his agent to read it, he did so
    rapidly, six times in succession, called the agent back
    and said: "I'll play this part any time, any place."

562. Calta, Louis. "*Equus* Voted Best Play by Drama Critics."
    New York Times 28 May 1975: 30.

563. Davis, Ken, and William Hutchings. "Playing A New Role:
    The English Professor as Dramaturg." *College
    English* 46.6 (Oct. 1984): 560-569.
    This is a discussion of experiences undergone, and
    conclusions reached, by the authors while serving
    separately as literary advisors for university theatre
    productions of *Romeo and Juliet* and *Equus*. Mr.
    Hutchings, who worked in this capacity for an *Equus*
    production at the University of Alabama at
    Birmingham, remarks in passing on some minor
    inconsistencies in the character of Alan. (The boy's
    detailed knowledge of certain literary and historical

passages, as well as his reference to ballet dancers, would seem to belie Dysart's description of an almost illiterate youth whose only source of culture is "pop" television.)

564. Deford, Frank. "Peter Shaffer's *Equus* Celebrates the Horse as an Awesome Pagan Idol." *Sports Illustrated* 3 Mar. 1975: 9.

565. [Dexter, John, interviewed by Ronald Hayman.] "John Dexter: Walking the Tightrope of Theatrical Statement." *Times* (London) 28 July 1973: 9.

The director of *Equus* talks with Hayman around the time of the play's London opening. Though he discusses briefly his directorial contribution to *Royal Hunt*, Dexter's comments focus mainly on his role in nurturing *Equus* from its earliest stages through opening night. He asserts that it was he who devised the concepts of the masks, the stylized actor-horses, and the onstage audience seating. He also claims the credit for having suggested two major script improvements:

   (1) the use of a less naturalistic time sequence (a decision which led, among other things, "to that first image of a boy caressing a horse")
   (2) the development of Dysart's character by asking the playwright to engage in the process of "digging into himself"

566. [Dexter, John, interviewed by Gordon Gow.] "The Struggle: An Interview with John Dexter." *Plays and Players* Nov. 1979: 14-16.

Director Dexter's remarks include a lengthy description of the evolution of various stylized devices for his production of *Equus*, especially the masks for the actors portraying horses.

567. Edwards, Bill. "Award for *Equus.*" *Variety* 6 Apr. 1977: 119.
    A news report on the play's having received the Los Angeles Drama Critics Award.

568. Gruen, John. "*Equus* Makes Star of Peter Firth." *New York Times* 27 Oct. 1974: section 2; 1, 5.

569. Gussow, Mel. "Burton Finds a New Stage to Conquer." *New York Times* 27 Feb. 1976: 16.
    An interview with Richard Burton as he assumes the role of Dysart in *Equus.*

570. Guthrie, Constance. "National Resource." *Newsweek* 84 (11 Nov. 1974): 121.
    This article focuses on Anthony Hopkins and his success in the role of Dysart. *Equus* is called "that rarest of rarities, a serious play that's a smash hit."

571. Haupt, John. "Rethinking *Equus* Heads." *Theatre Crafts* May/June 1979: 24-25, 84.
    The process of designing the horse masks for a production at Miami's Coconut Grove Playhouse is described. The design team's decision was to move away from John Napier's original London (and Broadway) concept of "leather and aluminum" and toward "a totally metallic look."

572. Kerr, Walter. "Off-Broadway Fades Victoriously." *New York Times* 17 Aug. 1975: section 2; 1, 5.
    Kerr believes that the Off-Broadway "movement" of the 1950s and 1960s has come to an end. Yet its explorations into the Theatre of the Absurd and its experiments under the guidance of Peter Brook, Jerzy Gratowski, Julian Beck and Judith Malina have left a rich legacy, of both content and style, that has now reached Broadway in such adventurous plays as *Equus.* Kerr notes several earlier Off-Broadway

"innovations" utilized in *Equus*: the seating of a portion of the audience onstage, the use of masks both to assist performers and as decor, and the ritualistic presentation of the actors who play horses.

573. Klossowicz, Jan; Jerzy Koenig; Jerzy S. Sito; and Elzbieta Wysinka. *"Equus*: czli mechanizm sukcesu." *Dialog: Miesiencznik Poswiecony Dramaturgii Wspolczesnej: Teatralnej, Filmowej, Radiowej, Telewizyjnej* (Warsaw) 23.8 (1978): 146-152.

574. Lerner, Max. "The Best Plays." *New York Post* 9 May 1975: 41.
    A feature story on two award winning-plays: Albee's Pulitzer-winner, *Seascape,* and Shaffer's Tony-winner, *Equus.* Lerner contends that both plays are worthy of their awards and uses them to illustrate the fact that though some deserving plays (*Equus*) are popular successes, others (*Seascape*) are not.

575. Simons, Piet. *"Equus*: Verslag van een beleving." *Ons Erfdeel: Algemeen-Nederlands Tweemaandelijks Cultureel Tijdschrift* (Rekkem, Belgium) 18.1 (1975): 125-126.

576. Wimble, Barton. "Maryland Ballet Premieres Shaffer's *Equus.* " *New York Daily News* 24 Mar. 1980: 27.
    A report on the imminent opening of a dance version of the play entitled "Equus: The Ballet." It is noted that Shaffer himself has collaborated on the scenario with Israeli choreographer Domy Reiter-Soffer, who hopes that the ballet will extend the ritualistic theatricalism of the play to achieve "mythic proportions."

SCHOLARLY ESSAYS (Play)
[Includes items from psychoanalytic journals]

577. Baldwin, Helene L. "*Equus*: Theater of Cruelty or Theater Sensationalism?" *West Virginia University Philological Papers* 25 (Feb. 1979): 118-127.
     The writer attempts to assess *Equus* by the standards of Artaud's ideas on a "theatre of cruelty." Though Shaffer (and director Dexter) have admitted the influence of Artaud, such an exclusively theoretical analysis seems forced at best. The writer concludes by agreeing with Jack Richardson's review in *Commentary* [see entry #534] that the script of *Equus* is a banal soap opera and has been made to succeed only by virtue of John Dexter's sensational staging.

578. Berman, Jeffrey. "*Equus*: 'After Such Little Forgiveness What Knowledge?'" *Psychoanalytic Review* 66.3 (1979): 407-422.
     Berman begins by explaining that Shaffer's play rests on an "unresolvable paradox": Alan's cure equals his dehumanization (or, social normality equals abnormality from a higher philosophical point of view). The remainder of this article amounts to an attack on Shaffer's faulty ideas about psychoanalysis and false notions about his own motives in writing the play (the writer maintains that there is ample evidence that the underlying emotion of the play is repressed homosexual love). Berman concludes by asserting that Dysart's problem is "not that he knows too much for his own good, but that he knows too little [for Alan's good]."

579. Beyer, M. "Peter Shaffer's *Equus* and the Paradox of the Healthy Sick Man and the Sick Healthy Man." *Forum Modernes Theater* 2.2 (1987): 154-169.

An interpretation, in German, of the play. The
writer uses extensive quotes from Shaffer's text as
support.

580. Brewer, Colin. "Psychiatry and Contemporary Thoughts
on the Nature of Mental Illness: Don't Frighten the
Horses." [*Equus* and other films discussed] *World
Medicine* 13.7 (1978): 51-52.

581. Burland, J. Alexis. "Discussion of Papers on *Equus*."
*International Journal of Psychoanalytic
Psychotherapy* 5 (1976): 501-506.
     Burland's contribution is apparently intended as
an objective, moderator's view of the four other papers
on Shaffer's play published in this issue. It indeed
begins in a neutral tone, pointing out that (1) it may
not be wise to apply psychoanalytic procedures to
fictional characters, and (2) "Mr. Shaffer was not
primarily interested in depicting a psychiatric case
study." However, Burland eventually admits that he
sides with Dr. Sanford Gifford (who authored the
controversial Op-Ed piece in the *New York Times*
titled "A Psychoanalyst Says Nay to *Equus*," for
which, see #593). Applying psychoanalytic
interpretations both to the fictional characters of
Equus and to their creator, he concludes that the
"passion" experienced by Alan and admired by Dysart
"can be understood as a subjective sense of infantile
omnipotence" [emphasis supplied by Burland]. To
support his view that the playwright has upheld
infantile (presumably deluded) ideals, the writer
supplies information on Shaffer's personal life: "The
fact that, as reported in the *New York Times*, the
young actor who played Alan . . . lived with the
playwright points even further to the creation of
reality from fantasy." Burland concludes with the
observation that, in the case of *Equus*, the audience is
"asked to witness a self-inflating, even auto-erotic

event" and is shortly thereafter "tricked into being a sychophilic participant in the reality the playwright has created." [This issue of the *Journal* contains four other articles on *Equus*, also by teachers or practitioners of clinical psychotherapy; see #594, #595, #617, and #618.]

582. Cerny, Lothar. "Peter Shaffer's *Equus.* " Pages 157-170 in *Englische Literatur der Gegenwart* [festschrift]. Ed. by Rainer Lengeler. Dussendorf: Bagel, 1977.

583. Chandhuri, Una. "The Spectator in Drama/Drama in the Spectator." *Modern Drama* 27 (1984): 281-298.
     Along with several other plays, *Equus* is discussed.

584. Clum, John M. "Religion and Five Contemporary Plays: The Quest for God in a Godless World." *South Atlantic Quarterly* 77.4 (Autumn 1978): 418-432.
     Clum defines the theme of *Equus* as "the creation of a Dionysian religion in a highly rational world." He maintains that such a theme "reflects the Christian world's inability to integrate sexuality and religion." He briefly examines similar thematic strains in *The Royal Hunt of the Sun*.

585. Corbally, John. "The *Equus* Ethic." *New Laurel Review* 7.2 (1977): 53-58.
     Corbally's article, as its title suggests, is a critique of the play's ethical position rather than its value as a work of art. Its starting point is the contention that, in *Equus*, "not only does Shaffer suggest that beneath a veneer of social convention man is a raving lunatic beast, but he seems to applaud the fact." An examination of this premise leads the writer to conclude that the play advocates "a wholesale tearing down of an ordered society, but . . . offers no sound

architectural model for rebuilding . . . [and] seems to opt for chaos."

586. Corello, Anthony V. "*Equus*: The Ritual Sacrifice of the Male Child." *Psychoanalytic Review* 73.2 (Summer 1986): 191-211.

Corello takes this opportunity to diagnose psychoanalytically both leading character Dysart and author Shaffer. According to this theory, Alan's character is virtually non-existent, serving no function in the play except as a mirror for, and a target of, Dysart's "unresolved transference issues." Corello concludes that Dysart is afflicted with a "narcissistic disorder of the self" and displays "archaic" feelings and perceptions of reality. Dysart's (and Shaffer's) disdain for the psychiatric profession is sharply taken to task.

587. Davies, D. Russell. "Alienation, Detachment and Reconciliation." *Community Schools Gazette* (Oswestry, England) 68.9 (1974): 537-545.

Mentions *Equus* briefly.

588. Dean, Joan F. "The Family as Microcosm in Shaffer's Plays." *Ball State University Forum* 23.1 (1982): 30-34.

The writer claims that the treatment of family relationships in works by Shaffer "epitomizes his handling of institutions" (i.e., institutions, including families, are systematic, therefore corrupt, and will stifle or pervert the genuine human impulses of individuals). Works examined are: *Five Finger Exercise, The Public Eye, Royal Hunt, White Lies, Shrivings,* and *Equus.* She sees *Five Finger Exercise* as the "prototype" for her thesis and describes its basic plot structure: "An outsider triggers an examination of the problems which lie beneath the superficial tranquillity maintained for propriety's sake." It is a pattern which she finds repeated in

Shaffer's later works, notably in the case of Alan's family in *Equus*.

589. Deneulin, Alain. "*Equus*." *Kunst en Cultuur* (Brussels) 1 Apr. 1976: 14-16.

590. Ebner, I. Dean. "The Double Crisis of Sexuality and Worship in Peter Shaffer's *Equus.*" *Christianity and Literature* 31.2 (Winter 1982): 29-47. This is one of the few reviews from theological or religious periodicals to come out strongly in favor of the play. Ebner praises Shaffer for admonishing his audience not to settle for the easily-repeated slogans of organized religion, but to go on exploring until they find the "undivided Reality" of a genuine spiritual life. He also appreciates Shaffer's willingness to depict honestly both "the crisis of sexuality" and "our fundamental need to worship." The final assessment: *Equus* is a modern classic which merits serious study by literary critics.

591. Gabbard, K. "Updike, Shaffer, and the Centaurs." *Helios* 14.1 (1987): 47-58.

592. Gianakaris, C.J. "Theatre of the Mind in Miller, Osborne, and Shaffer." *Renascence* 30 (Autumn 1977): 33-42. Compares *After the Fall*, *Inadmissible Evidence*, and *Equus* as studies of middle-aged men of "the professions" in search of personal integrity. Gianakaris's "theatre of the mind" concept is of some interest as a way of approaching these protagonist-as-narrator psychological dramas (and, in fact, could also be applied to Shaffer's later *Amadeus* and *Yonadab*).

593. Gifford, Sanford. "A Psychoanalyst Says Nay to *Equus*."
    New York Times 15 Dec. 1974: section 2; 5.
    Gifford, faculty member at the Harvard Medical
    School, is moved to deliver a lengthy Op-Ed article
    condemning *Equus* as a "play [which] paints a picture
    of the psychoanalytic process that demands a
    professional response." He contends that Shaffer is not
    only ignorant of the processes of psychotherapy but
    distorts them for unworthy ends, and that the audience
    is "promised some significant glimpse of the truth and
    left with a bogus or trivial message."

594. Gifford, Sanford. "'Pop' Psychoanalysis, Kitsch, and the
    'As If' Theater: Further Notes on Peter Shaffer's
    Equus. *International Journal of Psychoanalytic
    Psychotherapy* 5 (1976): 463-471.
    Gifford follows up his critique published by the
    New York Times in December, 1974 [see #593]. He
    complains that Shaffer's writing is manipulative and
    exploitative with a "high proportion of conscious
    artifice [and] a pervasive sense of insincerity." The
    label which should be applied to the play is "kitsch,"
    rather than "an unsuccessful . . . attempt at high art."
    The term "kitsch," explains Gifford, is properly applied
    when the author's motive is not to produce a work of
    artistic integrity but to achieve "a sensation." "*Equus*,"
    as he describes it, "can be identified as kitsch . . .
    because it fails the traditional Aristotelian test of
    tragic catharsis." [This issue of the *Journal* contains
    four other articles on *Equus*, also by teachers or
    practitioners of clinical psychotherapy; see #581,
    #594, #612, and #613.]

595. Glenn, Jules. "Alan Strang as an Adolescent: A
    Discussion of Peter Shaffer's *Equus*." *International
    Journal of Psychoanalytic Psychotherapy* 5
    (1976): 473-487.

Glenn is a therapist-author with a special interest in the psychology of twins. Although he begins by admitting that there are pitfalls in psychoanalyzing the products of an artistic creation, he interprets Alan "as if he were a real person." He considers the play "not realistic" in its depiction of the progress of Alan's therapy; but he finds it "vivid and compelling," in part because it shows Alan "regressing to a narcissistic state [involving] desires to fuse, to have a double, and to be a twin." [This issue of the *Journal* contains four other articles on *Equus,* also by teachers or practitioners of clinical psychotherapy; see #581, #594, #617, and #618.]

596. Greiff, Louis K. "Two for the Price of One: Tragedy and the Dual Hero in *Equus* and *The Elephant Man.*" Pages 64-77 in *Within the Dramatic Spectrum* (Lanham, Maryland: University Presses of America, 1986).

597. Hamilton, James W. "*Equus* and the Creative Process." *Journal of the Philadelphia Association for Psychoanalysis* 6 (1979): 53-64.

598. Hays, Peter L. "Shaffer's Horses in *Equus:* The Inverse of Swift's." *Notes on Contemporary Literature* 17.4 (Sept. 1987): 10-12.

599. Herzenstein, Guido. "Peter Shaffer: *Equus.*" Pages 499-516 in *Studi inglesi: Raccolta di saggi e ricerche, Series 5* (Bari: Adriatica, 1978).

600. Jensen, Marvin D. "Teaching Interpersonal Communication Through Novels, Plays and Films." Paper presented at Meeting of the Conference on Culture and Communication (Philadelphia, PA, Apr. 1981).

Equus is among the literary works and motion
pictures discussed as tools for teaching communication
skills.

601. Jones, Anne Hudson. "Thomas Szasz' Myth of Mental
Illness and Peter Shaffer's *Equus.*" Pages 282-290 in
*Proceedings of Asclepius at Syracuse: Thomas
Szasz, Libertarian Humanist* [festschrift], ed. by
M.E. Grenander (Albany, New York: Institute for
Humanistic Studies, State University of New York,
1980).

602. Jones, A.H. "Psychiatrists on Broadway, 1974-1982."
Literature and Medicine 4 (1985): 128-140.
Includes a discussion of *Equus.*

603. Kaplan, Morris Bernard. "*Equus*: A Psychiatrist
Questions His Priestly Powers." *Hastings Center
Report* 5.1 (Feb. 1975): 9-10.
Kaplan, a staff consultant on ethics for the
Hastings Center, is described in an introductory note
as "philosopher, lawyer, playgoer." His article describes
the plot of *Equus* and considers the grounds for the
controversy it has generated among psychotherapists.
His comments are even-handed and penetrating. He
enumerates the key issues with which the play deals:
"the adequacy of the medical model, the values implicit
in concepts of normality and mental health, the use of
therapy to deal with socially deviant behavior, and the
possibility of a human need to transcend the limits of
secular rationality." Though Shaffer's treatment of
these themes is open to question from health
professionals, Kaplan concludes, the play is valuable
for exposing important and rarely discussed issues to
the general public. Finally, he endorses the work as "a
powerful theatrical presentation of the personal and
professional crisis of Martin Dysart."

604. Klein, Dennis. "Literary Onomastics in Peter Shaffer's *Shrivings* and *Equus*." *Literary Onomastics Studies* 7 (1980), 127-138.
     An essay on the possibly intentional symbolism of the character names Shaffer has chosen for *The Battle of Shrivings* and *Equus*.

605. Klein, Dennis A. "Peter Shaffer's *Equus* as a Modern Aristotelian Tragedy." *Studies in Iconography* 9 (1983): 175-181.

606. Lee, James. "*Equus*, Round Three." *Exchange* 2 (Spring 1976): 49-59.
     According to Lee, the opening night reviews for *Equus*, most of which were raves, constitute "Round One;" and he sees as "Round Two" the wave of critical backlash of harsh objections that came later. "Round Three," says Lee, is an attempt to take the critical journey full circle: a defense of *Equus* against its severest detractors, such as Dr. Sanford Gifford [see #593 and #594].

607. Lee, Ronald J. "Jungian Approach to Theatre: Shaffer's *Equus*." *Psychological Perspectives* 8.1 (Spring 1977): 10-21.

608. Loomis, Jeffrey B. "As Margaret Mourns: Hopkins, Goethe, and Shaffer on 'Eternal Delight.'" *Cithara* 22.1 (Nov. 1982): 22-38.
     Includes a discussion of *Equus*.

609. Lynch, William F. "What's Wrong with *Equus*?" *America* 133 (13 Dec. 1975): 419-422.
     In a lengthy and detailed article, theologian Lynch supports his dislike for *Equus* by comparing it unfavorably with Euripides' *Bacchae*. Both plays, he says, deal with the conflict between the Dionysian ideal of passion and the Apollonian ideal of

rationality. Whereas Euripides' treatment depicts both the glory and the horror of Dionysius, Shaffer's is fraudulently simplistic and "ovational" in support of the Dionysian impulse.

610. May, William F. "From Obscurity to Center Stage: Playwrights, Patients, and Professionals." *Hastings Center Report* 11.6 (Dec. 1981): 24-30.
   In a brief report on several recent plays dealing with doctor-patient relationships, May describes *Equus* psychiatrist Dysart as "a convenient symbol, if one wants to undercut the claims of modern medical therapy."

611. Miles, John A. "*Equus* and the Death of Psychiatry." *Parabola* 1.3 (Summer 1976): 100-105.
   In a "review" of the published text of the play, Miles does not attempt to analyze the script in depth but uses it, instead, as a springboard for reflections (with numerous quotations from other works) on the so-called "death of psychiatry."

612. Miner, Michael D. "Grotesque Drama in the '70s." *Kansas Quarterly* 12.4 (Fall 1980): 99-109.
   Briefly discusses *Equus* along with six other New York productions of the decade: *Dracula*, *The Effects of Gamma Rays on Man-in-the-Moon Marigolds*, *Dawn*, *Duck Variations*, *Night of the Tribades*, and *Dirty Linen*. Miner defines "the grotesque" as "an aesthetic motif composed of the fused images of the inanimate and the animate." *Equus*, he explains, is encompassed by this rubric, because of its extensive animal (equine) imagery, and especially because of its blinding-the-horses sequence.

613. Plunka, Gene A. "The Existential Ritual: Peter Shaffer's *Equus*." *Kansas Quarterly* 12 (Fall 1980): 87-97.

Plunka states that, as a playwright, Shaffer "takes an existential approach every time." This pattern is defined as a searching on the part of major characters for "their own identity in life, free from the control of the Other." *Equus* is accordingly described as a work which combines "an existential and sexual search for identity with a ritualistic representation of spiritual freedom." Among the writer's conclusions is the designation of Alan as "a perfect anti-hero for [the 1970s] . . . never conforms to his environment . . . a unique personality surrounded by role-players and phonies . . . [who] turns inward to find his identity."

614. Radavich, David A. "Using Drama in the Composition Class." Paper presented at the 37th Conference on College Composition and Communication (New Orleans, LA, Mar. 13-15, 1986).
    This paper cites *Equus* as a useful model.

615. Rice, Julian C. "*Equus* and the True Jungian Symbol." *International Journal of Symbology* 7.2 (July 1976): 60-65.

616. Sanchez Arnosi, Milagros. "Acerca de *Equus*, de Peter Schaffer [sic]." *Arbor: Revista general de investigacion y cultur* 93 (Mar. 1976): 121-124.
    This article, in Spanish, sets out to offer an analysis and appreciation of a play by one of the modern English dramatists "least known in Spain." Unlike most commentators, Sanchez Arnosi treats the character of Alan as equal, or superior, in importance and complexity to Dysart. However, the structure of the play, he claims, is based on Dysart's "fragmented monologue." In conclusion, he describes *Equus* as a work of great literary and theatrical beauty.

617. Slutzky, Jacob E. "*Equus* and the Psychopathology of
Passion." *International Journal of Psychoanalytic
Psychotherapy* 5 (1976): 489-500.
Slutzky, a private practitioner of clinical
psychology, analyzes both major characters. Dysart's
mental illness is thought to be demonstrated by his
"pathological inhibition of passion [and] envy of Alan's
passion, his . . . 'countertransference,' and his choice
of abreaction as a form of therapy." The writer ends by
suggesting that *Equus* "can be seen as a deeply
moving artistic portrayal of very powerful resistance to
psychotherapy." [This issue of the *Journal* contains
four other articles on *Equus*, also by teachers or
practitioners of clinical psychotherapy; see #581,
#594, #595, and #618.]

618. Stamm, Julian. "Peter Shaffer's *Equus*—A Psychoanalytic
Exploration." *International Journal of
Psychoanalytic Psychotherapy* 5 (1976): 449-461.
Stamm analyzes not only Alan and Dysart but also
their author. He contends that, "in the creative
process, instinctual tension and/or conflict is the
driving, motivating force." Succeeding arguments
attempt to demonstrate that *Equus* "articulates the
author's fantasies in mythopoetic terms." Along the
way, Stamm refers to the play as "brilliant." [This issue
of the *Journal* contains four other articles on *Equus*,
also by teachers or practitioners of clinical
psychotherapy; see #581, #594, #595, and #617.]

619. Terrien, Samuel. "*Equus*: Human Conflicts and the
Trinity." *Christian Century* 94.18 (18 May 1977):
472-476.
A discussion of *Equus* from a "trinitarian" point
of view. The work is considered to be "a study of the
starvation for transcendence." Although it is praised
insofar as it "compels audiences to ask the ultimate
meaning of life," it is condemned for misreading the

basic demands of Judaism and Christianity. Terrien
sees the play's potential benefit as a warning against
the "danger of misunderstanding the doctrine of the
Trinity" (and leading one to realize that God the
Father is not to be read as a tyrannical parent figure,
nor is God the Son a paradigm for youthful Marxist
rebelliousness, nor is God the Spirit a symbol for
emotional intoxication). The character of Hesther
Salomon is upheld as a "model of Hebraco-Christian
sanity."

620. Timm, Neil. "*Equus* as a Modern Tragedy." *West
Virginia University Philological Papers* 25 (Feb.
1979): 128-134.
     The writer offers a wholehearted endorsement of
the play, both as pure theatre ("a triumph of
imagination and humanity") and as certifiable modern
tragedy (comparing it favorably on this score to *Death
of a Salesman*).

621. Vandenbroucke, Russell. "*Equus*: Modern Myth in the
Making." *Drama and Theatre* 12.2 (Spring 1975):
129-133.
     Though largely an investigation of the play's
"mythical" aspects, this article also offers a warm
appreciation of *Equus* ("the apogee of Mr. Shaffer's
work to date"). After offering the premise that a myth
must always "contain elements of ritual, religion, and
ceremony," Vandenbroucke recounts the plot of the
play in an effort to demonstrate these components.

622. Walls, Doyle W. "*Equus*: Shaffer, Nietzsche, and the
Neuroses of Health." *Modern Drama* 27.3 (Sept.
1984): 314-323.
     Walls sets forth an analysis of the play based on
the "strict definition" of the Apollonian-Dionysian
conflict as outlined by Nietzsche in *The Birth of
Tragedy*.

623. Welsh, J.M. "Dream Doctors as Healers in Drama and Film: A Paradigm, an Antecedent, and an Imitation." *Literature and Medicine* 6 (1987): 117-127.

624. Witham, Barry B. "The Anger in *Equus*. " *Modern Drama* 22.1 (Mar. 1979): 61-66.
Witham delivers a scholarly critique. He concludes that the play's "theatrical fireworks cannot mask its muddled logic and tired philosophy."

LETTERS TO THE EDITOR (Play)

625. Marowitz, Charles. Letter to the Editor. *Village Voice* 15 Sept. 1975: 4.
Marowitz writes to second Voice critic Julius Novick's "distrust" of *Equus*. He agrees that there is much that is admirable in Shaffer's works. But he likewise supports the view that, even though Shaffer often "opts for exoticism," he is basically a conventional playwright who does not fully persuade with his exoticisms.

626. "Yeas and Nays for *Equus*." *New York Times* 5 Jan. 1975: section 2; 5.
Four letters responding to Dr. Gifford's Op-Ed article condemning the play [see #588]. One letter-writer supports Gifford's views. The other three write in praise of *Equus*.

DISSERTATIONS AND THESES

627. Hammond, Gay Hobgood. "An Actress's Approach to the Role of Dora Strang in Peter Shaffer's *Equus*." M.A. Thesis, University of Louisville, 1984.

628. Hammond, James Brian. "A Director's Approach to Peter Shaffer's *Equus*: A Production Monograph." M.F.A. Thesis, University of Louisville, 1984.

629. Robbins, Leonard Henry. "Madness in Modern Drama." Ph.D. Dissertation, State University of New York at Binghampton, 1984. (DAI 45:2128)

630. Taylor-William, Dianne. "Directing Shadows: Drama and Psychodrama in Shaffer's *Equus*, Arrabal's *L'Architecte et l'empereur d'Assyrie*, and Weiss' *Marat/Sade*." Ph.D. Dissertation, University of Washington, 1981. (DAI 42:1627)

THE FILM

631. Lumet, Sidney, dir. *Equus* [film: "Screenplay by Peter Shaffer, based on his play of the same name"] with Richard Burton and Peter Firth, United Artists, 1977.

FILM REVIEWS

632. Anon. Review of film version of *Equus*. *Newsweek* 90 (24 Oct. 1977): 125.

A negative review which actually spends more time criticizing the original stage version than discussing the movie. While conceding the play and its film treatment "a certain amount of feverish power," the reviewer detects in them "a distressing amount of hot air." The chief complaint is that Shaffer's script is "too pat, too simplistic." This reviewer credits the movie with revealing the play's flaws, and performing in fact, "an act of devastating literary criticism."

633. Anon. Review of film version of *Equus*. *America* 137 (5 Nov. 1977): 314.

Here is a rare reviewer who prefers the film to the stage version: the play was "overly encumbered by [its specious] ideas." While not a "rave" (the film is described as "competent . . . mildly enjoyable"), this is essentially a favorable review, despite the fact that it describes as highly objectionable the realistic blinding of the horses during the final sequence.

634. Brien, Alan. "Metaphysician, Heal Thyself." *Sunday Times* (London) 23 Oct. 1977: 39.

Brien, who previously viewed the stage version, has little use for the movie or its writer. The film, he complains, "moves at a funereal pace" and is bogged down by its "confusing and repetitive" verbiage. In due course, the critic takes the opportunity to set forth a tally-sheet on the playwright: " . . . articulate, without quite striking eloquence, spectacularly theatrical, yet often un-dramatic, outrageous but finally conventional . . . " Shaffer is summed up as "a middle-brow enslaved by a magnificent obsession with high seriousness and poetic tragedy."

635. Canby, Vincent. "*Equus*: Film of a Different Color." *New York Times* 17 Oct. 1977: 39.

Canby suggests that the movie, because it is a realistic rather than stylized interpretation of Shaffer's play, makes possible a more accurate assessment of the text ("without being distracted by the dazzling theatricality"). He finds *Equus* revealed as "an extraordinarily skillful, passionate inquiry into the entire Freudian method." At the same time, however, he laments that the film's realism turns "what was once poetic and mysterious" into something far more "banal, anticlimactic." [The premise that the film exposes the true merits and demerits of the play is voiced by other critics; see especially Kauffmann, entry #645, and Rich, entry #649.]

636. Carroll, Kathleen. "*Equus* Just Plods Along." *New York Daily News* 17 Oct. 1977: 23.
    Carroll assigns the movie a rating of two and a half stars (which, considering the content of her review, is a generous allotment). She regards Shaffer's play as "a highbrow thriller" that was effective on the stage only because of its "novel staging."

637. Courant, Gerard. Review of film version of *Equus*. [In French] *Cinema* (Paris) 232 (Apr. 1978): 86-88.
    Courant, like a surprising number (though by no means all) of the French critics, responds favorably to the screen version.

638. Crist, Judith. "*Equus* Hobbles in with Poor Results." *New York Post* 17 Oct. 1977: 28.
    Crist discusses the play's theatricality, which she admires. As for the film, she criticizes Shaffer for delivering a screenplay that is "a verbatim transcript of his drama," and eventually concludes that the stage is the author's only appropriate medium.

639. D.G. Review of film version of *Equus*. [In French] *Cineaste* 8.2 (Fall 1977): page no. not available.
    The critic is virtually a chorus of one in suggesting that *Equus* gains in impact by being transferred to

the screen, calling it "the best of its kind [of psychological thriller] in years."

640. Davies, Russell. "Rider on the Beach." *Observer* (London) 23 Oct. 1977: 29.
     Davies admits that he didn't care for the play and likes the film less. Blame is assigned to Shaffer, rather than director Lumet (who is guilty of only a few "silly miscalculations").

641. Evans, J. Claude. "*Equus*: Double Binds and Bridles." *Christian Century* 95.12 (5 Apr. 1978): 367-372.
     The topic of this article is not so much the motion picture itself as the theme that mythical content is defeated by a literalist approach. The author argues that only "remembered myths and fantasies can contain the mystery of human existence." He therefore concludes that the stage version, with its suggestions of mythical memories, is a far more effective vehicle for "unlocking our need for transcendent reality" than is the motion picture with its "flat literalism." In passing, Evans offers an interesting explanation for the play's impact: "We are all Martin Dysarts . . . living in our 'normal' world . . . [but] yearning for the supernatural reality of ecstasy."

642. Gele, Claude. Review of film version of *Equus*. [In French] *Ecran* 69 (May 1978): 55-56.
     A largely favorable assessment of Lumet's motion picture. While noting that there are certain "ruptures of tone and style," the film is described as a very faithful adaptation of Shaffer's "excellent" play.

643. Haskell, Molly. "An Unstable Fable." *New York* 10 (7 Nov. 1977): 91.
     Haskell says that she cannot account for the popularity of the stage version of *Equus* and considers the film equally disappointing. She is

surprised to find that the naturalistic sequences added for the movie are less effective than the "staged passages," by which she means Burton's "soliloquy in installments."

644. Kael, Pauline. Review of film version of *Equus*. *New Yorker* 53 (7 Nov. 1977): 120-122.
     Kael has nothing good to say of either the film version or its stage predecessor. In her eyes, the film places "Shaffer's worst ideas on a pedestal." Due to its faithful rendition of the play's text, she says, the movie not only "suffers from literacy" but "sickens and dies from it."

645. Kauffmann, Stanley. "Ill Wind." *New Republic* 5 Nov. 1977: 24-26.
     The reviewer refers repeatedly to his conversations with noted literary critic Lionel Trilling. Kauffmann writes that he and Trilling regarded the success of the stage version of *Equus* as an instance of "the fact that inferior work often gets high praise." He now maintains that the film, "stripped of its theater paraphernalia," exposes the "dubiousness of the material." [The premise that the film exposes the true merits and demerits of the play is voiced by other critics; see especially Canby, entry #635, and Rich, entry #649.]

646. Kissel, Howard. Review of film version of *Equus*. *Women's Wear Daily* 17 Oct. 1977: 8.
     Kissel likes nothing about the movie and apportions the blame almost equally among director, star, and screenwriter. His "hook" for the review is blunt: "Everyone said it would be a mistake to film *Equus*, and everyone was right."

647. Murf. Review of film version of *Equus*. *Variety* 19 Oct. 1977: 25.

A favorable report on all aspects of the movie,
describing it as "an excellent example of 'film-as-
theatre.'"

648. Reed, Rex. "A Good & Decent *Equus*. " *New York
Daily News* 19 Oct. 1977: 79.
When he took his seat for a showing of the film,
Reed had not only seen the play, he had twice
reviewed it [see #531 and #532]. His original
complaint concerning the script, Dysart's unconvincing
and "chilling" final speech, is again registered. While
he concedes that Lumet has made "as good [a movie]
as possible" from Shaffer's material, Reed sees major
problems, especially the "boring" (ill-adapted to
cinematic terms) soliloquies.

649. Rich, Frank. "Horseplay." *Time* 110 (31 Oct. 1977): 91.
A complete pan, starting from the premise: "If
ever there was a play that has no business being a
movie, *Equus* is it." Rich maintains that Lumet's
fidelity to Shaffer's script "accentuates every flaw" in
the play, and that "all that remains is 2 1/2 hours of
talky debate about shopworn ideas." [The premise that
the film exposes the true merits and demerits of the
play is voiced by other critics; see especially Canby,
entry #635, and Kauffmann, entry #645.]

650. Sarris, Andrew. "Reining in the Prancers and the
Dancers." *Village Voice* 31 Oct. 1977: 45.
Sarris comes to the film without having seen the
play. His reaction is negative: "I do not like what the
script seems to be saying about 'passion' and
'normality' and the superiority of instinct over
intellect." To him, Alan's obsession with horses seems
silly. In fact, Sarris charges that it is "only through a
complete lack of humor that the text's horse worship is
not hooted off both stage and screen."

651. Sigal, Clancy. Review of film version of *Equus*.
Spectator (London) 29 Oct. 1977: 27.
A thorough pan of both the movie and its stage
predecessor. Sigal has arrived at the screening of the
film with the idea that the play (which he had read but
not previously seen) is "inflated claptrap." In his view,
Equus contains "some of the most meaningless
dialogue [he has] heard in years."

652. Simon, John. "Double Whammy." *National Review* 29
(9 Dec. 1977): 1444.
Equus is the second of two movies reviewed in
this issue, both of which are slammed (hence the
"whammy" of the headline). After delivering a
thorough bashing to *Looking for Mr. Goodbar*,
Simon continues: "Even more portentous a piece of
speciousness is *Equus*." Shaffer's play is described as
"highly though undeservedly successful." Simon claims
that the work "can be read . . . as a thinly veiled paean
to pederasty." Being more naturalistic than its stage
predecessor, the film version is condemned for lending
"added repugnancy and preposterousness" to the
proceedings.

653. Sterritt, David. "A Deeply Memorable, Troubling
Equus." *Christian Science Monitor* 27 Oct. 1977:
19.
A minority view: the film is not only "gripping"; it
"works even better on its own terms than did the
original play."

FILM VERSION—FEATURE STORIES

654. Burke, Tom. "Suddenly, I Knew How to Film the Play."
New York Times 24 July 1977: section D; 9, 20.

An interview with director Sidney Lumet on the evolution of his approach to filming *Equus*. For Lumet, Shaffer's play is about "duality, Jekyll and Hyde, Apollonian versus Dionysian thought."

Chapter Ten

Amadeus

THE TEXT

The complete text of *Amadeus* is included in *The Collected Plays of Peter Shaffer* [see #144] and in other single editions and anthologies, three of which are listed below. (Shaffer's screenplay has not yet been published.)

655. Shaffer, Peter. *Amadeus*. London: Andre Deutsch, 1980.
   This is the text of the play as originally produced in London.

656. Shaffer, Peter. *Amadeus*. New York: Harper and Row, 1981.
   This edition contains the play as revised for the Broadway production and includes a preface by Shaffer.

657. Cornish, Roger, and Violet Ketels, ed. *Landmarks of the British Theatre; II: the Seventies*. London: Methuen, 1985.

Contains the (revised) text of the play and an eight-
page essay on Shaffer.

PLAY REVIEWS

A. Reviews: Original London Production.
Opened at the Olivier Theatre on November 2, 1979.

658. Barber, John. "Mozart Depicted as a Popinjay." *Daily
     Telegraph* (London) 5 Nov. 1979: 15.
     Aside from registering a mild complaint about its
     wordiness, Barber is noncommittal on the subject of
     the quality of Shaffer's play. He does, however,
     express enthusiasm for the two principal performers
     and Peter Hall's direction.

659. Billington, Michael. "Divining for a Theme." *Manchester
     Guardian* 5 Nov. 1979: 11.
     Billington finds *Amadeus* "for half its length . . .
     [an] exquisitely gripping . . . big, bold, theatrical play."
     He complains, however, that the last act is jarringly
     out of step with what has preceded it, and he wishes
     "Shaffer had not tried to elevate the play into a
     majestic homily on the death of a god."

660. Dace, Tisit. Review of *Amadeus*. *Soho Weekly News*
     20 Aug. 1980: 51-52.
     A report on the London production for the benefit
     of New Yorkers who will soon have the opportunity of
     seeing the play on Broadway. Dace calls *Amadeus* a
     skillful and ingenious comedy which "mustn't be
     missed."

661. Esslin, Martin. Review of *Amadeus*. *Plays and Players*
     27.2 (Nov. 1979): 20, 27-28.

While Esslin considers the play's theme to be bold and potentially of profound interest, he concludes that neither Shaffer's form nor his language measure up to the challenge of his tremendous subject matter.

662. Fenton, James. "Can We Worship This Mozart?" *Sunday Times* (London) 23 Dec. 1979: 43.

The most scathing of all the denunciations of Shaffer's play, with special vehemence reserved for the dramatist's treatment of Mozart. Shaffer is described as "a very, very bad dramatist, indeed—perhaps the worst serious English dramatist since John Drinkwater." Fenton's critical summation has achieved a kind of notoriety in its own right: "[The play is] a perfectly nauseating load of—to use a word much loved by Peter Shaffer—shit."

663. Fenton, James. Note in reply to a Letter to the Editor. *Sunday Times* (London) 6 Jan. 1980: 15.

Fenton defends his review of *Amadeus* and attempts to clarify a point: "I do not object to [the use of obscenity per se] . . . What I object to is the use of obscenity to define the character of Mozart, to make him both banal and offensive."

664. Geist, Kenneth L. "Was Mozart Murdered?" *After Dark* Oct. 1980: 32-33.

The greater portion of this review is devoted to the question of historical accuracy. Geist's opinion is that *Amadeus* is "full of theatrical pleasures" but is "unpersuasive as biography."

665. Grant, Steve. "Much Ado About Mozart." *Observer* (London) 11 Nov. 1979: 16.

Grant declares that, despite "minor lapses," the play is "marvelously engrossing."

666. Green, J.G. "A Year in London." *Canadian Theatre Review* no. 31 (Summer 1981): 136-143.
     Includes a brief review of *Amadeus*, which the reviewer says, "demonstrates [Shaffer's] range, diversity, and fundamental good craftsmanship."

667. Hepple, Peter. "*Amadeus* at the Olivier." *Stage and Television Today* (London) 8 Nov. 1979: 9.
     A brief, favorable review. Hepple generalizes on Shaffer's career and stature: " . . . what he lacks in quantity [of plays written], he makes up for with immaculate craftsmanship and a wonderful flair for theatrical effect."

668. King, Francis. "If Music Be the Food of Hate." *Sunday Telegraph* (London) 11 Nov. 1979: 12.
     King is uneasy with the subject matter of *Amadeus*, claiming that "Mr. Shaffer unduly belittles [Mozart]." He asserts, however, that Peter Hall's staging and Paul Scofield's performance are splendid. As a result of their efforts, "the play never for one moment fails to hold the attention."

669. Levin, Bernard. "Clearing Up the Eternal Mystery of Mozart." *Times* (London) 6 Dec. 1979: 14.
     In a lengthy and well-reasoned piece, Levin defends *Amadeus* against the charges of historical inaccuracy and cheap sensationalism which have been lodged against it. He maintains that Shaffer has succeeded in fulfilling "his tremendous, his colossal theme, in language of great strength and deceptively obvious subtlety." He concludes that many London critics have "widely and grossly under-valued" the play.

670. Nightingale, Benedict. "Obscene Child." *New Statesman* 9 Nov. 1979: 735.
     Amadeus is described as "a didactic melodrama, very characteristic of Shaffer." It is judged a failure on

the grounds of Shaffer's treatment of the two central
characters: the depiction of Mozart is criticized as "too
vague, general and mindlessly rhapsodic," while the
portrayal of Salieri is called an "outrageous
implausibility." Nightingale adds that "without [Paul
Scofield as Salieri] to rivet and mesmerise us, Mr.
Shaffer's lavish argosy would simply sink."

671. Panter-Downes, Mollie. "Letter from London." *New
    Yorker* 10 Mar. 1980: 138-140.
    Panter-Downes reports that the play is remarkably
effective and notes that—considering the dominance of
Salieri—"in form, it is practically a one-man narrative."

672. Taylor, John Russell. Review of *Amadeus*. *Drama* 135
    (Jan. 1980): 48-49.
    Taylor's reactions are mixed. He finds the beginning
section of the play disastrously long and confused, "as
if Shaffer has thought of three or four possible
openings and then used all of them." He complains, as
well, of the playwright's tendency "to over-verbalise
everything." On the credit side of the ledger, he admits
that *Amadeus* "has the core, more than the core, of a
very workable play," and that, "for quite a bit of its
length it does, dammit, work."

673. Toynbee, Polly. "Slow Motion." *Spectator* (London) 10
    Nov. 1979: 26.
    Having found that its only moving moments "were
when Mozart's music was played," Toynbee suggests
that *Amadeus* "should have been a musical." She
admits finding the opening section of the play "crisp
and enjoyable" but complains that during the last two
hours of playing time Shaffer "has nothing more to
say." Salieri's constantly addressing the audience also
comes under attack, a device which she contends is so
overworked that it rapidly becomes boring. She

concludes: " . . . this is hardly a play at all, but more of a narration."

674. Young, B.A. Review of *Amadeus*. *Financial Times* (London) 5 Nov. 1979: 15.
    A negative verdict is given. The play is found unimaginative and stilted, as "hollow as a cartoon-strip."

B. Reviews: New York Production.
Opened at the Broadhurst Theatre on December 17, 1980.

675. Asahina, R. "Shaffer's *Amadeus* and the Alienation Effect." *Hudson Review* 34.2 (1981): 263-268.
    Asahina deems *Amadeus* "much more sophisticated than Shaffer's earlier plays" because in it the playwright's fascination with "theology and psychoanalysis" is linked with Brechtian alienation effects (deliberately theatrical disruptions of the narrative flow). But he judges the play a failure, citing John Simon as one who has accurately perceived its hollowness. Like Simon, he points disdainfully to the work's "homoerotic elements." Asahina ends by maintaining that *Amadeus*, beneath its slick theatrical veneer, "is really about amour-propre of a particularly twisted kind."

676. Barnes, Clive. "*Amadeus*: A Total Triumph." *New York Post* 18 Dec. 1980: 39.
    Barnes recalls that when he saw the London production he found *Amadeus* enormously theatrical and considered it Shaffer's best play. Now he likes it even more. The revisions have given it more weight and deeper dramatic dimensions. He calls the New York production "a total, iridescent triumph." [This item, along with nine other reviews, is reprinted in *New York Theatre Critics' Reviews*, for which see

#702 below. Barnes continued to praise the play
through a number of follow-up reviews, entries #677-
680. It therefore came as something of a surprise when
he published a piece in 1984 vehemently denouncing
the Academy Award bestowed on the movie version,
for which see #781.]

677. Barnes, Clive. "Change Aids *Amadeus*." *New York Post*
31 Dec. 1980: 17.
Barnes states his case for preferring the revised,
Broadway version to the original London production.
He describes the revision process as a collaboration
between Shaffer and director Peter Hall, resulting in
"a myriad of small re-writes and a few major
insertions." In summing up, he characterizes the New
York production as more dramatic and direct.

678. Barnes, Clive. "Following the *Amadeus* Score: Wood
Plays Salieri." *New York Post* 17 Dec. 1981: 36.
An appreciation of the performance by John Wood
(who has replaced Ian McKellen) in the leading role.

679. Barnes, Clive. "Looking at Langella in *Amadeus*." *New
York Post* 26 July 1982: 20.
In reviewing another new group of principal actors
(whom he praises), Barnes again lauds Shaffer's script.
This time special emphasis is given to the dramatist's
understanding of the world of music and musicianship,
about which "Shaffer writes with sybilline clarity."

680. Barnes, Clive. "*Amadeus* Going Strong." *New York
Post* 8 Jul. 1983: 17.
Barnes reviews the latest in a long succession of
acting pairs to essay Salieri and Mozart: David Birney
and Mark Hamill.

681. Beaufort, John. "Mozart Murdered? Unlikely, but It Makes for an Unusual Play." *Christian Science Monitor* 22 Dec. 1980: 19.
This review deals principally with the controversial nature of the play. The quality of *Amadeus* is not assayed beyond a brief reference to it as "complex, darkly probing, [and] richly theatrical." [This item, along with nine other reviews, is reprinted in *New York Theatre Critics' Reviews*, for which see #702 below.]

682. Brustein, Robert. "The Triumph of Mediocrity." *New Republic* 184 (17 Jan. 1981): 23.
An especially vitriolic slam at both play and playwright. Brustein sees this work as a craftsmanly dramatist's all-too-obvious attempt to lend noble stature to the theme of (Salieri's) cultured mediocrity outdone by (Mozart's) raw talent. Brustein takes offense at the fact that *Amadeus* permits its audience to feel superior to a man of genius (while Shaffer, according to Brustein, is feeling superior to his audience). The final verdict: the play is over-inflated costume drama masquerading as tragedy.

683. Brustein, Robert. *Who Needs Theatre: Dramatic Opinions*. New York: Atlantic Monthly Press, 1987.
Contains, on pages 186-190, a reprint of Brustein's *Amadeus* review ("The Triumph of Mediocrity") originally published in *New Republic*. [See #677 above.]

684. Cunningham, Dennis. Review of *Amadeus*. WCBS-TV, New York City Channel 2, 17 Dec. 1980.
Though Cunningham admits that the play is "not without flaws," he praises it enthusiastically: "a theatrical wonder." [This item, along with nine other reviews, is reprinted in *New York Theatre Critics' Reviews*, for which see #702 below.]

685. Cushman, Robert. "Exporting *Amadeus*." *Observer*
(London) 25 Jan. 1981: 32.
Cushman maintains that the much-publicized re-
writes have made no essential difference. He charges
that the play's major flaw is not intellectual, as others
critics have claimed, but structural (". . . it has no
second act"). In his opening, he identifies the two
critical "sins" of which Shaffer reviewers are invariably
guilty: the adoption of a tone which is either
patronizing or senselessly ecstatic.

686. Diether, Jack. Review of *Amadeus*. *East Side Express*
15 Jan. 1981: 13.
This is basically a plot rehash with cast notes. It
says nothing of the quality of the play except to put
forth a minor complaint concerning its historical
inaccuracies and to judge that it deserves a long run.

687. Feingold, Michael. "Eine Kleine Nicht Musik." *Village
Voice* 24-30 Dec. 1980: 82-83.
A relentless pan. The leading character is rejected
as an "unending stream of mediocrity." The playwright
is similarly dismissed. Feingold describes Shaffer's
dialogue as being "every bit as wrongheaded and
schematic as his thinking."

688. Gelatt, Ronald. "Peter Shaffer's *Amadeus*: A
Controversial Hit." *Saturday Review* 7 (Nov. 1980):
11-14.
In a review of *Amadeus* during its pre-Broadway
tryout in Washington, D.C., Gelatt recounts the critical
controversy surrounding the play in London. He
vouches for Shaffer's credentials as a serious musical
scholar, referring to the playwright's background as a
piano student and his later tenure as a music critic.
Shaffer is characterized as a rare writer of "the play of
ideas."

689. Gill, Brendan. "Bargaining with God." *New Yorker* 29
     Dec. 1980: 54.
     This is no pan, though it has the tone of one. It is,
     rather, a limply favorable review, which grudgingly
     concedes that Shaffer is a clever writer who has
     written another "brainy, thriller-like" play.

690. Harvey, Stephen. Review of *Amadeus*. *Nation* 232 (17
     Jan. 1981): 59.
     The play is condescendingly dismissed as "a dollop
     of swanky uplift from abroad . . . [which] manages to
     flatter the audience for its presumed musical
     erudition."

691. Hughes, Catherine. Review of *Amadeus*. *America* 144
     (24 Jan. 1981): 62.
     Though the bulk of this single page review is
     devoted to describing the content of the play, high
     praise is bestowed. *Amadeus* is found to make
     demands and offer rewards "on a level only rarely
     experienced on Broadway."

692. Hummler, Richard. Review of New Cast in *Amadeus*.
     Variety 23 Dec. 1981: 70.
     Having seen the play in London, the critic finds
     that, on second inspection, *Amadeus* looks even
     better than before. He deems it a thoughtful and
     challenging work and upholds it as proof that drama of
     high quality can still prosper on Broadway.

693. Kalem, T.E. "Blood Feud." *Time* 118 (29 Dec. 1980): 57.
     Kalem admires the play but considers it less
     compelling than either *Royal Hunt* or *Equus*. He
     suggests that *Amadeus* shares (and overworks) the
     theme of these earlier plays: "the death of God, the
     need for God, the rage against God if he does exist."
     [This item, along with nine other reviews, is reprinted

in *New York Theatre Critics' Reviews*, for which see #702 below.]

694. Kauffmann, Stanley. "Shaffer's Flat Notes." *Saturday Review* Feb. 1981: 78-79.
     Kauffmann sees little worthy of praise and regrets that a potentially fertile dramatic idea has been undermined by tricky devices, preening witticisms, and uncertainties of tone.

695. Kerner, Leighton. "Who Is This Salieri Guy and Why Are We Talking About Him?" *Village Voice* 24-30 Dec. 1980: 81.
     The New York version of the play is judged "marvelous," even though the reviewer preferred the London production, having found Paul Scofield vastly superior to Ian McKellen in the role of Salieri.

696. Kerr, Walter. "Waiting for an Ingenious Twist That Never Comes." *New York Times* 4 Jan. 1981: section 2; 3, 12.
     A lengthy discussion of what Kerr considers the fatal flaw undermining his otherwise great admiration for the play. If Shaffer had dealt with Salieri's conflict (simultaneous admiration and detestation of Mozart) forthrightly, he might have written a play of genuine "dramatic weight."

697. Kissel, Howard. Review of *Amadeus*. *Women's Wear Daily* 19 Dec. 1980: 17.
     The reviewer objects to the fact that Shaffer's interpretation of Mozart—a portrayal that Kissel likens to Bugs Bunny—tends to justify Salieri's scheming. In short, this is an unremitting pan, which prominently refers to the play's "speciousness." [This item, along with nine other reviews, is reprinted in *New York Theatre Critics' Reviews*, for which see #702 below.]

698. Kroll, Jack. "Mozart and His Nemesis." *Newsweek* 29
    Dec. 1980: 58.
    A condescending smack at the playwright. Kroll
    suggests that *Amadeus* only proves that Shaffer has
    mastered the art of writing the quintessential "Shaffer
    play," which the critic defines as "large" in every
    external way, but "essentially superficial." [This item,
    along with nine other reviews, is reprinted in *New
    York Theatre Critics' Reviews*, for which see #702
    below.]

699. Larson, Janet Karsten. "*Amadeus*: Shaffer's Hollow
    Men." *Christian Century* 98.18 (20 May 1981):
    578-583.
    Larson comes out in passionate opposition to the
    philosophical stance of the play, which she describes as
    "the scarecrow spirit of Salieri/ Shaffer's cynicism."
    She deprecates "the *Equus* formula" of combining
    "religious themes, voyeurism and violence, a mildly
    learned title—plus black comedy and operatic effects."

700. McClatchy, J.D. Review of *Amadeus*. *Yale Review*
    73.1 (Autumn 1983): 115-122.

701. Morrison, Hobe. Review of *Amadeus*. *Variety* 24 Dec.
    1980: 62.
    Morrison finds the play artfully written and
    thoroughly engrossing but also calls it (without
    elaboration) "emotionally arid."

702. *New York Theatre Critics' Reviews* 41.20 (Week of
    15 Dec. 1980): 64-70.
    Contains reviews listed here as entries #706, #676,
    #684, #697, #693, #715, #717, #698, #684, and #711.

703. Novick, Julius. "Mozart and Shaffer's Craft." *Village
    Voice* 24-30 Dec. 1980: 82.

Although this is a favorable critique, Novick makes a slighting reference to the work as "this season's snob hit" and couples his notes of praise with a reminder of the play's "occasional preposterousness."

704. Paul. Review of *Amadeus* [Washington tryout]. *Variety* 301 (19 Nov. 1980): 84.
The play is considered "wondrously sardonic."

705. Pit. Review of *Amadeus*. *Variety* 14 Nov. 1979: 90, 92.
A favorable report, but one which includes a slighting summation: " . . . a clever, provocative and playful stunt."

706. Rich, Frank. Review of *Amadeus*. *New York Times* 18 Dec. 1980: C17.
Rich disapproves on several counts: writing dismissed as un-Mozartian, secondary characters treated as mere plot pawns or one-joke caricatures, and an unsatisfactory series of "blurred multiple endings." Nevertheless, he ends by admitting that, thanks to the "triumphant production . . . the flaws don't mar the excitement." [This item, along with nine other reviews, is reprinted in *New York Theatre Critics' Reviews*, for which see #702 above.]

707. Rich, Frank. "*Amadeus*, with Three New Principals." *New York Times* 17 Dec. 1981: C22.
Warm appreciation for the three actors who have recently assumed major roles in the Broadway production: John Wood, Peter Firth, and Amy Irving.

708. Rich, Frank. "The Stage: *Amadeus* with American Principals." *New York Times* 1 June 1982: C10.
Another look at the play on the occasion of the leading roles being assumed, for the first time, by two American actors: Frank Langella as Salieri and Dennis Boutsikaris as Mozart. Rich finds fault with both

performers but decides that "it says a lot about Mr. Shaffer's script that *Amadeus* often works as an entertainment, even when the passion is cut out from under the visual spectacle and verbal gloss."

709. Rosenwald, Peter J. "*Amadeus*: Who Murdered Mozart?" *Horizon* 23.2 (Feb. 1980): 33.
       This is not so much a review as a piece of reportage on the recent opening of the play. Rosenwald praises the work, calling it "marvelous theatre."

710. Sauvage, Leo. Review of *Amadeus*. *New Leader* 64 (26 Jan. 1981): 17.
       A mixed, though predominately negative, report. The characterization of Mozart is found "impossible to accept." Sauvage marvels at the play's power to "simultaneously beguile us with its style and repel us with its flawed thinking."

711. Siegel, Joel. Review of *Amadeus*. WABC-TV, New York City Channel 7, 17 Dec. 1980.
       An all-out rave. Siegel declares the play "brilliantly conceived and beautifully executed." [This item, along with nine other reviews, is reprinted in *New York Theatre Critics' Reviews*, for which see #702 above.]

712. Simon, John. "'Amadequus,' or Shaffer Rides Again." *New York* 29 Dec. 1980/5 Jan. 1981: 62-63.
       Simon does not hesitate to trash the play. After proclaiming the piece "a goddamned middlebrow masterpiece," he proceeds to disdain each aspect of the script, from its "barbershop metaphysics" and "shoddy invention" to its "cutesy conceits" and "obvious jokes."

713. Tillman, W.N. Review of *Amadeus*. *Theatre Journal* 33.3 (1981): 406-407.

Reporting on its pre-Broadway run in Washington, D.C., Tillman finds in *Amadeus* a few blemishes (such as the chorus effects supplied by the Venticelli characters) and "much to praise." He is especially taken with the Mozart characterization ("a marvelous fusion of history and imagination") and ends by calling the play "a masterpiece."

714. Wallach, Allan. "Peter Shaffer's Portrait of Mozart." *Newsday* (Long Island, NY) 18 Dec. 1980: Part 2; 48.
Wallach's opinion is largely favorable, emphasizing the play's "vividly theatrical" appeal. He adds, however, that "Shaffer weakens his case by overstating it . . . making [Mozart] a buffoon." He concludes that, though *Amadeus* does not delve deeply into the mysterious processes of genius, it is nonetheless "spellbinding," thanks to Peter Hall's direction and, especially, to Ian McKellan's "glittering performance" as Salieri.

715. Watt, Douglas. "*Amadeus* Questions the Gift of Genius." *New York Daily News* 18 Dec. 1980: 63.
Watt has reservations, especially in regard to a few "vulgar episodes" which he considers inaccurate and unnecessarily demeaning to the Mozart character. On the whole, however, he finds the play fascinating, "a good show on its own terms." He is one of several critics who term the work a "monodrama" (depending so hugely as it does on Salieri's role as principal-and-narrator). [This item, along with nine other reviews, is reprinted in *New York Theatre Critics' Reviews*, for which see #702 above.]

716. Watt, Douglas. "New Wood Sheen on *Amadeus*." *New York Daily News* 17 Dec. 1981: 100.
In looking again at the play, on the occasion of John Wood's replacing Ian McKellen as Salieri, Watt reiterates misgivings about "Shaffer's contrivances, especially his sometimes excessive use of melodrama."

717. Wilson, Edwin. "Peter Shaffer's Astigmatic View of God." *Wall Street Journal* 19 Dec. 1980: 25.
    The title of this piece may not prepare the reader for what is, in fact, a rave review. *Amadeus* is declared the most ingenious and engrossing play the reviewer has seen "in some time." [This item, along with nine other reviews, is reprinted in *New York Theatre Critics' Reviews*, for which see #702 above.]

C. Reviews: London Revival.
Opened at the Olivier Theatre on July 2, 1981.

718. Amory, Mark. Review of *Amadeus*. *Spectator* (London) 3 July 1981: page no. not available.
    In a review of the revived and revised National Theatre production, Amory's reappraisal of the play is unenthusiastic ("for middle brows only"). Shaffer's stature is summed up by assigning him an "honorable position, formerly held by Somerset Maugham . . . at the top of the second class." [This item, along with seven other reviews is reprinted in *London Theatre Record*, for which see #723 below.]

719. Barber, John. Review of *Amadeus*. *Daily Telegraph* (London) 3 July 1981: page no. not available.
    Barber detects relatively little change in the revised version and continues to find the play "totally absorbing." [This item, along with seven other reviews is reprinted in *London Theatre Record*, for which see #723 below.]

720. De Jongh, Nicholas. Review of *Amadeus*. *Manchester Guardian* 3 July 1981: 11.
    De Jongh responds warmly. He especially praises the play's "strong ironies." As for the revisions, they strike him as merely serving to heighten Salieri's

fanatical hatred of Mozart. [This item, along with seven other reviews is reprinted in *London Theatre Record*, for which see #723 below.]

721. Fenton, James. "*Amadeus*: The Version According to Broadway." *Sunday Times* 5 July 1981: 39.
   The opening paragraph explains that, in view of the fact that Shaffer has so thoroughly revised his play, the critic must in fairness withdraw his earlier objections. Having thus invited the fly into his web, Fenton announces that he will "begin again" to assess the work and proceeds to do so tersely: "This play is tripe."

722. Hurren, Kenneth. Review of *Amadeus*. *What's On in London* [Date and page no. not available.]
   Hurren concludes that Shaffer's revisions have "softened" the characterization of Mozart and that the result is a combination of "gains and losses" (it is now more plausible but less theatrically arresting). However, on the whole, he says, *Amadeus* "remains a marvellous evening in the theatre." [This item, along with seven other reviews is reprinted in *London Theatre Record*, for which see #723 below.]

723. *London Theatre Record* 1.14 (2-15 July 1981): 329-332.
   Contains reviews listed here as entries #718, #720, #729, #725, #719, #724, #727, and #722.

724. Say, Rosemary. Review of *Amadeus*. *Sunday Telegraph* (London) 5 July 1981: page no. not available.
   This is another re-review of the play in light of the new London cast and revised, post-Broadway script. Say now considers the play, as revealed by "less accomplished actors" in the key roles, to be "a beautifully constructed piece of writing for the theatre that catches the eye and the ear but not the heart."

[This item, along with seven other reviews is reprinted in *London Theatre Record*, for which see #723 above.]

725. Shulman, Milton. Review of *Amadeus*. *New Standard* (London) 3 July 1981: page no. not available.
Shulman praises Shaffer's revisions, especially those resulting in a version of Mozart's character which is less coarse. [This item, along with seven other reviews is reprinted in *London Theatre Record*, for which see #723 above.]

726. Taylor, John Russell. "Plays in Performance." *Drama* 142 (Autumn 1981): 34.
A brief review of the re-opened and revised National Theatre production with Frank Finlay as Salieri. The script is described as "a model" for the writing of historical plays. Taylor considers the revisions resulting from the New York production to have strengthened the script, turning it into a consistent "ironic comedy" by eliminating "the strivings for tragic significance" which made the original version at times pretentious. He congratulates Shaffer for his dedication in re-writing what was already a vastly successful work.

727. Tinker, Jack. Review of *Amadeus*. *Daily Mail* (London) 3 July 1981: page no. not available.
Tinker is not favorably impressed by the play's post-Broadway revisions. While he recognizes that the new interpretation is likely to be more commercially successful, he finds it less painful, less moving, and "much less of an eternal puzzle as to the vagaries of the Almighty." [This item, along with seven other reviews is reprinted in *London Theatre Record*, for which see #723 above.]

728. Wardle, Irving. Review of *Amadeus*. *Times* (London)
     3 July 1981: 11.
     On seeing the re-opened and revised version,
     Wardle's highly favorable opinion is unchanged.

729. Young, B.A. Review of *Amadeus*. *Financial Times*
     (London) 5 July 1981: page no. not available.
     A brief appraisal of the post-Broadway re-opening
     at the National Theatre. Young praises Peter Hall's
     "splendid" production but writes that he "can't pretend"
     that he admires the play. [This item, along with seven
     other reviews is reprinted in *London Theatre
     Record*, for which see #723 above.]

D. Reviews: Other Productions.

730. Anon. (ed.). "La Presse." *Avant Scene Theatre* 709
     (1982): 41-43.
     In French. A compilation of partial and complete
     reviews delivered by the Parisian press on the Theatre
     Marigny production of *Amadeus* (which opened
     January, 1982), directed by Roman Polanski, who also
     appeared as Mozart, with Francois Perier as Salieri.
     The reviewers are Francois Chalais (*France-Soir*);
     Jean-Jacques Gautier (*Le Figaro*); Robert Kanters
     (*L'Express*); Pierre Marcabru (also *Le Figaro*);
     Michel Mourlet (*Valeurs Actuelle*); Flavie Solerieu
     (*Aspects de la France*); Philippe Tesson (*Le
     Canard Enchaine*); Guy Verdot (*La Nouvelle
     Republique*); and Jules Vigneron (*La Croix*). [This
     entire issue is devoted to *Amadeus*. It includes the
     French text of the play as produced at the Marigny, a
     revision in French of Shaffer's "Figure of Death"
     article (for which, see #108), and a brief biographical
     sketch of the playwright.]

731. Aragones, J.E. Review of *Amadeus*. *Nueva Estafeta* No.40 (1982): 118-119.

732. Baniewicz, E. Review of Warsaw production of *Amadeus*. *Theatre en Pologne* 23.12 (1981): 3-10. This is a lengthy review of the production at the Na Woli Theatre, directed by Roman Polanski (who also starred as Mozart). Its attitude toward the play is gently condescending. *Amadeus* is upheld as proof that a play of middling quality, which is nonetheless well constructed and written with theatrical imagination, can provide an excellent vehicle which is "much favored by actors and enjoyed by audiences."

733. Camp, Andre. "Pieces policieres ou policiees." *Avant Scene Theatre* 706 (1982): 46-48. [In French.] A review of three entries in the 1982 Parisian theatrical season, including the Theatre Marigny production of *Amadeus*, directed by Roman Polanski. [For additional reviews of this version see #730 above.]

734. Carleton, Don. Review of *Amadeus*. *Drama* No. 141 (Summer 1981): 39. A brief review of the National Theatre's touring version of *Amadeus* as seen in Bristol. While referring to the production as a "delight," Carleton suggests that one leaves the theatre feeling that the play has "[fallen] short of some greater potential achievement."

735. Kruntorad, P. Review of *Amadeus*. *Theater Heute* April 1981: 24.

736. Tarjan, T. Review of *Amadeus*. *New Hungarian Quarterly* 23.87 (1982): 186-190.

737. Trauth, V. Review of *Amadeus*. *Theater der zeit* 40.8
     (1985): 44.

738. Wagner, M. Review of *Amadeus*. *Osterreichische
     Musik Zeitschrift* 36.7-8 (1981): 415-416.

NEWS REPORTS AND FEATURE STORIES

739. Anon. "*Amadeus* Is Best Play . . . " *Variety* 30 Jan.
     1980: 89.
     A brief report on the play's winning the London
     Evening Standard Award as "Best Play of 1979."

740. Apple, R.W., Jr. "Portrait of Mozart as a Loudmouth."
     New York Times 11 Nov. 1979: section 2; 8.
     A description of the critical controversy
     surrounding the London production of *Amadeus*
     (centering on Shaffer's depiction of Mozart).

741. Callow, Simon. *Being an Actor*. New York: St. Martin's
     Press, 1984.
     Callow's autobiography provides, on pages 84-86
     and 94-98, an intriguing inside view of the original
     London production of *Amadeus*. The actor's account
     of his involvement begins with a telephone call from
     John Dexter (whom he had never met) asking if he'd
     like to play Mozart; it ends with a description of his
     performance after the play is well into its run at the
     National Theatre. Though Callow's research convinced
     him that the excesses of the character were historically
     at least partially true ("Mozart, if you like, glimpsed by
     lightning"), he found it impossible for much of the
     rehearsal period to make it credible that "the little
     beast . . . had written a note of the [great] music." A
     key to playing the part came to him when he read a

passage from the memoirs of the composer's brother-in-law Josef Lange: "I can understand that so exalted an artist can, out of a deep veneration for his Art, belittle and as it were expose to ridicule his own personality." Callow then saw that "every word, every gesture that [Shaffer] had written was consonant with the man." [Dexter, Shaffer's original choice for director, was unable to agree with the playwright on, among other things, financial terms and was replaced by Peter Hall prior to the start of rehearsals.]

742. Darnton, Nina. "Polanski on Polish Stage Amid Political Upheaval." *New York Times* 18 Oct. 1981: section 2; 8.

Commentary on Roman Polanski's involvement as both director and actor in a production of *Amadeus* at Warsaw's Na Woli Theatre. Of special interest is an account of Polanski's unusual interpretation of the role of Mozart. Instead of stressing the composer's beastly childishness, Polanski portrays him with restraint, as a naive rebel. Darnton maintains that this sympathetic treatment renders Salieri's intrigues against Mozart "all the more tragic."

743. Gianakaris, C.J. "Fair Play: Shaffer's Treatment of Mozart in *Amadeus.*" *Opera News* 46.13 (1982): 18, 36.

Gianakaris examines the historical accuracy of the playwright's interpretation of the composer as "an obscene child." He concludes that Shaffer "has followed factual sources to a remarkable degree" in presenting "an authentic, candid portrait."

744. Gruber, G. "Gibt es ein neues Mozart-Bild?" ["Is There a New Image of Mozart?"] *Acta Mozartiana* 33.3 (Aug. 1986): 37-43.

A discussion, in German, of the revisionist view of the composer which has been promulgated largely by Shaffer's *Amadeus*.

745. Hummler, Richard. "*Amadeus* Is New Installment in N.Y. Times Preview Serial." *Variety* 301 (24 Dec. 1980): 63, 66.
A news story on the recently inaugurated and controversial *Times* policy of reviewing previews rather than opening night performances.

746. Kirby, F.E. "Bach as a Character for Peter Shaffer." *Piano Quarterly* 130 (1985): 44-48.
Kirby demonstrates the potency of *Amadeus* as a source of inspiration for "revisionist" ideas concerning classical composers other than Mozart. The light-hearted premise of this piece is that there are mysteries and possible scandals surrounding the true story of Bach's life which could provide fodder for Shaffer's pen.

747. Loney, G.M. "Recreating *Amadeus*: An American Team Recreates John Bury's Designs." *Theatre Crafts* 15.3 (Mar. 1981): 10.
An account of the painstaking process of duplicating the original London scenery and properties for the Broadway production.

748. Luddy, Thomas E. Review of *Amadeus*. *Library Journal* 106 (1 Apr. 1981): 811.
Reviewing the text of the play published by Harper in 1981, Luddy refers to it as "a glorious achievement . . . highly recommended for most [library collections]."

749. [McKellen, Ian, interviewed by Harold C. Schonberg.] "Villain of *Amadeus* Is Hero of Broadway." *New York Times* 19 Dec. 1980: C3.

An interview with McKellen focusing on his portrayal of Salieri. Among points of interest is McKellen's revelation that it was his idea to begin the New York production with a 20-minute pre-show section in which Salieri sits on stage in his wheelchair, back to audience, virtually motionless.

750. Morley, Sheridan. "Who Killed Mozart?" *Playbill* Nov. 1980: 6-10.
    Morley outlines the controversy among London critics which greeted the original production over the Mozart characterization. He goes on to discuss the question of the historical accuracy of the play, concluding that, though there will continue to be disagreements over the depiction of Mozart, "*Amadeus* towers above other new plays of its time."

751. Nightingale, Benedict. "In London, the Talk Is of *Amadeus*." *New York Times* 23 Dec. 1979: section 2; 5, 15.
    A tally of the conflicting opinions of London critics. Nightingale wonders whether Shaffer's work "deserves the great acting of Paul Scofield."

752. "1979 Awards." *Plays and Players* Jan. 1980: 12-23.
    This article records the results of P&P's annual critics' poll. Eighteen London critics provide brief articles surveying the season and cast votes for the "Best Play." The winner, *Amadeus*, garners the votes of eight critics (John Barber of the *Daily Telegraph*, Felix Barker of the *Evening News*, Michael Billington of the *Guardian*, Clive Hirshhorn of the *Sunday Express*, Kenneth Hurren of *What's On in London*, Jack Tinker of the *Daily Mail*, J.C. Trewin of the *Illustrated London News*, and Irving Wardle of the *Times*).

753. Otten, Allen L. "Arts Letter from London." *Wall Street Journal* 21 Dec. 1979: 13.
Reports on the controversy surrounding *Amadeus* among London critics and on the favorable verdict rendered by audiences.

754. Robertson, Nan. "When a Top British Actor Faces a Top Director, Electricity Crackles." *New York Times* 5 Nov. 1980: C25.
In this report on the Washington, D.C. rehearsals for *Amadeus*, interview materials are supplied by actor Ian McKellen and director Peter Hall. Shaffer contributes a few remarks, including a description of how he came to write the play and his commitment in it to "the enormous theme of the envy of genius by mediocrity [and] . . . the relevance of human goodness to art."

755. Schonberg, Harold. "Mozart's World: From London to Broadway." *New York Times* 14 Dec. 1980: section 2; 1, 35.
A story based on a joint interview with author Shaffer and director Hall, conducted during the pre-Broadway tryout of *Amadeus* in Washington, D.C. A major topic is the process by which re-writes have been made for the U.S. version.

756. Schonberg, Harold. "Mozart as 'A Silly Little Man.'" *New York Times* 2 Mar. 1980: section 2; 21, 27.
The *Times* music critic assesses the heated complaints made by London reviewers who found Shaffer's depiction of Mozart offensive. Schonberg defends the dramatist's credentials as a serious and knowledgeable student of music and musicians. The key facts brought forward are Shaffer's early training as a pianist, his continuing love of classical music, and his two-year tenure as a music critic. Schonberg

concludes: " . . . musicologically speaking . . . Mr.
Shaffer has done his homework."

757. Seeds, Dale E. "How to: Put the Frosting on *Amadeus.*"
Theatre Crafts 22 (Jan. 1988): 88-89.
A description of the problems encountered in
constructing the Baroque properties required for the
play.

758. Suzy. "Wolfgang Scores Again in London." *New York
Daily News* 20 Nov. 1979: 12.
Suzy reports on the enormous (and, in her opinion,
deserved) success of *Amadeus* at the National
Theatre.

759. Zakariason, Bill. "It's a Mystery, All Right, but Is It
Murder?" *New York Daily News* 17 Dec. 1980: 49.
One of many newspaper articles appearing at the
time of the New York opening of *Amadeus* dealing
with the "historical facts" concerning Salieri and
Mozart.

SCHOLARLY ESSAYS

760. Arens, K. "Mozart: A Case-Study in Logocentric
Repression." [Discusses *Amadeus*] *Comparative
Literature Studies* 23.2 (1986): 141-169.

761. Bidney, M. "Thinking About God and Mozart: The
Salieris of Pushkin and Shaffer." *Slavic and East
European Journal* 30.2 (1986): 183-195.

762. Brunkhorst, Martin. "Die Rekonstruktion der
vergangenheit bei Heiner Kipphardt und Peter
Shaffer." [Discusses *Amadeus*] *Der*

Deutschunterricht (Seelze, W. Germany) 36.3 (June 1984): 51-59.

763. Gianakaris, C.J. "A Playwright Looks at Mozart: Peter Shaffer's *Amadeus*." *Comparative Drama* 15.1 (1981): 37-53.

This is essentially a plot synopsis with references to the historical facts of the case. Gianakaris proposes that Shaffer has achieved a fair degree of historical accuracy and has successfully applied his research to the development of the theme: " . . . how does one respond to a world without rationality or fairness [or] universal order . . . ?"

764. Gianakaris, C.J. "Shaffer's Revisions in *Amadeus*." *Theatre Journal* 35.1 (1983): 88-101.

A lengthy inquiry into the evolution and profitability of script revisions Shaffer made on the occasion of transferring the London production to Broadway. Gianakaris concludes that the original version was improved by the changes and suggests that a major component of Shaffer's "genius" is his "will to . . . make again."

765. Gillespie, M. "To Make Whatever God There Is." *Claudel Studies* 9.2 (1982): 61-70.

766. Hristic, Jovan. "Mocart, Salijeri i jos poneki." *Knjizevnost* (Belgrade, Yugoslavia) 72.7-8 (July-Aug. 1981): 1446-1450.

767. Huber, Werner, and Hubert Zapf. "On the Structure of Peter Shaffer's *Amadeus*." *Modern Drama* 27.3 (Sept. 1984): 299-313.

The authors provide a wide-ranging view of the play's structural components, including (1) its "leitmotivs" and other musical elements and (2) its use of structural devices common to "epic theater,

analytical drama, classical tragedy and comedy . . .
[etc.]." The piece concludes with the assertion that
Amadeus displays "a degree of thematic and
structural complexity which makes it, beyond its
sensational popularity, a dramatic masterpiece in its
own right."

768. Jones, D.R. "Peter Shaffer's Continued Quest for God in
     Amadeus." *Comparative Drama* 21.2 (1987): 145-
     155.
       Jones compares Salieri to two previous Shaffer
     protagonists, Pizarro and Martin Dysart. All three, he
     maintains, have "experienced God, but . . . cannot
     confirm Him."

769. Klein, Dennis A. "*Amadeus*: The Third Part of Peter
     Shaffer's Dramatic Trilogy." *Modern Language
     Studies* 13.1 (Winter 1983): 31-38.
       Klein's paper endeavors to present a case for
     viewing *Amadeus* as the end-piece in a trilogy which
     also includes *Royal Hunt* and *Equus*. The word
     "trilogy" is used as a peg on which to hang a discussion
     of the similarity of themes and techniques in the three
     plays. Klein somewhat lamely attempts to identify
     other Shaffer "trilogies," among them the
     "truth/identity trilogy" of *Black Comedy-White
     Lies-White Liars*.

770. Mikels, F.X., and J. Rurak. "Finishing Salieri: Another
     Act to *Amadeus.*" *Soundings* 67.1 (1984): 42-54.

771. Nottingham, William J. "Why Did God Love Mozart?"
     [On *Amadeus*] *Christian Century* 42 (21 June
     1982): 195-196.

772. Soria, Dorle J. "Peter Shaffer: His *Amadeus* Explores
     Grand Themes." *High Fidelity* 31 (Aug. 1981): MA6.

773. Sullivan, William J. "Peter Shaffer's *Amadeus*: The
     Making and Un-Making of the Fathers." *American
     Imago* 45.1 (Spring 1988): 45-60.
        Sullivan contends that the play is "a study of the
     love of God." He goes on to point out "two exquisite
     ambiguities: (1) we cannot tell . . . whether we are
     dealing with a loving God who embraces his creatures,
     or with the love which the creature directs at his God;
     and (2) the definition of 'love' is de-sentimentalized by
     being inextricably bound to the destructive power of a
     transcendent will."

774. Terrien, Samuel. "*Amadeus* Revisited." *Theology
     Today* 42 (Jan. 1986): 435-443.

775. Thomsen, Christian W., and Gabriele Brandstetter.
     "Mozart und Salieri: Das schauspiel als oper:
     Uberlegungen zu Peter Shaffers *Amadeus*."
     Anglistik und Englischunterricht (Bochum, W.
     Germany) 16 (1982): 191-210.

776. Townsend, Martha A. "*Amadeus* as Dramatic
     Monologue." *Literature-Film Quarterly* 14.4
     (1986): 214-219.
        This paper is devoted to supporting the contention
     that Shaffer's play bears significant points of
     resemblance to the dramatic monologues in verse of
     Robert Browning. The chief source used in defining
     the genre for purposes of comparison is Robert
     Langenbaum's *The Poetry of Experience: The
     Dramatic Monologue in Modern Literary
     Tradition*.

777. Wes, M.A. "The Mystery Surrounding the Death of
     Mozart: Analysis and New Documents." *Maatstaf*
     33.11 (1985): 95-113.

778. Wootton, C. "Literary Portraits of Mozart." *Mosaic* 18.4 (Fall 1985): 77-84.

LETTERS TO THE EDITOR, (LONDON) TIMES

779. Goodwin, John. Letter to the Editor. *Sunday Times* (London) 30 Dec. 1979: 10.
    Goodwin, head of the National Theatre's press office, responds to *Sunday Times* critic James Fenton's attack on *Amadeus* [see #662] by praising the play as "a work of rare power." He also denies Fenton's assertion that the National Theatre attempted to influence the *New York Times*'s London critic, Benedict Nightingale, to write favorably of *Amadeus* and actually caused him to lose his job when he turned in an unfavorable review.

780. Oestricher, Paul. Letter to the Editor. *Times* (London) 10 Dec. 1979: 13.
    Oestricher thanks Bernard Levin for his insightful article on *Amadeus* [see #669]. He reminds readers that, like Shaffer, Karl Barth also wrestled with the problem of "the divine mystery of Mozart" and "concluded that although when the angels sing for God they sing Bach, when they sing for pleasure they sing Mozart, and God eavesdrops."

781. Poyser, I. Letter to the Editor. *Sunday Times* (London) 30 Dec. 1979: 10.
    In a letter taking issue with Fenton's negative review of *Amadeus* [see #662], Poyser admits that the play has weaknesses but lauds it as "one of the best theatre productions for many a year."

LETTER TO THE EDITOR, NEW YORK TIMES

782. Lauder, Rev. Robert E. "Focus of Current Drama: the
Human and the Divine." *New York Times* 18 Oct.
1981: section 2; 8.
Lauder writes that *Amadeus*, like *Equus* before
it, "won't bear much critical reflection." He compares
the play unfavorably to three other less acclaimed
works of the same Broadway season.

THE FILM

783. Forman, Milos, dir., *Amadeus* [film: "Screenplay by
Peter Shaffer, based on his play of the same name"],
with F. Murray Abraham and Tom Hulce, Orion
Pictures, 1984.

FILM REVIEWS

784. Adair, Gilbert. Review of film version of *Amadeus*.
Sight and Sound Spring 1985: 142.
A review which, while never stating its objections
clearly, proceeds to pan the film by implication. The
critic likens the two leading characters to "Bugs Bunny
and Elmer Fudd" and the entire movie to "a cartoon of
the eighteenth century." [This item, along with twelve
other reviews, is reprinted in *Film Review
Annual—1985*, for which see #801 below.]

785. Anon. Review of film version of *Amadeus*. *People
Weekly* 22 (1 Oct. 1984): 14.

The film is called a "mixed blessing." Its chief success is held to be its lavish musical score. On other counts, notably a pace described as plodding, the movie is compared unfavorably to the play which inspired it.

786. Ansen, David. Review of film version of *Amadeus*. *Newsweek* 104 (24 Sept. 1984): 85.

Although Ansen sees in the film several imperfections (particularly its lack of tension), he nevertheless admires it as a "big, generous, flawed movie." [This item, along with twelve other reviews, is reprinted in *Film Review Annual—1985*, for which see #801 below.]

787. Archibald, Lewis. "The Music Never Disappoints; The Story Only Sometimes Does." *Aquarian Weekly* 26 Sept. 1984: 5.

In a review of the film version of *Amadeus* by the rare critic who has not seen the play, the verdict is mixed, but largely negative. Shaffer is accused of "casual pontificating" and of having drawn too broad a contrast between Mozart and Salieri to sustain credibility.

788. Barnes, Clive. "One Man's *Amadeus* Is Another Man's Elephantiasis." *New York Post* 27 Apr. 1985: 11.

Outraged when *Amadeus* is handed the Oscar as "Best Picture," theatre critic Barnes is spurred to write about the film. He contends that, by reducing it to another "pompous Hollywood composer-epic," the creators have perpetrated "a total botching of the excellent original play." He maintains that "a more pretentious, over-inflated, overwrought, over-none-too-soon piece of nonsense is difficult to imagine." [This was a somewhat surprising turnaround; Barnes had bestowed lavish praise on the play, for which see entries #676-680.]

789. Benson, Sheila. Review of film version of *Amadeus*.
     Los Angeles Times 19 Sept. 1984: Calendar, 1.
       A favorable verdict: " . . . enthralling film." [This
     item, along with twelve other reviews, is reprinted in
     Film Review Annual—1985, for which see #801
     below.]

790. Blake, Richard A. Review of film version of *Amadeus*.
     America 151 (13 Oct. 1984): 210.
       An unqualified rave. Blake likens the experience of
     viewing the film to onion-peeling (which mystics use as
     a metaphor in attempting to communicate the
     importance of "essence" and the concept that the whole
     may be greater than the sum of its parts). He
     concludes by pronouncing the work "the most powerful
     film I have seen in a long time."

791. Canby, Vincent. Review of film version of *Amadeus*.
     New York Times 19 Sept. 1984: C23.
       Canby acknowledges that Shaffer and Forman have
     "made the right decisions" in adapting the play for the
     screen (especially the decisions to use Prague locations
     and to add sequences from Mozart's operas). "Never
     for a moment," he writes, "does this *Amadeus* seem
     like a filmed play." Yet the reviewer complains that
     "something has been lost in the transition" which
     makes the movie less impactful than its stage parent.
     [For Canby's follow-up on these points, see #792.]

792. Canby, Vincent. "Stage and Screen Go Their Separate
     Ways." *New York Times* 30 Sept. 1984: section 2; 1,
     19.
       In lengthy reflections on the film version of
     Amadeus, Canby proceeds from the premise that
     each medium affords a fundamentally different set of
     resources and potentials. He argues that the severe
     restrictions of the stage "make possible a kind of
     language you will respond to nowhere else."

Playwrights should not "adapt to" these limitations, but should "soar over" them to achieve "a heightened, poetic . . . experience that cannot be duplicated by movies." Canby congratulates Shaffer on his new screenplay: "*Amadeus* is certainly a movie, not a photographed play." Yet the critic regrets that on the screen some of the play's impact has been lost. He refers to the stage set as "the prison of Salieri's obsession" and contends that, by departing from this unifying space, the film loses its way in a bewilderingly complicated series of realistic locales and "just sort of wanders to its conclusion."

793. Carroll, Kathleen. "Great *Amadeus* Music Redeems a Shrill Story." *New York Daily News* 19 Sept. 1984: 40.
    Carroll rejects the film's plot line and its "one-note" characterization of Mozart. Nonetheless, she recommends it on the basis of its "saving grace," the great composer's great music, splendidly performed.

794. Cart. Review of film version of *Amadeus*. *Variety* 316 (5 Sept. 1984): 12.
    The pleasures of the film are seen as its sumptuous production values, especially the Prague location photography. The reviewer notes, however, that the screen treatment's naturalism proves less effective than the stage version's stylization.

795. Combs, Richard. Review of *Amadeus*. *Monthly Film Bulletin* Jan. 1985: 14.
    A mixed review, leaning to the favorable, which includes a lengthy discussion of the process by which a stage play is converted to the medium of cinema. [This item, along with twelve other reviews, is reprinted in *Film Review Annual—1985*, for which see #801 below.]

796. Corliss, Richard. Review of film version of *Amadeus*.
   Time 124 (10 Sept. 1984): 74.
   High praise for the film: " . . . grand, sprawling
   entertainment." [This item, along with twelve other
   reviews, is reprinted in *Film Review Annual—1985*,
   for which see #801 below.]

797. Craft, Robert. "B-Flat Movie." *New York Review* 11
   Apr. 1985: 11-12.
   Timed to coincide with the Academy Awards
   presentations, this review faults the film version of
   Amadeus for its historical inaccuracies, its "premise,"
   and its handling of Mozart's music. In a final
   paragraph, Craft somewhat ruefully admits that the
   audience members with whom he watched the film
   responded enthusiastically.

798. Denby, David. Review of film version of *Amadeus*. *New
   York* 17 (24 Sept. 1984): 93.
   Denby confesses that he has "painfully divided
   feelings" about the film. He finds some sections
   "charming and inventive," others "pitifully trashy a la
   Ken Russell." The final third of the film is described as
   a "lurid disaster," and Shaffer himself is characterized
   as "an author of overemphatic middlebrow problem
   plays." [This item, along with twelve other reviews, is
   reprinted in *Film Review Annual—1985*, for which
   see #801 below.]

799. Edelstein, David. Review of film version of *Amadeus*.
   Village Voice 25 Sept. 1984: 63.
   As *Voice* pans go, this one is delivered with
   unusual restraint. Edelstein correctly predicts that the
   film will "clean up at the Academy Awards." His
   reasoning: the typical Academy voter "thinks like
   Salieri," which is to say that he "thinks small, selfish,
   and mediocre thoughts." The reviewer insists, however,
   that "anyone who regards creation as a complex

process . . . will find *Amadeus* an outrage." [This item, with twelve other reviews, is reprinted in *Film Review Annual—1985*, for which see #801 below.]

800. Elitzik, Paul. Review of film version of *Amadeus*. *Cineaste* 14.1 (1985): 60.
Largely a plot synopsis; includes a brief, favorable assessment of the film. [This item, along with twelve other reviews, is reprinted in *Film Review Annual—1985*, for which see #801 below.]

801. *Film Review Annual—1985*. Englewood, NJ: Jerome S. Ozer Publisher, 1985.
Reviews of *Amadeus*, pages 43-57; includes reprints of reviews by Sterritt [see #814], Elitzik [see #800], Frumkes [see #803], Benson [see #789], Combs [see #795], Denby [see #798], Reed [see #811], Seligsohn [see #812], Ansen [see #786], Adair [see #784], Corliss [see #796], Edelstein [see #799], and Kissel [see #808].

802. French, Philip. "A Matter of Divine Injustice." *Observer* (London) 20 Jan. 1985: 43.
French warns that the film "bears about as much resemblance to the stage version as Kurosawa's *Throne of Blood* does to *Macbeth*." Yet he concedes that the "radical adaptation" works and goes so far as to declare the movie version psychologically stronger than the play.

803. Frumkes, Roy. Review of film version of *Amadeus*. *Films in Review* April 1985: 246.
A tepidly favorable review. Frumkes calls the movie version "rather sedate." He would have preferred to see Mozart's story given the "Ken Russell" treatment. [This item, along with twelve other reviews, is reprinted in *Film Review Annual—1985*, for which see #801 above.]

804. Gow, Gordon. Review of film version of *Amadeus*.
     Films 5.2 (Feb. 1985): 32-33.
          A rave. "Sumptuous and engrossing . . . Forman's
     best film . . . a superlative transition from stage to
     screen."

805. Hornak, Richard. Review of film version of *Amadeus*
     [on videotape]. *Opera News* 50.34 (15 Feb. 1986): 34.
          Hornak is one of a relatively small number of
     critics who believe that *Amadeus* was at its best in its
     original form and deteriorated with each of Shaffer's
     two succeeding re-writes. His view in brief:
          (1) The original London version of the play in
              1979 was splendid. It "explored the ageless
              theme of the tragedy that befalls an
              otherwise pious man who dares strike a
              bargain with God."
          (2) The 1980 Broadway re-writes were
              undertaken "in a desperate attempt to
              make the complex work more acceptable to
              hit-hungry New York." In the process
              "much of Shaffer's Miltonic vision [was]
              seriously compromised."
          (3) The film version of 1984, though it won
              eight Academy Awards, is "banal, simple-
              minded."
     In his only kind words for the movie, Hornak praises
     conductor Neville Marriner and his instrumentalists
     and vocalists.

806. Kael, Pauline. Review of film version of *Amadeus*. *New
     Yorker* 29 Oct. 1984: 22.
          A mixed but predominately unfavorable report.
     Kael finds "nothing but confusion at the heart of the
     movie" and suggests that the director and screenwriter
     have unintentionally produced another version of an
     old story: the genius who isn't appreciated and dies in
     poverty. It is the basic appeal of this story, she

speculates, that "probably saves the movie from being a disaster."

807. Kauffmann, Stanley. Review of film version of *Amadeus*. *New Republic* 191 (22 Oct. 1984): 30.

While presenting a largely favorable review, Kauffmann makes it clear that he has but middling regard for both the stage and film versions of this work. He considers the play cheapened by spurious theatrical conceits. The film, he maintains, fares better but suffers from excessive length and an obviously contrived ending.

808. Kissel, Howard. Review of film version of *Amadeus*. *Women's Wear Daily* 18 Sept. 1984: 28.

Having turned in a negative review of the play nearly four years earlier [see #697], Kissel now trains his guns on the film. He faults it for its "gross oversimplifications" and regards it as "terribly close to Hollywood musical biography." In much of his assessment, he harks back to the stage version, complaining, for instance, that "The play answers the questions it asks so neatly, so prissily, it never engages us on a deep level." [This item, along with twelve other reviews, is reprinted in *Film Review Annual—1985*, for which see #801 above.]

809. O'Brien, Tom. Review of film version of *Amadeus*. *Commonweal* 19 Oct. 1984: 557.

A favorable report. O'Brien, who has not seen the stage version, finds the film "moving" and declares that its weaknesses are redeemed by the glorious music.

810. Perry-Camp, Jane. Review of film version of *Amadeus*. *Eighteenth Century Life* 9.1 (Oct. 1984): 116-122.

A point-by-point refutation of the "historical accuracy" of Shaffer's depiction of Mozart. While admitting that Shaffer himself has described his work not as history but as "a fantasia based on fact," the writer suggests that the proper course, in that case, would have been to adopt Mann's approach in *Death in Venice*: change the names of the principals to remove all confusion of fact with fiction. Perry-Camp characterizes Shaffer's conception of Mozart as "a new, revised, and flattened paperdoll guaranteed to differ from the romantic nineteenth century porcelain model."

811. Reed, Rex. Review of film version of *Amadeus*. *New York Post* 19 Sept. 1984: 93.

Reed delivers a mixed review. He complains of the movie's "painfully dull stretches," also of its use of "too much Mozart music" and its length. He sums up by quipping, "There's nothing wrong with *Amadeus* that a good pair of scissors couldn't fix." [This item, along with twelve other reviews, is reprinted in *Film Review Annual—1985*, for which see #801 above.]

812. Seligsohn, Leo. Review of film version of *Amadeus*. *Newsday* 19 Sept. 1984: part II; 57.

Referring to the stage version as a "victory of style over substance," Seligsohn reports that the film is "entertaining on a number of levels" but fails to find an essential chord which would "elevate it above the commonplace." [This item, along with twelve other reviews, is reprinted in *Film Review Annual—1985*, for which see #801 above.]

813. Simon, John. Review of film version of *Amadeus*. *National Review* 36 (19 Oct. 1984): 56.

This is an unmitigated pan in the slashing Simon manner, in which it is deplored that a bad play has been turned into a movie that is "immeasurably worse." Simon charges that the theme of the play is Shaffer's lamentation of his own mediocrity (via his surrogate, Salieri).

814. Sterritt, David. Review of film version of *Amadeus.*
     Christian Science Monitor 20 Sept. 1984: 27.
     A highly favorable report, calling *Amadeus* "one of
     the year's most imposing movies—rowdy, funny,
     suspenseful, and sometimes very moving." [This item,
     along with twelve other reviews, is reprinted in *Film
     Review Annual—1985,* for which see #801 above.]

815. Thomson, David. "Salieri, Psycho." *Film Comment* 21:1
     (Jan.-Feb. 1985): 70-75.
     Thomson insists that, despite its polished surface,
     the film is a fraud. "How long," he asks, "can you listen
     to that music and settle for Peter Shaffer's mannered
     agony over its giddy composer and his wicked
     mastermind agent?" He considers the movie's message
     ("if art comes without plodding it must be a gift from
     above") "an insult to Mozart."

816. Williamson, Bruce. Review of film version of *Amadeus.*
     Playboy 31 (Nov. 1984): 18.
     A rave review for the film and for Shaffer, who is
     praised for daring to transform a brilliant play into a
     vastly different work in order to present its ideas in
     cinematic terms.

FILM VERSION: NEWS AND FEATURE STORIES

817. Ansen, David. "The Return of the Native." *Newsweek*
     102 (11 July 1983): 41.
     A report, based on interviews, concerning the
     return of *Amadeus* director Milos Forman to his
     native Prague. "The real stars of *Amadeus,* " Forman
     says, "are Mozart's music and Prague's 18th century
     architecture." One section of Ansen's piece is devoted
     to comments by Shaffer on the problems of adapting

for the screen. He mentions the addition of a key
character (Mozart's father, Leopold) and the creation
of two entirely new and important scenes: (1) a
sequence in which the dying Mozart dictates his
'Requiem' to Salieri (2) another in which a parody-
pastiche of Mozart's operas, devised by Schikaneder, is
performed.

818. Castro, A. "*Amadeus* and the Oscars of Hollywood."
Insula 40.461 (1985): 14.
A brief commentary on the Academy Awards and a
complaint concerning the arbitrary process by which
they are made.

819. Holdenfield, Chris. "The Czech Bounces Back." *Rolling
Stone* 27 Sept. 1984: 19.
An extensive interview with Milos Forman, who
discusses the making of *Amadeus*. Several
paragraphs deal with Forman's favorable impressions
of Shaffer and a description of the collaborative
methods by which they arrived at the screen version of
the play.

820. Kakutani, Michiko. "How *Amadeus* Was Translated from
Play to Film." *New York Times* 16 Sept. 1984:
section 2; 1, 20.
In a lengthy article based on an interview with
Shaffer, we learn that the playwright was at first
reluctant to adapt his work for the motion picture
screen. Once he had been persuaded to do so, he
underwent a six-month period of intense pre-
production collaboration with director Milos Forman.
Their primary aim: "switching emphasis from verbal to
visual."

821. Kamm, Henry. "Milos Forman Takes His Cameras and
Amadeus to Prague." *New York Times* 29 May
1983: section 2; 3.

Forman is interviewed (as is Shaffer, briefly) during a flight from Rome to Prague, where he is to begin work on the film. Though most of the piece is devoted to Forman, the subject of his collaboration with Shaffer is mentioned. Shaffer is quoted as saying that the film is to be primarily the work of Forman ("MY *Amadeus* is the play").

822. Lee, Nora. "Miroslav Ondricek and *Amadeus.*" *American Cinematographer* Apr. 1985: 94-101.

An interview, via interpreter, with Ondricek in his home in Prague, including material on his experiences while serving as Director of Photography on *Amadeus.*

823. Shaffer, Peter. "Paying Homage to Mozart." *New York Times* 2 Sept. 1984: magazine section; 22-23, 27, 35, 38.

On the occasion of the film premiere of *Amadeus,* Shaffer delivers a personal, and impressively knowledgeable, tribute to Mozart. A line he wrote for Salieri which was cut prior to the first production, he says, expresses his own sentiments: "The God I acknowledge lives, for example, in bars 34 to 44 of Mozart's 'Masonic Funeral March.'"

824. Smith, Ronn. "Designing History." *Theatre Crafts* 18 (Mar. 1984): 12-18.

Film production designer Patrizia Von Brandenstein is interviewed. She compares her problems in designing *Amadeus* to those she faced in the contemporary drama *Silkwood.*

825. Toubiana, S. "Conversation with Milos Forman Regarding *Amadeus.*" *Cahiers du Cinema* 365 (1984): 9-12.

826. Von Rhein, John. "On Film, a More Musical *Amadeus.*" *New York Daily News* 24 Oct. 1982: 13.

A story on the play's transition to film, written in the early stages of production. It focuses on the pains being taken by Shaffer and others to avoid the usual tendency of cinematic biographers to romanticize their subjects beyond recognition.

827. Watkins, Roger. "Zaentz High on Back-end Deals as *Amadeus* B.O. Tops $90-mil." *Variety* 321 (20 Nov. 1985): 6.
    A report on the financial success of the film version of *Amadeus*.

FILM VERSION: LETTERS TO THE EDITOR
[Note: All letters cited below (other than Shaffer's) are apparently intended by the writers to refer to both the stage and screen versions of *Amadeus*. However, since they date from 1989, it may be judged that the writers have been influenced more recently, and perhaps more strongly, by the film adaptation than by its stage predecessors.]

828. Barzun, Jacques. Letter to the Editor. *New York Times* 1 July 1989: 22.
    The eminent teacher-critic refers only indirectly to Shaffer and his play. He applauds Menotti's *Times* article of June 10 [see #829], while differing with it vigorously on a single point: Barzun considers it unwise, or simply irrelevant, to approach the question of an artist's stature from a moral perspective.

829. Menotti, Gian Carlo. "I Forgive Goethe, Tolstoy and, Above All, Mozart." *New York Times* 10 June 1989: 27.
    Having recently directed a Spoleto Festival production of *The Marriage of Figaro*, Menotti is

spurred to express his opposition to "the common image of Mozart . . . made popular by the play and film *Amadeus*." A sharp distinction is drawn between Mozart, whose inspirations were brilliantly crafted and clothed in "conventional style," and today's self-acclaimed musical "geniuses," whose works are without discipline and whose "only effort is to shock." Menotti also deplores the current tendency "to try to understand artists by delving into their private lives rather than into their works. "Must we then forgive the artist," he asks, "for his failures as a man?" His reply is: "It all depends on how great the artist is." According to Menotti, magnificent artists such as Mozart are due limitless pardon, "in exchange for the splendors with which they have enriched the world and because of the torment their work must have cost them."

830. Shaffer, Peter. "Letter to the Editor." *New York Times* 14 Oct. 1984: 8.

A response to a letter to the *Times* suggesting that Franz Xaver Sussmayr (the historical personage who attempted to steal the credit for Mozart's *Requiem*) would have made a more appropriate villain for Shaffer's *Amadeus* than Salieri. Shaffer, displaying considerable musical erudition, lightheartedly writes that assigning Sussmayr's story to Salieri represents merely one of many cases of playwriting pilferage: Salieri, in fact, acts out events from the lives of several historical figures, among them Da Ponte, Leutgeb, and Count Walsegg.

831. Stapleton, Rev. Scott. Letter to the Editor. *New York Times* 1 July 1989: 22.

Writing in support of Menotti's Op-Ed page article of June 10, Rev. Stapleton agrees that Shaffer has "demeaned" Mozart. His letter focuses on the contrast between the "sufferings" of (historical) Mozart and

Salieri (as depicted by Shaffer), Mozart's having been for art's sake, while Salieri's were selfish, "bitter and sullen."

832. Steinhauer, Jules Verne. Letter to the Editor. *New York Times* 19 August 1989: 22.

Another attempt to "set the record straight" as to the historical facts concerning Mozart.

Chapter Eleven

Yonadab

THE TEXT

833. Shaffer, Peter. *Yonadab*. New York: Harper and Row, 1987.

PLAY REVIEWS

London Production.
Opened at the Olivier Theatre on December 4, 1985.

834. Barber, John. Review of *Yonadab*. *Daily Telegraph* (London) 6 Dec. 1985: page no. not available.
 A mixed report. Barber opens with a powerful tribute: "The huge imagination of Peter Shaffer is one of the glories of the modern stage." *Yonadab*, he maintains, demonstrates many of the playwright's

virtues. Nevertheless, the work proves disappointing.
At the heart of the matter, says Barber, is the misuse
of the title character, whose "skeptical commentaries"
so often undercut the play's "great events." [This item
is reprinted, along with 15 other reviews of the play, in
London Theatre Record, for which see #851
below.]

835. Billington, Michael. Review of *Yonadab*. *Manchester
Guardian* 6 Dec. 1985: 10.
   The verdict on *Yonadab* is negative: " . . . curiously
unsatisfying drama." Billington sees as its major flaw a
lack of suspense. Much of the review is devoted to
reflections on the relationship of *Yonadab* to
Shaffer's other plays. In theme, for example, it echoes
"all his major work": a conflict between "cold
calculation and dangerous ecstasy with God as the
invisible protagonist." *Yonadab* himself is upheld as
the most recent in a succession of characters who are
"obsessed by other men's passion or capacity to
become divine instruments." The others, according to
Billington's theory, include Pizarro in *Royal Hunt*,
Gideon in *Shrivings*, Dysart in *Equus*, and Salieri
in *Amadeus*. The critic ends with a plea to the
author: "I wish he would temporarily banish God from
his theatrical vocabulary." [This item is reprinted,
along with 15 other reviews of the play, in *London
Theatre Record*, for which see #851 below.]

836. Chaillet, Ned. Review of *Yonadab*. *Wall Street
Journal* 15 Dec. 1985: page no. not available.
   A mixed review. Although Chaillet concedes that
Shaffer "retains his canny sense of rhetoric," he finds
the play too often "stiffly schematic" and lacking in
dramatic conflict. [This item is reprinted, along with 15
other reviews of the play, in *London Theatre
Record*, for which see #851 below.]

837. Connor, John. Review of *Yonadab*. *City Limits* (London) 20 Dec. 1985: page no. not available.
Connor accuses Shaffer of trying to give the impression that "weighty ideas are bounding all over the place," when he is, in fact, not "saying anything more than the obvious." [This item is reprinted, along with 15 other reviews of the play, in *London Theatre Record*, for which see #851 below.]

838. Coveney, Michael. Review of *Yonadab*. *Financial Times* (London) 5 Dec. 1985: page no. not available.
A unmistakable thumbs down. The material is described as "dramatically tenuous"; the title character, "a bore." [This item is reprinted, along with 15 other reviews of the play, in *London Theatre Record*, for which see #851 below.]

839. Cropper, Martin. "Fear of Sacrilege." *Times* (London) 25 June 1986: 19.
An unrelentingly negative review. To begin with, Cropper complains, the genre itself is faulty ("there is something inherently and inescapably ludicrous about staging Bible stories"). The plot is likewise contemptible ("key incidents are handled [with] . . . woeful clumsiness"). Finally, the baseness of the title character ("combining the less attractive aspects of Iago and Uriah Heep"), is compounded by his running commentary on the events of the play, an "obtrusive and lowering device which pretends to do more than it does, and succeeds in undoing a good deal more."

840. Edwards, Christopher. "Dramatic Sterility." *Spectator* (London) 14 Dec. 1985: 41-42.
The reviewer detects in Shaffer no particular skills as a dramatist, by which he means the ability to create "life and tension and character through dialogue." Looking back, Edwards dismisses *Equus* and *Amadeus* as cold and external exercises whose only

achievement is a "stylish fluency." *Yonadab* is
characterized as yet more calculating and lifeless than
its predecessors and is accounted a thorough failure.

841. Fisher, J. Review of *Yonadab*. *Theatre Journal* 39.1
(1987): 108-109.
A favorable, though not enthusiastic, opinion of the
play is presented.

842. Hepple, Peter. "Shaffer and a Dark Corner of the Bible."
Stage and Television Today (London) 12 Dec.
1985: 11.
Hepple is one of the few critics to offer an
unreserved welcome to Yonadab, finding it "never less
than enthralling to listen to."

843. Hiley, Jim. Review of *Yonadab*. *Listener* (London) 12
Dec. 1985: page no. not available.
This piece focuses not so much on the particular
play as the stature of the playwright. Hiley enumerates
Shaffer's strengths: he deals with interesting and
important ideas, the canvases on which he works are
large ones, his plays are brilliantly actable, and he sets
out to please the popular audience (often resorting to
wisecracks and four-letter words). However, in the
end, Hiley maintains, Shaffer comes off as a "sly
illusionist," and the spectator always knows "what he's
up to." As for his rank among playwrights, Hiley makes
him the subject of broad comparison: "[He] would like
to be a spiritualised Brecht; instead, he's an exotic
Arnold Wesker, with better gags." [This item is
reprinted, along with 15 other reviews of the play, in
London Theatre Record, for which see #851
below.]

844. Hirschhorn, Clive. Review of *Yonadab*. *Sunday
Express* (London) 8 Dec. 1985: page no. not
available.

A favorable review. The critic reports that, in
Yonadab, "Shaffer's favorite theme of 'consuming
heat' . . . versus 'consuming cold' . . . is vividly
expressed." [This item is reprinted, along with 15 other
reviews of the play, in *London Theatre Record*, for
which see #851 below.]

845. Hornby, R. "The London Theater, Summer 1986."
     Hudson Review 39.4 (1987): 635-643.

846. Hurren, Kenneth. Review of *Yonadab*. *Mail on
     Sunday* (London) 8 Dec. 1985: page no. not available.
        Hurren parodies pseudo-biblical jargon to pan
     Yonadab: "And the multitude were respectful to
     Shaffer's eloquence. But only some were persuaded by
     him." [This item is reprinted, along with 15 other
     reviews of the play, in *London Theatre Record*, for
     which see #851 below.]

847. Jameson, Sue. Review of *Yonadab*. London
     Broadcasting no date.
        The reviewer approves: " . . . an entertaining and
     thought-provoking evening." [This item is reprinted,
     along with 15 other reviews of the play, in *London
     Theatre Record*, for which see #851 below.]

848. Joffee, Linda. "New Peter Shaffer Play Is Profound But
     Lacks Punch." *Christian Science Monitor* 18 Mar.
     1986: 29-30.
        In her review of *Yonadab*, Joffee delivers an
     intriguing appraisal of Shaffer's aims,
     accomplishments, and failings through the twenty-
     eight-year span of his career. The critic begins by
     acknowledging that "this formidable British playwright
     has already made his mark on 20th century drama."
     She argues, however, that "what remains an open
     question . . . is the overall value of his brand of
     theatricality." Her analysis includes the view   that

Shaffer ("unlike most dramatists today") has based all his major works on "one obsession: religious belief." In *Yonadab,* she finds that this theme is "at times deeply thought-provoking but lacks punch." At the same time, she speculates that the play "has all the signs of being an important steppingstone to more inspired things."

849. King, Francis. Review of *Yonadab. Sunday Telegraph* (London) 8 Dec. 1985: page no. not available.
    Mixed comments: while the play has "fine moments," it is on the whole "boring." King lays some of the blame at the door of Peter Hall, whose direction he calls "dainty and hygenic" [sic]. [This item is reprinted, along with 15 other reviews of the play, in *London Theatre Record,* for which see #851 below.]

850. Kroll, Jack. "Four from the London Stage." *Newsweek* 107 (13 Jan. 1986): 65.
    Includes a brief, positive appraisal of *Yonadab*: " . . . once again [Shaffer] explores the battle between the mundane and the transcendent . . . . For me, this is Shaffer's most daring, most personal, most honest play."

851. *London Theatre Record* 5.25/26 (Productions from 4-31 Dec. 1985): 1211-1217.
    Reprints reviews listed here as entries #864, #846, #843, #855, #847, #849, #852, #834, #835, #858, #861, #853, #836, #844, #837, and #838.

852. Mackenzie, Suzie. Review of *Yonadab. Time Out* (London) 12 Dec. 1985: page no. not available.
    A bluntly unfavorable review. The work is condemned for having "no informing intellect at work" and on the grounds that "no demand is made of the audience to engage at any level." [This item is reprinted, along with 15 other reviews of the play, in

London Theatre Record, for which see #851
above.]

853. Nathan, David. Review of *Yonadab*. *Jewish Chronicle*
13 Dec. 1985: page no. not available.
    The work is described as "a typical Shaffer play,"
one in which "a brilliant sense of theatre . . . [is]
supported by a set of fairly simple ideas, some of them
suspect." [This item is reprinted, along with 15 other
reviews of the play, in *London Theatre Record*, for
which see #851 above.]

854. Nightingale, Benedict. "Peter Shaffer Creates Another
Envious Outsider." *New York Times* 22 Dec. 1985:
section 2; 5, 16.
    Nightingale begins by conceding that "whatever else
Peter Shaffer may lack, it isn't courage." Nevertheless,
the playwright's current attempt to cope with a great
theme on a large canvas (*Yonadab*) is judged a
failure. The critic complains that Shaffer's treatment
of the material lacks vitality and plausibility. Its
language, he says, ranging from high-flown archaisms
to anachronistic modern quips, verges on the "silly." Of
interest to followers of Shaffer's career is
Nightingale's theory that, "emotionally, *Yonadab* is
kin to Salieri . . . to Dysart . . . to Pizarro," all four
representing variations on a single theme: "the envious
outsider, seeking to control others he feels to be in
some way more gifted, more blessed, more central to
the workings of an unjust universe." It is the fate of
this archetypal character, suggests Nightingale, that he
"seeks but finds neither faith nor ecstasy."

855. Nightingale, Benedict. Review of *Yonadab*. *New
Statesman* 110 (13 Dec. 1985): 31.
    Nightingale, like several other critics, seizes the
opportunity provided by *Yonadab* to assess the
author's work in toto. He begins by asking, "Isn't it

time Shaffer got over his weakness for florid, gasping rhetoric . . . ?" He expands on this theme and quotes a few lines to buttress it. In concluding remarks, however, he adopts a more complimentary (though equally condescending) tone: "In a world of mainly thin plays on monochrome subjects, isn't there a cranky heroism in the way he leaps across the centuries feverishly banging away at grand metaphysical themes . . . ?" Concerning *Yonadab*, Nightingale merely complains that the title character "dominates the evening without being very plausible or interesting in himself." [This item is reprinted, along with 15 other reviews of the play, in *London Theatre Record*, for which see #851 above.]

856. Peter, John. "The Art of the Voyeur." *Sunday Times* (London) 8 Dec. 1985: 43.
    Peter expresses disapproval both of *Yonadab* and its author. The play is described as "a long, louche literary entertainment which relates to serious drama rather as Little Red Riding Hood relates to anthropology." As for Shaffer, he is represented as a playwright whose works are "theatrical without being dramatic . . . [his] art is the art of glossing and elaboration."

857. Pit. Review of *Yonadab*. *Variety* 11 Dec. 1985: 138.
    A negative review, in which the play is held to be "unredeemed by piercing vision, or even good old rousing melodrama."

858. Ratcliffe, Michael. "An Attack of Brotherly Love." *Observer* (London) 8 Dec. 1985: 25.
    A thoroughly unfavorable response from Ratcliffe, who complains that in *Yonadab* ideas take precedence over people and that lecture-demonstration serves as a substitute for drama. He ends by dismissing it as "pseudo-tragedy." [This item is reprinted, along

with 15 other reviews of the play, in *London Theatre Record*, for which see #851 above.]

859. Rich, Frank. "A Mixed Array of Dramas in London." *New York Times* 29 May 1986: C19.
    A brief report on current theatre fare in the British capital. Rich's response to *Yonadab* is largely negative: "Only at the violent end of each act does the drama emit the characteristic Shaffer heat." The critic speculates that the script might benefit from "a more intimate production" than the one it has received at the National.

860. Ross, Chris. "Peter Shaffer's *Yonadab.*" *The World and I* Mar. 1986: 320-321.
    Ross disapproves, insisting that, though "ambiguity . . . may be one hallmark of genius," the ambiguity of form and idea in *Yonadab* is "unsatisfying."

861. Shulman, Milton. Review of *Yonadab*. *Standard* (London) 5 Dec. 1985: page no. not available.
    Shulman finds the play overwritten and pretentious ("perfumed biblical bosh trying to smell like something pungent and significant"). [This item is reprinted, along with 15 other reviews of the play, in *London Theatre Record*, for which see #851 above.]

862. Sinclair, Clive. "The Voyeur Viewed." *Times Literary Supplement* (London) 20 Dec. 1985: 1457.
    The theme of this article is Shaffer's failure to translate successfully Dan Jacobson's novel (*The Rape of Tamar*) into theatrical terms. Sinclair particularly regrets Shaffer's decision to retain the novel's narrative device: "[the character] Yonadab as a storyteller."

863. Thomsen, Christian W. "Die Hohe Schule des Voyeurismus." *Theater Heute* 4 (April) 1986: 44-45.

A review, in German, of the National Theatre's London production of *Yonadab*.

864. Tinker, Jack. Review of *Yonadab*. *Daily Mail* (London) 5 Dec. 1985: page no. not available.
This is one of the very few reviews of the play which can be categorized as a "rave." According to Tinker, the work "produces a stunning effect." Shaffer is lauded as one of the few current playwrights whose products "gnaw relentlessly into our conscience." [This item is reprinted, along with 15 other reviews of the play, in *London Theatre Record*, for which see #851 above.]

865. Wardle, Irving. "Spy of History." *Times* (London) 5 Dec. 1985: 12.
After a lengthy plot synopsis, Wardle briefly turns his attention to Shaffer's writing. *Yonadab* is condemned on the grounds that "it lays claim to ultimate questions of man's place in the universe and reduces them simply to a theatrical structure." Though the critic concedes that the drama holds the audience's attention, he argues that it fails to awaken the spectator "to the mysteries and possibilities of human destiny."

866. Watt, Douglas. "He Shouldn't Be Saying This." *New York Daily News* 10 July 1986: 57.
Watt has seen the play after the introduction of script revisions and following Patrick Stewart's taking over from Alan Bates in the title role. He writes that, without Stewart's magnificent performance, "there wouldn't be much of a play."

867. Wilson, Edwin. "Two on the Aisle in Britain." *Wall Street Journal* 1 Aug. 1986: 15.
Includes a short review of *Yonadab*. Wilson finds the play "seriously flawed": Shaffer has attempted to

deal with "too many themes" while "not sufficiently developing any of them."

NEWS REPORTS AND FEATURE STORIES

868. Barnes, Clive. "Britain's Theaters." *New York Post* 9 Aug. 1986: 13-14.
    Barnes gives a brief report on *Yonadab*'s mixed reception at the hands of both the London critics and its audiences.

869. De Jongh, Nicholas. "Viennese Reject Shaffer Play." *Guardian* (Manchester) 8 Feb. 1986: 2.
    A report on the decision by Austrian officials to reject the National Theatre's production of *Yonadab* as an entry in their "Britain in Vienna" celebrations, in favor of Congreve's *Love for Love*. Shaffer's play is thought "unsuitable fare for the President of Austria and his wife, not to mention their guests the Prince and Princess of Wales."

870. Wolf, Matthew. "Peter Shaffer, Creator of *Amadeus*, Suffers Dramatic Flop with *Yonadab*." *Chicago Tribune* 5 Jan. 1986: section 13; 6-7.

SCHOLARLY ESSAY

871. Klein, Dennis A. "*Yonadab*: Peter Shaffer's Earlier Dramas Revisited in the Court of King David." *Comparative Drama* 22.1 (Spring 1988): 68-78.
    Klein compares *Yonadab* to three other works by Shaffer: *Royal Hunt*, *Equus*, and *Amadeus*. He

finds similarities on three fronts: (1) the protagonist-as-narrator device, (2) recurring motives or themes ("voyeurism and a quest for divinity"), and (3) the concluding lament for an empty future (as in Yonadab's final words: " . . . attached to the tree of Unattachment . . . Who can cut me down?").

Chapter Twelve

Lettice and Lovage

THE TEXT

872. Shaffer, Peter. *Lettice and Lovage: A Comedy.*
New York: Harper and Row, 1989.

PLAY REVIEWS

A. Reviews: Original London Production.
Opened at the Globe Theatre, Oct. 27, 1987.

873. Anon. Report on London theatre scene. *New York Times* 25 Feb. 1988: C28.
    In a capsule review, *Lettice* is condemned on the grounds of its length and its triviality. Maggie Smith's performance, which is called "camp," is said to render the play "as stylized as Kabuki."

874. Asquith, Ros. Review of *Lettice and Lovage*. *City Limits* (London) 11 Nov. 1987: page no. not available.
    Asquith applauds Shaffer's latest effort: " . . . a classy comedy." [This item is reprinted, along with eighteen other reviews of the play, in *London Theatre Record*, for which see #890 below.]

875. Barnes, Clive. "Shaffer's *Lettice* Cool Salad of a Play." *New York Post* 22 Sept. 1988: 38.
    Essentially, a favorable appraisal which describes the work as "yet another eccentric variation on [Shaffer's] theme of eccentricity." The charms of the piece are enumerated, but the whole is found to be insubstantial.

876. Billington, Michael. "Lord Peter's Whimsy." *Guardian* (Manchester) 29 Oct. 1987: 22.
    Billington expresses mixed reactions to *Lettice*. On the one hand, he rejoices that Shaffer has "banish[ed] God from his vocabulary" [see entry #835 for Billington's review of *Yonadab*], and that the new work is "whimsically enjoyable" in a manner that recalls *The Public Eye*. On the other hand, the critic regrets that the secondary role of Lotte has not been "built up" and that the theme of truth vs. lies is not "dug deeper into." [This item is reprinted, along with eighteen other reviews of the play, in *London Theatre Record*, for which see #890 below.]

877. Bonner, Hilary. Review of *Lettice and Lovage*. *Daily Mirror* (London) 30 Oct. 1987: page no. not available.
    A rave, with equal praise awarded to Maggie Smith for her performance as Lettice and to Shaffer for composing "a comedy full of wit and originality . . . a sheer joy." [This item is reprinted, along with eighteen other reviews of the play, in *London Theatre Record*, for which see #890 below.]

878. Chand, Paul. "Shaffer's Got His Wits About Him." *Stage and Television Today* (London) 5 Nov. 1987: 15.

Chand applauds *Lettice and Lovage* as "a comedy to rank with the smartest . . . [that] puts the West End back on the map."

879. Couling, Della. Review of *Lettice and Lovage*. *Tablet* (London) 14 Nov. 1987: page no. not available.

Although Couling exults that, "at last," she has found a new play that she can "thoroughly recommend," she concludes with the observation that "it is all preposterous nonsense, of course." [This item is reprinted, along with eighteen other reviews of the play, in *London Theatre Record*, for which see #890 below.]

880. Edwards, Christopher. "A Touch of Spice." *Spectator* (London) 31 Oct. 1987: 51.

Edwards finds *Lettice* "compulsively funny viewing" but also refers to it as "middle-brow, middle-class entertainment, the sort of play Peter Shaffer has always been writing."

881. Grant, Steve. Review of *Lettice and Lovage*. *Time Out* (London) 4 Nov. 1987: page no. not available.

Grant approves of Shaffer's latest effort, calling it the playwright's "lightest, wittiest, and most accessible play in years." [This item is reprinted, along with eighteen other reviews of the play, in *London Theatre Record*, for which see #890 below.]

882. Hiley, Jim. Review of *Lettice and Lovage*. *Listener* (London) 5 Nov. 1987: page no. not available.

Hiley is less than enthusiastic about Shaffer's "wonkily constructed vehicle for Maggie Smith." The two leading characters, he complains, talk too much and "have very little worth hearing to say." [This item is reprinted, along with eighteen other reviews of the play, in *London Theatre Record*, for which see #890 below.]

883. Hirschhorn, Clive. Review of *Lettice and Lovage*. *Sunday Express* (London) 1 Nov. 1987: page no. not available.
An unqualified rave for Shaffer, who is called "brilliant and canny," and for his new comedy, which is hailed as "one of the sharpest, wittiest, most passionate and elegant plays of the year." [This item is reprinted, along with eighteen other reviews of the play, in *London Theatre Record*, for which see #890 below.]

884. Hoyle, Martin. Review of *Lettice and Lovage*. *Financial Times* (London) 28 Oct. 1987: page no. not available.
Hoyle concentrates on Maggie Smith's performance in what he calls "a one-woman show." [This item is reprinted, along with eighteen other reviews of the play, in *London Theatre Record*, for which see #890 below.]

885. Hurren, Kenneth. Review of *Lettice and Lovage*. *Mail on Sunday* (London) 1 Nov. 1987: page no. not available.
A rave for Maggie Smith's performance ("a constant delight") which maintains that, without her, the play would be "a lesser thing . . . if indeed it could exist at all." [This item is reprinted, along with eighteen other reviews of the play, in *London Theatre Record*, for which see #890 below.]

886. Jameson, Sue. Review of *Lettice and Lovage*. London Broadcasting 28 Oct. 1987.
Though Jameson maintains that the play is "more than a vehicle," she devotes the entire review to a paean of praise for Maggie Smith in the title role and

offers no assessment of Shaffer's contribution to the proceedings. [This item is reprinted, along with eighteen other reviews of the play, in *London Theatre Record*, for which see #890 below.]

887. Jones, Dan. Review of *Lettice and Lovage*. *Sunday Telegraph* (London) 1 Nov. 1987: page no. not available.

A plot synopsis without much discussion of the play's merits. [This item is reprinted, along with eighteen other reviews of the play, in *London Theatre Record*, for which see #890 below.]

888. Kemp, Peter. Review of *Lettice and Lovage*. *Independent* (London) 29 Oct. 1987: page no. not available.

In this brief and unenthusiastic review, Kemp roguishly credits Maggie Smith's performance with making "a very stagey meal . . . out of Shaffer's burlesque fare." [This item is reprinted, along with eighteen other reviews of the play, in *London Theatre Record*, for which see #890 below.]

889. Kissel, Howard. "So Veddy, Veddy Classy." *New York Daily News* 5 Jan. 1988: 33.

A report on the London theatre scene, including commentary on Maggie Smith's performance in *Lettice and Lovage* (without reference to the quality of the play).

890. *London Theatre Record* 7.22 (Productions from 22 Oct.-4 Nov. 1987): 1384-1390.

Includes reprints of reviews listed here as entries #885, #881, #901, #884, #882, #886, #888, #887, #883, #876, #877, #899, #891, #902, #893, #895, #874, #896, and #879.

891. Morley, Sheridan. "All Her Yesterdays." *Punch* 4 Nov.
     1987: 67.
        While Morley praises the play, he expresses
     reservations about its structure: " . . . a weird and
     wondrously ramshackle . . . extraordinarily baroque,
     rambling comedy . . . [with] eccentric, if usually
     enjoyable tangents . . . [which] goes nowhere very
     specific." [This item is reprinted, along with eighteen
     other reviews of the play, in *London Theatre
     Record*, for which see #890 above.]

892. Morley, Sheridan. Review of *Lettice and Lovage*.
     Plays and Players Dec. 1987: 16-17.
        In a review which is almost identical to the one he
     delivered in *Punch* [see entry #891 above], Morley
     concludes, "At its best, this is a very odd love story and
     at its worst it's simply a yelp of pain from someone
     who can't get the modern world to make any kind of
     sense on her own exotic scale of values."

893. Nathan, David. Review of *Lettice and Lovage*. *Jewish
     Chronicle* (London) 6 Nov. 1987: page no. not
     available.
        Nathan maintains that Shaffer has written an
     "admirable comedy . . . [which] finally collapses on a
     manifestly impossible conclusion." [This item is
     reprinted, along with eighteen other reviews of the
     play, in *London Theatre Record*, for which see
     #890 above.]

894. Nightingale, Benedict. "Peter Shaffer Turns on the
     Laughing Gas." *New York Times* 22 Nov. 1987:
     section 2; 5, 20.
        This is a moderately favorable report, in which
     Nightingale congratulates Shaffer for having "happily
     recovered his sense of humor." He complains, however,
     that the work is flawed by the author's tendency to
     sentimentalize not only the characters and their

relationships but also his theme of England's lost greatness.

895. Osborne, Charles. Review of *Lettice and Lovage*. *Daily Telegraph* (London) 29 Oct. 1987: page no. not available.
    Approval for all aspects of the project. Shaffer's script is described as "an original, highly entertaining, and intelligent comedy." [This item is reprinted, along with eighteen other reviews of the play, in *London Theatre Record*, for which see #890 above.]

896. Paton, Maureen. Review of *Lettice and Lovage*. *Daily Express* (London) 29 Oct. 1987: page no. not available.
    The review is devoted entirely to Maggie Smith's performance. [This item is reprinted, along with eighteen other reviews of the play, in *London Theatre Record*, for which see #890 above.]

897. Peter, John. "Sugaring a Bitter Pill." *Sunday Times* (London) 1 Nov. 1987 62.
    Peter finds a great deal in *Lettice* that is praiseworthy: the play "has a real theme; it can look pain straight in the face; it is hilariously and unsparingly observant . . . Shaffer's writing is immensely assured: he skirts the ridiculous with . . . exquisite precision." Ultimately, however, the experience proves disappointing: the comedy "ends in a pink, ingratiating glow of hope which leaves me incredulous and unmoved."

898. Pit. Review of *Lettice and Lovage*. *Variety* 4 Nov. 1987: 84.
    A mixed review. The play is described as "a zany farce that also has thoughtful humor and uplifting concerns." While Shaffer shows himself "in less than

top form," his "literate, witty language" is considered a "treat," as is Maggie Smith's performance as Lettice.

899. Ratcliffe, Michael. Review of *Lettice and Lovage. Observer* (London) 1 Nov. 1987: 22.
    A favorable opinion of the play is given along with an enthusiastic tribute to Maggie Smith, who "leads us to the land beyond belief." [This item is reprinted, along with eighteen other reviews of the play, in *London Theatre Record*, for which see #890 above.]

900. Rogoff, Gordon. Note on *Lettice and Lovage. Village Voice* 9 Feb. 1988: 99.
    A capsule review is included among Rogoff's personal observations on the current London theatre scene. He finds *Lettice* a "delightfully ramshackle comedy" and congratulates Shaffer on "single-handedly reviving the type of leisurely English comedy that expired when Oscar [Wilde] was crucified."

901. Tinker, Jack. Review of *Lettice and Lovage. Daily Mail* (London) 28 Oct. 1987: page no. not available.
    Tinker raves about Maggie Smith's performance and, at considerably less length, praises Shaffer's script. [This item is reprinted, along with eighteen other reviews of the play, in *London Theatre Record*, for which see #890 above.]

902. Wapshott, Tim. Review of *Lettice and Lovage. Today* (London) 29 Oct. 1987: page no. not available.
    A brief, enthusiastic endorsement is offered: " . . . a perfect vehicle for Miss Smith." [This item is reprinted, along with eighteen other reviews of the play, in *London Theatre Record*, for which see #890 above.]

903. Wardle, Irving. Review of *Lettice and Lovage*. *Times* (London) 28 Oct. 1987: 21.

Wardle finds the theme of the play both important and heretofore "theatrically neglected." He describes that theme as an appeal to "the buried rage of Londoners towards the mutilation inflicted on their city by postwar planners." The treatment is judged "original and often hilarious." However, the critic expresses two major reservations. First, "as a play about the past, it is always coming to a stop for memory speeches." Second, "the two characters are of decidedly unequal interest . . . every scene is stolen by Miss Smith."

904. Wardle, Irving. "Much Improved." *Times* (London) 17 Nov. 1988: 20.

Wardle takes a second look at the play a year after its opening, as the major roles change hands. He approves of the re-writes made by Shaffer, "which enliven the comic detail and secure a better balance between the parts." He also praises Geraldine McEwan, who has replaced Maggie Smith as Lettice, noting that her "appearance of porcelain-like fragility belied by steely determination..is applied here to maximum advantage."

905. Watt, Douglas. Remarks on *Lettice and Lovage*. *New York Daily News* 20 July 1988: 36.

Watt is not impressed with the play, deeming it a "slight" and "prissy" comedy. He suspects that the production's success is entirely dependent on having a "deft and daft" comedienne in the title role.

906. Wolf, Matthew. "West End Reunion: Peter Shaffer's New Play Is His Gift to Maggie Smith." *Chicago Tribune* 15 Nov. 1987: section 13; 22.

This is essentially a news story which encompasses a brief review of *Lettice and Lovage*. Wolf emphasizes the reunion of Shaffer (as playwright) and Smith (as star) for the first time since *Private Ear/Public Eye*. While conceding that the show "has the smell of a hit", he finds Maggie Smith's performance a bit overdone and considers the "murder subplot" in Act Three "idiotic."

B. Reviews: New York Production.
Opened at the Barrymore Theatre, Mar. 25, 1990.

907. Barnes, Clive. "Maggie the Magnificent." *New York Post* 26 Mar. 1990: 23.
    Barnes joins his fellows in glorifying Smith's performance but establishes himself as virtually a chorus of one by bestowing lavish praise on the play. While criticizing its third act (a "letdown"), he describes *Lettice* as "one of the most scintillating and witty Broadway comedies in years." [This item, along with eight other reviews of the play, is reprinted in *New York Theatre Critics' Reviews*, for which see entry #916.]

908. Beaufort, John. "Maggie Smith's Brilliant Comic Inventions Brighten Broadway." *Christian Science Monitor* 2 Apr. 1990: 10.
    Beaufort raves about Maggie Smith as Lettice but praises Shaffer only by implication in a reference to the work's "verbal delights." [This item, along with eight other reviews of the play, is reprinted in *New York Theatre Critics' Reviews*, for which see entry #916.]

909. Disch, Thomas M. Review of *Lettice and Lovage*. *Nation* 7 May 1990: 644.
    Disch is favorably impressed with Shaffer's "self-effacing" efforts in providing "the great and inimitable Maggie Smith [with] one of her signature roles." The

script is labeled "that rarest of commodities, a comedy both genteel and consistently funny in a range from droll to hilarious."

910. Feingold, Michael. "La Triviata." *Village Voice* 3 Apr. 1990: 101.

Feingold pronounces *Lettice and Lovage* Shaffer's "best play since *Five Finger Exercise*," but the gloss is dulled considerably when he goes on to describe *Exercise* as "that amusing piece of trash." *Lettice* serves as a launching pad for a harsh evaluation of the playwright's 30-year-career, an assessment which ends with the theory that Shaffer should have contented himself all along with writing diverting and unpretentious theatre pieces, instead of such "important . . . middlebrow" works as *Royal Hunt*, *Equus*, and *Amadeus*.

911. Henry, III, William A. Review of *Lettice and Lovage*. *Time* 2 Apr. 1990: 71.

Henry reviews *Lettice and Lovage* along with *The Grapes of Wrath* and *Cat on a Hot Tin Roof* under the heading, " . . . Three Powerful Dramas." The piece concentrates not on Shaffer, but on his play as "in spirit . . . a one-woman show" and "a showcase for Dame Maggie Smith."

912. Hluchy, Patricia, and Brian D. Johnson. Review of *Lettice and Lovage*. *Maclean's* 28 May 1990: 62.

913. Humm. Review of *Lettice and Lovage*. *Variety* 28 Mar. 1990: 103,108.

Praise is bestowed in equally lavish portions on stars Smith and Tyzack and on playwright Shaffer, whose work is described as "an irresistible light comedy . . . a model of boulevard playmaking craftsmanship."

914. Kissel, Howard. "Smith's Lettice: A Star in Her Element."
     New York Daily News 26 Mar. 1990: 31.
         Kissel defines the play as an old-fashioned "star
     vehicle" and adds that, "if anyone can justify a 'star
     vehicle,' it's Maggie Smith." Shaffer's work is not
     examined beyond a brief analysis toward the end of the
     review: " . . . at heart the play is a celebration of the
     imagination, a celebration of the art of theater." [This
     item, along with eight other reviews of the play, is
     reprinted in *New York Theatre Critics' Reviews*,
     for which see entry #916.]

915. Kroll, Jack. "The Prime of Dame Maggie." *Newsweek* 2
     Apr. 1990: 54.
         Like most of his fellow critics, Kroll devotes his
     review to a paean of praise for actress Smith. His
     appraisal of Shaffer's writing is confined to a
     tantalizingly brief and equivocal final paragraph: " . . .
     here's a pure draft of high-styled Wildean comedy . . .
     Well, yes and no. It . . . squeaks through, because
     Shaffer is a masterly craftsman and, more important,
     Smith is a masterly comedienne."

916. *New York Theatre Critics' Reviews* 51.3 (Week of 5
     Mar. 1990 [sic . . . date incorrect by 3-4 weeks]): 340-
     346.
         Reprints reviews listed here as entries #919, #914,
     #923, #924, #925, #908, #915, #907, and #920.

917. Oliver, Edith. "To the Ladies." *New Yorker* 9 Apr. 1990:
     80.
         Oliver follows the path beaten out by her
     colleagues, devoting the bulk of her article to the
     pleasures of Maggie Smith's "indelible" acting style.
     Shaffer's work is largely ignored, although some
     reservations are expressed about a third act which
     "slides into foolishness." On the whole, however, Oliver

delivers an enthusiastic endorsement, calling the play "a source of continuous delight."

918. O'Malley, Thomas P. Review of *Lettice and Lovage*. *America* 21 Apr. 1990: 410.

O'Malley is not entirely entranced with Shaffer's script, which he describes as "a fragile piece," but he shares his colleagues' extreme fondness for Smith's "simply extraordinary" acting in the title role.

919. Rich, Frank. "One and Many Maggie Smiths." *New York Times* 26 Mar. 1990: C11.

Rich admires Maggie Smith's "extravagant" portrayal of Lettice, a performance, however, for which he can find only "a modest excuse" in Shaffer's play. *Lettice and Lovage* is described as "essentially a high camp, female version of the archetypal Shaffer play"—in other words, a story, exemplified by *Equus* and *Amadeus*, "in which two men, one representing creativity and ecstatic passion and the other mediocrity and sterility, battle for dominance." [This item, along with eight other reviews of the play, is reprinted in *New York Theatre Critics' Reviews*, for which see entry #916.]

920. Siegel, Joel. Review of *Lettice and Lovage*. WABC-TV. 25 Mar. 1990.

Glowing approval for Smith's star turn and her vehicle, which is called a "brilliant comedy." [This item, along with eight other reviews of the play, is reprinted in *New York Theatre Critics' Reviews*, for which see entry #916.]

921. Simon, John. Review of *Lettice and Lovage*. *New York* 9 Apr. 1990: 102.

Simon regards *Lettice* as proof that Shaffer is at his best when he "does not reach beyond his true métier [as] the solid *boulevardier*." This, however, is prologue to another of the critic's devastating put-downs of the playwright: "The play is not even superior, civilized situation comedy . . . [but] a *mere* vehicle for two brilliant performers." Not content with slighting the quality of the writing, Simon chastises Shaffer for lacking the courage to permit the story to develop into what, at heart, it seems to be—a "love story between two women."

922. Stearns, David Patrick. "Lettice Catches Smith in Her Prime." *USA Today* 26 Mar. 1990: 20.
    A rave for Maggie Smith: " . . . one of the most sublimely funny people alive." The play is accounted coarser and "broader" as a result of rewrites following the original London opening. Stearns sums up by referring to Lettice's abhorrence of "the mere," saying of the play, " . . . it's merely hilarious, which isn't such a bad thing except that it's—you know—'mere.'"

923. Watt, Doug. "Second Thoughts on First Nights." *New York Daily News* 30 Mar. 1990: page no. not available.
    Briefly following up his 1988 review of the London production [see #905 above], Watt continues to praise actress Smith and director Michael Blakemore. He refers to Shaffer only indirectly, by mentioning that he finds the re-written ending more "logical" than that of the earlier version, which seemed to him "hastily contrived." [This item, along with eight other reviews of the play, is reprinted in *New York Theatre Critics' Reviews*, for which see entry #916.]

924. Wilson, Edwin. "Maggie Smith's Tour de Force." *Wall Street Journal* 2 Apr. 1990: A11.
    As the headline suggests, this is another review devoted almost exclusively to extolling the virtues of the star's performance. The reviewer also bestows a few words of praise on the play, but he thinks Act

Three becomes "silly" and "far-fetched." [This item,
along with eight other reviews of the play, is reprinted
in *New York Theatre Critics' Reviews*, for which
see entry #916.]

925. Winer, Linda. "A Tour of Maggie Smith's Catalog of the
Eccentric." *Newsday* 26 Mar. 1990: Part II; 2, 4.
   For this critic, as for so many others, Maggie
Smith's star turn represents the chief, if not the only,
reason for seeing *Lettice*. The performance is
described as "an enormous catalog of comic
affectations, quite shameless in its histrionics, but
charmingly so and never close to boring." Winer
echoes the sentiments of her colleagues in
downgrading Shaffer's contribution: " . . . the kind of
leisurely, old-fashioned, cockle-warming granny play
that could have been entertaining matinees anytime in
the last 40 years." [This item, along with eight other
reviews of the play, is reprinted in *New York Theatre
Critics' Reviews*, for which see entry #916.]

NEWS REPORTS AND FEATURE STORIES

926. Anon. "Arts Diary." *Times* (London) 17 Oct. 1987: 21.
   A report on the impending London premiere of
Shaffer's new comedy, featuring the two Burmese cats
("Fortnum and Mason") who share the role of Lettice's
pet. Also mentioned is the play's 100,000 pound box
office "take" during its pre-London tryout at the
Theatre Royal in Bath.

927. Anon. "National's Hat Trick." *Times* (London) 19 Nov.
1988: 2.

Reports that three National Theatre productions
have won Evening Standard Drama Awards, among
them *Lettice and Lovage* for "best comedy."

928. Anon. "Times Diary." *Times* (London) 19 Feb. 1988: 14.
A commentary on Maggie Smith's performance in
Lettice: " . . . the great comic actress of our time . . .
demonstrates that comedy can be as profoundly
moving and revealing as tragedy . . . a gem always to
be treasured."

929. Kerr, Walter. "About a Poinsettia and a Woman with Five
Hands." *New York Times* 22 Apr. 1990: section 2;
5-6.
In one of his lengthy Sunday "Stage View" pieces for
the Arts and Leisure section of the *Times*, Kerr
praises the "wonderful" Maggie Smith and her amazing
inventory of gestures in *Lettice and Lovage* but
wonders why so little has been said about the play.
Though he finds it interesting, he suggests that "there
is something about [it] that isn't quite in register." The
four Act One versions of Lettice's history of Fustian
House, he contends, "don't vary enough for us to
justify the time and space spent on them." He also
complains that "the 'color [vs. drabness]' theme and
the comedy playing around it tend to take turns instead
of linking arms and advancing upon us in force."

930. Rogoff, Gordon. "Broadway Redux." *Connoisseur* Jan.
1989: 32.
This item is of interest not only for its capsule
review of *Lettice* but also as an example of incorrect
reporting. In it, Rogoff announces that "tickets are
available by phone this month" for performances "at
the Plymouth Theatre." The article is listed in The
Magazine Index as a "review" of the Broadway
production. As events proved, *Lettice and Lovage*

did not reach New York during the 1989 season, due to
an injury to star Maggie Smith.

SCHOLARLY ESSAY

931. Gianakaris, C.J. "Placing Shaffer's *Lettice and Lovage*
in Perspective." *Comparative Drama* 22.2 (Summer
1988): 145-161.
Gianakaris attempts to reveal the threads of theme
and style which link *Lettice* to Shaffer's earlier
works. For example, he sees the temperamental and
philosophical clashes of Lotte and Lettice as being in
the tradition of Shaffer's earlier antagonists, such as
Pizarro/ Atahuallpa, Dysart/Alan, and Salieri/Mozart:
an Apollonian authority-figure vs. a Dionysian free-
spirit. Gianakaris concludes that "all aspects of
Lettice and Lovage have appeared previously in
works by Peter Shaffer."

Index

All references are to page numbers, not to entry numbers.

Adair, Gilbert 215
Adam, Peter 36
Amadeus ix, xvii, xviii, xx,
    xxi, xxvii, 3, 5, 6, 10, 11,
    15-18, 20, 22, 26, 38-42, 44,
    51, 166, 185-228, 232, 233,
    241, 253, 255
Amory, Mark 200
Ansen, David 216, 224
Apple, R.W., Jr. 205
Aragoncs, J.E. 204
Archibald, Lewis 216
Arens, K. 210
Armistead, Claire 43
Artaud, Antonin 27, 28, 107,
    108, 162
Asahina, R. 190
Asquith, Ros 244
Aston, Frank 56
Atkinson, Brooks 57
Bail [*Variety* reviewer] 130

Balance of Terror, The
    xxiv, 46, 47
Balch, Jack 57
Baldwin, Helene L. 162
Baniewicz, E. 204
Barber, John 138, 186, 200,
    231
Barker, Felix 86, 112, 130
Barnes, Clive 14, 116, 142,
    143, 157, 190, 191, 216,
    241, 244, 252
Barzun, Jacques 227
Bassett, Abe 157
Battle of Shrivings, The
    viii, xx, xxvi, 11, 13, 15, 18,
    31-33, 40, 43, 44, 51, 129-
    135, 138, 152, 170
Beaufort, John 58, 143, 191,
    252
Beckerman, Bernard 10
Beckley, Paul V. 66

Benedictus, David 90
Benjamin, Philip 112
Benson, Sheila 217
Berman, Jeffrey 162
Beyer, M. 162
Bidney, M. 210
Billington, Michael xxi, 138, 186, 208, 232, 244
Black Comedy vii, viii, xvi, xx, xxv, xxvi, xxvii, 4, 9, 10, 13, 16, 30, 31, 44, 111-127, 132, 152, 196, 212
Blake, Richard A. 217
Bolton, Whitney 8, 58, 73, 95, 104, 117
Bonner, Hilary 244
Bosworth, Patricia 158
Boucher, Anthony 47
Brandstetter, Gabriele 213
Brewer, Colin 163
Brien, Alan 53, 90, 91, 177
Brisson, Frederick 64
Brukenfeld, Dick 143
Brunkhorst, Martin 210
Brustein, Robert 96, 192
Bryden, Ronald 86, 91, 112, 123, 130
Buckley, Peter 42
Buckley, Tom 36
Buckroyd, P. 15
Bunce, Alan N. 117
Burke, Tom 182
Burland, J. Alexis 163
Callow, Simon 205
Calta, Louis 158
Camp, Andre 204
Canby, Vincent 82, 109, 177, 217
Carleton, Don 127, 204

Carpenter, Charles A. 3
Carroll, Kathleen 81, 82, 109, 178, 218
Cart [*Variety* reviewer] 218
Castro, A. 225
Cerny, Lothar 164
Chagrin, Claude 99, 104
Chaillet, Ned 232
Chambers, Colin 38
Chand, Paul 245
Chandhuri, Una 164
Chapin, Louis 96
Chapman, John 58, 74, 96, 97, 117
Chiari, J. 10
Christiansen, Richard 74
Christie, Ian 138
Clum, John M. 164
Clurman, Harold xxi, 53, 58, 70, 74, 97, 117, 143
Cocks, Jay 82
Cohen, Marshall 97
Cohen, Nathan 97
Cohn, Ruby 106
Colby, Ethel 74
Coleman, Robert 59, 74
Colvin, Clare 43
Combs, Richard 218
Connor, John 233
Cooke, Richard P. 59, 75, 118
Corbally, John 164
Corello, Anthony V. 165
Corliss, Richard 219
Couling, Della 245
Courant, Gerard 178
Coveney, Michael 233
Craft, Robert 219
Crist, Judith 178
Cropper, Martin 233

Crosby, John 91
Crowther, Bosley 66, 81
Cunningham, Dennis 192
Curt. [*Variety* reviewer] 113
Cushman, Robert 125, 138, 193
Dace, Tisit 186
Dallas, Ian 8
Darnton, Nina 206
Dash, Thomas R. 53, 59, 75
Davies, Russell 139, 165, 179
Davis, Ken 158
Dawson, Helen 139
Day, Doris M. 127
Dean, Joan F. 15, 165
Deford, Frank 159
De Jongh, Nicholas 200, 241
Denby, David 219
Deneulin, Alain 166
Devlin, Diana 79
Dexter, John 34, 104, 105, 156, 159, 162, 205
Diether, Jack 193
Disch, Thomas M. 252
Dissertations and theses vi, viii, 20, 176
Driver, Tom F. 59
Ebner, I. Dean 166
Edelstein, David 219
Edwards, Bill 160
Edwards, Christopher 233, 245
Elitzik, Paul 220
Elsom, John 10
Equus viii, xiii, xvii, xviii, xx, xxi, xxvi, xxvii, 3-5, 9-12, 15, 16, 18-20, 22, 26, 33-37, 40, 44, 105, 137-183, 194, 196, 212, 215, 232, 233, 241, 253, 255
Esslin, Martin 92, 186

Evans, J. Claude 179
Fallon, James 42
Feingold, Michael 193, 253
Fenton, James 187, 201
Field, Rowland 60
Film versions of Shaffer's plays viii, ix, xxiv, xxv, xxvi, xxvii, 7, 27, 66-67, 82-83, 109-110, 127, 176-182, 215-227
Five Finger Exercise vi, xvii, xix, xx, xxiv, 13, 15, 18, 19, 22, 23, 27, 39, 44, 51-67, 70, 76, 131, 132, 146, 165, 253
Follow Me xvii, xxvi, 81
Forman, Milos 41, 215, 224-226
French, Philip 123, 130, 220
Frost, David 113
Frumkes, Roy 220
Funke, Phyllis 30
Gabbard, K. 166
Garstenauer, Maria 106
Gascoigne, Bamber 71, 87
Gassner, John 10, 75, 98
Gaver, Jack 27, 98
Geist, Kenneth L. 187
Gelatt, Ronald 40, 193
Gelb, Barbara 30
Gele, Claude 179
Gellert, Roger 71
Gianakaris, C.J. 16, 166, 206, 211, 259
Gibbs, Patrick 53
Gielgud, John xix, 9, 44, 57, 64, 134
Gifford, Sanford 167
Gill, Brendan 144, 194

Gillespie, M. 211
Gilliatt, Penelope 82, 92, 113
Glenn, Jules 11, 16, 106, 167
Goodwin, John 214
Gottfried, Martin 75, 99, 118,
    139, 144, 145
Gow, Gordon 221
Grant, Steve 156, 187, 245
Green, J.G. 188
Greer, Edward G. 145
Greiff, Louis K. 168
Gruber, G. 206
Gruen, John 160
Gussow, Mel 35, 118, 160
Guthrie, Constance 160
Hall, Peter xix, 11, 28, 39, 186,
    188, 191, 199, 203, 206,
    209, 236
Hamilton, James W. 168
Hammerschmidt, Hildegard
    107
Hammond, Gay Hobgood 176
Hammond, James Brian 176
Harvey, Stephen 194
Haskell, Molly 179
Haupt, John 160
Hayes, Richard 60
Hayman, Ronald 12, 15
Hays, Peter L. 168
Heilpern, John 44
Henry, William A., III 253
Hepple, Peter 188, 234
Hering, Doris 99
Herzenstein, Guido 168
Hewes, Henry 60, 75, 92, 99,
    105, 119, 145
Higgins, John 41
Hiley, Jim 234, 245

Hinchliffe, Arnold P. 12
Hinden, M. 17
Hipp, Edward Sothern 60, 76,
    99, 100, 119
Hirsh, Samuel 30
Hirschhorn, Clive 234, 246
Hluchy, Patricia 253
Hobson, Harold 71, 93, 113,
    115, 131, 139
Holdenfield, Chris 225
Hope-Wallace, Philip 48, 53,
    113, 123, 131
Hornak, Richard 221
Hornby, R. 235
*How Doth the Little
    Crocodile?* xxiii, 45
Hoyle, Martin 246
Hristic, Jovan 211
Huber, Werner 211
Hughes, Catherine 140, 194
Hughes, Elinor 25
Hummler, Richard 194, 207,
    253
Hurren, Kenneth 126, 140,
    201, 235, 246
Hutchings, William 158
Hutton, Brian G. 80
Jacobson, Dan 41, 239
Jameson, Sue 235, 246
Jensen, Marvin D. 17, 168
Joffee, Linda 235
Johnson, Brian D. 253
Jones, A.H. 169
Jones, Anne Hudson 169
Jones, D.R. 212
Jones, Dan 247
Kael, Pauline 109, 180, 221
Kakutani, Michiko 225

Kalem, T.E. 146, 194
Kalson, Albert E. 140
Kamm, Henry 225
Kaplan, Morris Bernard 169
Kauffmann, Stanley 12, 146, 180, 195, 222
Kavanagh, P.J. 40
Kemp, Peter 247
Keown, Eric 54, 72
Kerensky, Oleg 12
Kerner, Leighton 195
Kernodle, George 107
Kerr, Walter 60, 76, 100, 114, 141, 147, 160, 195, 258
King, Francis 188, 236
Kingston, Jeremy 87, 123, 132, 141
Kirby, F.E. 207
Kissel, Howard 34, 83, 147, 180, 195, 222, 247, 254
Klein, Dennis A. 3, 4, 17, 170, 212, 241
Klossowicz, Jan 161
Knapp, Bettina L. 107
Knight, Arthur 83
Knox, Collie 135
Knussen, Oliver 105
Kretzmer, Herbert 49, 72, 114, 124
Kroll, Jack 147, 148, 196, 236, 254
Kruntorad, P. 204
Lambert, J.W. 65, 87, 141
Lapole, Nick 80, 105
Larson, Janet Karsten 196
Lauder, Rev. Robert E. 215
Lawson, Wayne P. 20
Lee, James 170

Lee, Nora 226
Lee, Ronald J. 170
Lennartz, K. 156
Leonard, John 148
Lerner, Irving 108
Lerner, Max 161
Letters to the editor viii, ix, 145, 175, 214, 227
Lettice and Lovage ix, xx, xxi, xxii, xxviii, 5, 6, 43, 44, 243-259
Levin, Bernard xxi, 93, 114, 119, 188, 214
Lewis, Allan 13, 76
Lewis, Allen 80
Lewis, Emory 61, 76, 100, 120
Lewis, Peter 43, 124, 132
Lewis, Theophilus 61, 77, 100
Little, Stuart W. 23
Loftus, Joseph A. 23
London Theatre Record 200-203, 232-240, 244-250
Loney, Glenn 32, 98, 120, 207
Loomis, Jeffrey B. 170
Lounsberry, Barbara 18
Luddy, Thomas E. 207
Lumet, Sidney 37, 176, 179, 181, 183
Lumley, Frederick 13
Lynch, William F. 170
Lyons, Leonard 127
Mackenzie, Suzie 236
Mallett, Richard 83
Mann, Daniel 66
Marcus, Frank 132
Marowitz, Charles 13, 93, 94, 115, 175
Marriott, R.B. 21, 114, 132
May, William F. 171

McCarten, John 77, 100, 120
McClain, John 61, 77, 101
McClatchy, J.D. 196
McKellen, Ian 39, 191, 195,
    199, 209
Melly, George 83
Menotti, Gian Carlo 227
Merry Roosters Panto, The
    xxiv, 46, 48, 49
Messina, Matt 9
Michener, Charles 148
Mikels, F.X. 212
Miles, John A. 171
Miner, Michael D. 171
Mootz, William 148
Morgan, Derek 120
Morley, Sheridan 208, 248
Morrison, Hobe 62, 77, 101,
    120, 148, 196
Murf [*Variety* reviewer] 180
Myro [*Variety* reviewer] 94
Nadel, Norman 78, 101, 121
Nathan, David 124, 237, 248
National Theatre [of Great
    Britain] 9, 11, 157, 200,
    202-205, 210, 214, 240, 241,
    257
New York Theatre Critics'
    Reviews 57-59, 61-63, 74-
    79, 96, 101-103, 117-119,
    121, 122, 142-144, 146-148,
    150, 151, 153, 155, 190,
    192, 195-200, 252, 254-257
Nightingale, Benedict 87, 126,
    132, 156, 188, 208, 237, 248
Nottingham, William J. 212
Novick, Julius 149, 196
Oaks, Philip 33

O'Brien, Tom 222
Oestricher, Paul 214
Oliver, Edith 254
O'Malley, Thomas P. 255
Oppenheimer, George 29, 78,
    102, 121, 149
Osborne, Charles 249
Osorio de Negret, Betty 107
Pacheco, Patrick 149
Pad (And How to Use It), The
    vii, xvii, xxv, 80-81
Page, Malcolm 4
Panter-Downes, Mollie 54,
    189
Parser, Philip 47
Paton, Maureen 249
Paul [*Variety* reviewer] 197,
    214, 220, 245
Pearson, Kenneth 31
Pennel, Charles A. 18
Perry-Camp, Jane 222
Peter, John 238, 249
Pit [*Variety* reviewer] 141,
    197, 238, 249
Plunka, Gene A. 5, 20, 107,
    171
Podol, Peter L. 19, 107
Polanski, Roman 203, 204, 206
Pope, W. MacQueen 54
Pouteau, Jacques 133
Poyser, I. 214
Pree, Barry 25, 32
Prideaux, Tom 62, 80, 105, 121
Private Ear, The vii, xvi,
    xvii, xx, xxiv, xxv, 4, 8, 13,
    22, 25, 27, 43, 44, 69-80,
    132, 252
Probst, Leonard 149

Prodigal Father, The xxiv, 46
Pryce-Jones, Alan 78
Public Eye, The vii, xvi,
    xvii, xviii, xx, xxiv, xxvi, 4,
    8, 13, 16, 22, 25, 27, 30, 43,
    44, 69-83, 132, 152, 165,
    244, 252
Radavich, David A. 172
Rape of Tamar, The 41, 239
Ratcliffe, Michael 238, 250
Real, Jere 150
Reed, Carol 81
Reed, Rex 150, 181, 223
Rice, Julian C. 172
Rich, Alan 151
Rich, Frank 55, 110, 124, 181,
    197, 239, 255
Richardson, Jack 121, 151
Rissik, Andrew 106
Robbins, Leonard Henry 176
Roberts, Peter 88
Robertson, Nan 209
Rogoff, Gordon 9, 250, 258
Ross, Don 23
Rosten, N. 19
*Royal Hunt of the Sun,
    The* vii, xvii, xx, xxi, xxv,
    xxvi, 9, 10, 13, 15, 16,
    18-20, 22, 27-30, 35, 44, 85-
    110, 114, 116, 119, 131,
    132, 138, 141, 146, 159,
    164, 165, 192, 212, 232,
    241, 253
Rurak, J. 212
Rutherford, Malcolm 88, 94
Ryan, Thomas C. xvii, xxv, 80
Salem, Daniel 13

Salt Land, The xxiii, 46
Sanchez Arnosi, Milagros 172
Sanders, Kevin 151
Sarris, Andrew 181
Sauvage, Leo 198
Say, Rosemary 124, 201
Schickel, Richard 9
Schonberg, Harold 209
Schultz, Dieter 108
Seeds, Dale E. 210
Seligsohn, Leo 223
Shaffer, Anthony xxiii, 3, 11,
    31, 32
Shaffer, Peter
    WORKS: *see* individual titles
        [for a complete list of
        Shaffer's works, consult the
        Table of Contents, pages v-
        ix, or Chronology, pages
        xxiii-xxvii]
    adaptation of dialogue and
        bridging materials for
        Love for Love 9
    box-office success of his plays
        xx-xxi
    career as a screenwriter xvii-
        xviii, 16, 27, 31, 37, 40-42
    compared to other dramatists,
        Albee 146; Ayckbourne
        80; Barrie 133, 157;
        Beckett 12, 91; Bolt 89,
        134; Brecht 234; Coward
        54, 71, 79; Demarigny 19;
        Drinkwater 187; Eliot
        146; Giraudoux 71;
        Hampton 140; Kopit 108;
        MacLeish 146; Maugham
        200; Mortimer 72;

Shaffer, Peter, cont.
    Murdoch 130; O'Neill 17;
    Osborne 13, 22, 63; Pinero
    13, 53; Rattigan 22, 53;
    Shaw 131; Wesker 234;
    Whiting 87; Wilde 250
  controversy over his depiction
    of Mozart in *Amadeus*
    187, 195, 199, 205-211, 214,
    227-229
  controversy over his depiction
    of psychotherapy and
    psychotherapists in *Equus*
    145, 152, 162, 163, 165,
    167-169, 171, 173-176
  critics opposing him, *see*
    especially Brustein,
    Bryden, Fenton, Grant,
    Richardson, Simon, and
    Wetzsteon
  critics supporting him, *see*
    especially Hobson, Levin,
    and Nadel
  disappointment over failure of
    The Battle of Shrivings
    33
  early life (prior to establishing
    career as a playwright)
    xviii-xix, 5, 24, 38, 40-42
  experiments with LSD in 1960s
    32, 36
  his film versions used as
    pretexts to critique his
    plays 109, 177-182, 221-223
  homosexuality seen as a
    disguised theme of *Equus*
    and *Lettice and Lovage*
    145, 153, 256

  goals as a playwright 21, 28,
    29, 31, 33-34, 36, 40-41, 43-
    44
  mastery of technical skills as a
    playwright 9, 14, 63
  Month in the Country a
    plot source for *Five
    Finger Exercise* 15, 54-
    55
  nudity in *Equus* 157-158
  on Benjamin Britten 34
  on Carl Jung's ideas 36
  personal mannerisms 30
  private life 44
  revisions of his scripts 23, 25,
    39-40, 42, 43, 104, 123, 134-
    135, 184, 191, 202, 221
  ritualistic and symbolic devices
    in his plays 18, 20, 38, 159-
    160
  stature as a dramatist 9-10,
    17, 28, 71, 103, 104, 119,
    126, 151, 154, 193, 231, 237,
    245, 253
  twinship themes in plays,
    see Glenn, Jules
  unproduced or unfinished
    works 9, 26, 33, 128-129
  working methods as a
    playwright 25-26, 35, 36-
    37, 41-42
  working relationships with
    directors 11-12, 34-35, 159,
    225
  working relationships with
    actors 24-25
Sheed, Wilfred 102

Shrivings 18, 51; see also *The Battle of Shrivings*
Shorter, Eric 88, 125, 133
Shulman, Milton 49, 55, 72, 89, 95, 114, 116, 125, 133, 141, 202, 239
Siegel, Joel 198, 255
Sigal, Clancy 182
Simard, Rodney Joe 20
Simon, John xxi, 38, 96, 102, 152, 182, 190, 198, 223, 255
Simons, Piet 156, 161
Sinclair, Clive 239
Slutzky, Jacob E. 172
Smith, Maggie 43, 44, 243-247, 249-259
Smith, Michael 78, 102, 122
Smith, Ronn 226
Sontag, Frederick 152
Soria, Dorle J. 212
Spurling, Hilary 116, 125, 133, 156
Stacy, James R. 19
Stamm, Julian 173
Stapleton, Rev. Scott 228
Stasio, Marilyn 152
Stearns, David Patrick 256
Steinhauer, Jules Verne 229
Sterritt, David 83, 182, 224
Stoddart, Patrick 42
Sullivan, William J. 213
Suzy 210
Sydney, Edward 31
Tallmer, Jerry 35
Tarjan, T. 204
Taubman, Howard 79, 103
Taylor, John Russell xxi, 5, 6, 9, 13, 27, 29, 66, 189, 202

Taylor-William, Dianne 176
Terrien, Samuel 173, 213
Terry, Walter 106
That Was the Week That Was xxv, 46
Thomsen, Christian W. 213, 239
Thomson, David 224
Tillman, W.N. 198
Timm, Neil 174
Tinker, Jack 202, 240, 250
Tobias, Tobi 153
Topor, Tom 37
Toubiana, S. 226
Townsend, Martha A. 213
Toynbee, Polly 189
Trauth, V. 205
Trewin, J.C. 55, 72, 89, 115, 133
Troxel, Patricia Margaret 20
Trussler, Simon 108
Tynan, Kenneth 55, 62, 72
Vandenbroucke, Russell 174
Vidal, Gore 63
Von Rhein, John 226
Wagner, M. 205
Wallach, Allan 199
Walls, Doyle W. 174
Walsh, Michael 55
Wapshott, Tim 250
Wardle, Irving 126, 133, 134, 141, 203, 240, 251
Watkins, Roger 227
Watson, John Clair 20
Watt, Douglas 153, 154, 199, 240, 251
Watts, Richard, Jr. 63, 79, 89, 103, 104, 122, 142, 154

Weales, Gerald 154
Webb, W.L. 22
Weightman, John 154
Weiner, Bernard 155
Weise, Wolf-Dietrich 14
Wellworth, George 14
Welsh, J.M. 175
Wes, M.A. 213
West, Anthony 123
Westarp, K.H. 108
Wetzsteon, Ross 155
White Liars [The] vii, viii,
    xxvi, xxvii, 4, 16, 31, 44, 51,
    111, 123-127, 212
White Lies vii, xvi, xx, xxv, 4,
    16, 51, 111, 116-123, 125,
    165, 212
Whittaker, Herbert 63
Williamson, Bruce 224
Wilson, Edwin 155, 200, 240,
    256

Wimble, Barton 161
Winegarten, Renee 19
Winer, Linda 257
Winsten, Archer 67, 81
Witham, Barry B. 175
Withered Murder xxiii, 45,
    47
Wolf, Matthew 241, 251
Woman in the Wardrobe,
    The xxiii, 45
Wootton, C. 214
Worsley, T.C. 49, 55, 56, 73
Yonadab ix, xx, xxi, xxii,
    xxvii, 4, 7, 15, 41-43, 166,
    231-242
Young, B.A. 89, 115, 134, 142,
    190, 203
Zakariason, Bill 210
Zapf, Hubert 211
Zimmerman, Paul D. 110